Aristotle's Theology

The Primary Texts

Aristotle's Theology

The Primary Texts

Translated
With Introduction and Notes
By

C. D. C. Reeve

Hackett Publishing Company, Inc.
Indianapolis/Cambridge

Printed in the United States of America

25 24 23 22 1 2 3 4 5 6 7

For further information, please address
Hackett Publishing Company, Inc.
P.O. Box 44937
Indianapolis, Indiana 46244-0937

www.hackettpublishing.com

Cover design by Listenberger Design & Associates
Interior design by E. L. Wilson
Composition by Aptara, Inc.

Library of Congress Control Number: 20229334

ISBN-13: 978-1-64792-092-0 (cloth)
ISBN-13: 978-1-64792-081-4 (pbk.)
ISBN-13: 978-1-64792-093-7 (PDF ebook)

The paper used in this publication meets the minimum requirements of American National Standard for Information Sciences—Permanence of Paper for Printed Library Materials, ANSI Z39.48–1984.

∞

Contents

4. Later Intimations

5. Aristotle's God

6. The Gods and Us

7. The Gods in the Fragments

Preface

I have long wanted to write a book on Aristotle's theology, and on those gods of his, whom we do not fully meet until *Metaphysics* 12.7–10. To that end I began to assemble the scattered texts that I thought would prove most relevant to my endeavor. I arranged these in the canonical order in which one encounters them in Immanuel Bekker's *Aristotelis Opera* (Berlin, 1831 [1970]), or, in English, in Jonathan Barnes' *Revised Oxford Translation* (Princeton, 1984)—though omitting the dubious or spurious works.[1] Two things soon became apparent: first, that this was the right and natural order in which to present them and, second, that no book existed that presented them in it—or indeed in any other order. The second surprised me, but so too did the first. For what I saw was that Aristotle's gods reveal themselves by slow degrees, and only when fully revealed are we in a position to see their role in our lives.

At that point, as it seemed to me, all I needed to do was collect the most authoritative editions of the Greek texts, translate them as accurately and uniformly as possible into readable English, divide them under informative heads, and try to make sense of them. What sense I have made the reader will find in the Introduction, the notes that accompany the texts, and the Glossary, which explains key repeated terms and notions and identifies people referred to. As far as possible I let Aristotle explain himself by incorporating translations of other texts of his. For ease of location, all of these are listed in the Index of Quoted Passages. Material in brackets in the translated texts is added for clarification.

The Introduction, for its part, provides a brief biography of Aristotle and a way into his theology, which explains how and why it turns out to be identical to the science of being qua being, which Aristotle calls "primary science," or "primary philosophy," and which we call "metaphysics," after the Greek title of the work in which it is developed: *Ta Meta ta Phusika*. It also briefly compares Aristotle's god and God as we and some more familiar

1. Some passages from †*Magna Moralia* and ††*De Mundo*, though, do appear in the notes.

religions conceive of him. All discussion of traditional ancient Greek religion and its gods, however, is left to the pertinent notes.[2]

I have drawn on, and sometimes silently revised, translations first published in the New Hackett Aristotle Series, and I renew my thanks to all who helped with these. I also extend them to Justin Vlasits for allowing me to use his translation of the F fragments (forthcoming in the New Hackett Aristotle series). And I renew them, yet again, to ΔKE, the first fraternity in the United States to endow a professorial chair, and to the University of North Carolina for awarding it to me. The generous research funds that the endowment makes available each year have allowed me to travel to conferences and to acquire books, computers, and other research materials and assistance, most notably that of the eagle-eyed Sean Neagle, without which my work would have been much more difficult. Lastly, and very warmly, I thank my dear friend Pavlos Kontos for his generous assistance.

2. Interested readers should consult M. Segev, *Aristotle on Religion* (Cambridge, 2017). The immense influence of Aristotle on subsequent theology, in the West (on such figures as Augustine, Boethius, and Aquinas), and in the East (on Dionysius the Areopagite, Maximus the Confessor, and Gregory Palamas), is explored in D. Bradshaw, *Aristotle East and West: Metaphysics and the Division of Christendom* (Cambridge, 2004).

Abbreviations

Citations of Aristotle's works are standardly made, as they are in this book, to I. Bekker, *Aristotelis Opera* (Berlin: 1831 [1970]), in the canonical form of abbreviated title, book number (when the work is divided into books), chapter number, page number, column letter, and line number. A † indicates a work whose authenticity has been seriously questioned; †† indicates a work attributed to Aristotle but generally agreed not to be by him. The abbreviations used are as follows:

APo.	*Posterior Analytics*
APr.	*Prior Analytics*
Cael.	*De Caelo* (Moraux)
Cat.	*Categories*
DA	*De Anima* (Corsilius)
Div. Somn.	*Prophecy in Sleep* (Ross)
EE	*Eudemian Ethics*
Fr.	*Fragments* (Rose)
GA	*Generation of Animals*
GC	*Coming to Be and Passing Away* (Rashed)
HA	*History of Animals* (Louis)
IA	*Progression of Animals* (Falcon and Stavrianeas)
Int.	*De Interpretatione*
Juv.	*Youth and Old Age, Life and Death, and Respiration* (Ross)
Long.	*Length and Shortness of Life* (Ross)
MA	*Movement of Animals* (Primavesi and Corsilius)
Mem.	*Memory* (Ross)
Met.	*Metaphysics* (Bk. 7 Frede-Patzig; Bk. 12 Alexandru)
Mete.	*Meteorology* (Fobes)
†*MM*	*Magna Moralia* (Susemihl)
††*Mun.*	*De Mundo* (Thom)

NE	*Nicomachean Ethics*
PA	*Parts of Animals* (Louis)
Ph.	*Physics*
Po.	*Poetics*
Pol.	*Politics*
†*Pr.*	*Problems* (Mayhew)
Protr.	*Protrepticus* (Düring)
Rh.	*Rhetoric* (Kassel)
SE	*Sophistical Refutations*
Sens.	*Sense and Sensibilia* (Ross)
Somn.	*Sleep* (Ross)
Top.	*Topics* (Brunschwig)

I cite and translate the *Oxford Classical Texts* (OCT) editions of these works, except in the case of the editions indicated:

Alexandru, S. *Aristotle's Metaphysics Lambda* (Leiden, 2014).

Brunschwig, B. *Aristote Topiques Livres I–IV, Livres V–VIII* (Paris, 1967, 2007).

Corsilius, K. *Aristoteles Über die Seele: De Anima* (Hamburg, 2017).

Düring, I. *Aristotle's Protrepticus: An Attempt at Reconstruction* (Göteborg, 1961).

Falcon, A., and Stavrianeas, S. *Aristotle on How Animals Move* (Cambridge, 2021).

Fobes, F. *Aristotelis Meteorologicorum Libri Quattor* (Cambridge, MA, 1919).

Frede, M., and Patzig, G. *Aristoteles Metaphysik Z: Text, Übersetzung und Kommentar* (Munich, 1988).

Kassel, R. *Aristotelis Ars Rhetorica* (Berlin, 1976).

Louis, P. *Histoire des Animaux* (Paris, 1964–1969).

———. *Les Parties des Animaux* (Paris, 1956).

Mayhew, R. *Aristotle: Problems* (Cambridge, MA, 2011).

Moraux, P. *Aristote: Du Ciel* (Paris, 1965).

Primavesi, O., and Corcilius, K. *Aristotle's: De Motu Animalium* (Hamburg, 2018).

Rashed, M. *Aristote: De la Génération et la Corruption* (Paris, 2005).

Rose, V. *Aristotelis Fragmenta*, 3rd ed. (Leipzig, 1886).

Ross, D. *Aristotle Parva Naturalia* (Oxford, 1955).

Susemihl, F. *Aristotelis Magna Moralia* (Leipzig, 1883).

Thom, J. *Cosmic Order and Divine Power: Pseudo-Aristotle, On the Cosmos* (Tübingen, 2014).

Other Abbreviations

DK = Diels, H., and Kranz, W., eds. *Die Fragmente der Vorsokratiker*, 6th ed. (Berlin, 1951).

TEGP = Graham, D. *The Texts of Early Greek Philosophy: The Complete Fragments and Selected Testimonies of the Major Presocratics* (Cambridge, 2010).

Introduction

Life and Works

Aristotle was born in 384 BC to a well-off family living in the small town of Stagira in northern Greece. His father, Nicomachus, who died while Aristotle was still quite young, was allegedly doctor to King Amyntas of Macedon. His mother, Phaestis, was wealthy in her own right. When Aristotle was seventeen his guardian, Proxenus, sent him to study at Plato's Academy in Athens. He remained there for twenty years, initially as a student, eventually as a researcher and teacher.

When Plato died in 347, leaving the Academy in the hands of his nephew Speusippus, Aristotle left Athens for Assos in Asia Minor, where the ruler, Hermias, was a patron of philosophy. He married Hermias' niece Pythias and had a daughter by her, also named Pythias. Three years later, in 345, after Hermias had been killed by the Persians, Aristotle moved to Mytilene on the island of Lesbos, where he met Theophrastus, who was to become his best student and closest colleague.

In 343, Aristotle seems to have been invited by Philip of Macedon to be tutor to the latter's thirteen-year-old son, Alexander, later called "the Great." In 335, Aristotle returned to Athens and founded his own institute, the Lyceum. While he was there his wife died and he established a relationship with Herpyllis, also a native of Stagira. Their son Nicomachus was named for Aristotle's father, and the *Nicomachean Ethics* may, in turn, have been named for him, as the *Eudemian Ethics*, in turn, may have been for Eudemus of Rhodes, a famous student of Aristotle's. In 323, Alexander the Great died, with the result that anti-Macedonian feeling in Athens grew stronger. Perhaps threatened with a formal charge of impiety, Aristotle left for Chalcis in Euboea, where he died twelve months later, in 322, at the age of sixty-two.

Legend has it that Aristotle had slender calves and small eyes, spoke with a lisp, and was "conspicuous by his attire, his rings, and the cut of his hair." His will reveals that he had a sizable estate, a domestic partner, two children, a considerable library, and a large circle of friends. In it Aristotle asks his executors to take special care of Herpyllis. He directs that his slaves be freed "when they come of age" and that the bones of his wife, Pythias, be mixed with his "as she instructed."

Although the surviving writings of Aristotle occupy almost 2,500 tightly printed pages in English, most of them are not works polished for publication but lecture notes and working papers. This accounts for some, though not all, of their legendary difficulty. It is unfair to complain, as a Platonist opponent did, that Aristotle "escapes refutation by clothing a perplexing subject in obscure language, using darkness like a squid to make himself hard to catch," but there is darkness and obscurity enough for anyone, even if none of it is intentional. There is also a staggering breadth and depth of intellect. Aristotle made fundamental contributions to a vast range of disciplines, including logic, metaphysics, epistemology, psychology, ethics, politics, rhetoric, aesthetics, zoology, biology, physics, and philosophical and political history. When Dante called him "the master of those who know," he was scarcely exaggerating.

What Theology Is

The word "metaphysics," as we saw in the Preface, is a near transliteration of the Greek phrase *ta meta ta phusika*, which means "the things or writings that are after *ta phusika*"—after the ones devoted to natural things. It is not Aristotle's term for anything, not even for the work—or the contents of the work—that now has it as its title. But because that title mentions *ta phusika*, Aristotle's *Physics* is where we might reasonably begin our search for what comes after it.

In the *Physics*, Aristotle's focus is on the world of nature (*phusis*), a world pretty much coincident with the sublunary realm, consisting canonically of matter-form (or hylomorphic) compounds, whose material component involves the sublunary elements—earth, water, air, and fire. Were these the only substances, the only primary beings, we learn in *Metaphysics* 6.1, the science of them would be the science that the *Metaphysics* wishes to investigate, which is referred to as theoretical wisdom, the science of being qua being, and the primary science or primary philosophy. But if there are other substances that are not composed of the sublunary elements, which are "eternal and immovable and separable," and so prior to natural ones, the science of them will be the science of being qua being (1026^{a}10–16).

That there must be such substances is argued already in *Physics* 8, and that the gods, including in particular *the* primary god, are among them is presupposed from quite early on also in the *Metaphysics*. Thus in *Metaphysics* 1.2 we hear that theoretical wisdom is the science of this god, both in having him as its subject matter and in being the science that is in some sense his science.[1] When it is argued in *Metaphysics* 12.9 that he must be "the active understanding [that] is active understanding of active understanding" (1074^{b}34–35), we see how much *his* it is, since actively understanding itself—contemplating itself in an exercise of theoretical wisdom—is just what Aristotle's god *is*. While this is no doubt difficult to understand, Aristotle's argument for it is so probing and resourceful that we can come to understand it—or, at any rate, see why he thought it the only available option.

With just this much on the table there is already a puzzle whose difficulty is increased by special doctrine. Aristotle usually divides the bodies of knowledge he refers to as *epistêmai* ("sciences") into three types: theoretical, practical, and productive (crafts). When he is being especially careful, he also distinguishes within the theoretical sciences between the *strictly* theoretical ones (astronomy, theology), as we may call them, and the natural ones, which are like the strictly theoretical ones in being neither practical nor productive, but unlike them in consisting of propositions that—though necessary and universal in some sense—hold for the most part rather than without exception (*Met.* 6.1.1025^{b}25–1026^{a}30). The science of the soul, as a result, has an interestingly mixed status, part strictly theoretical (because it deals with understanding, which is something divine), part natural (because it deals with perception and memory and other capacities that require a body) (*DA* 1.1.403^{a}3–^{b}16).

When science is focally discussed in the *Nicomachean Ethics*, however, Aristotle is explicit that if we are "to speak in an exact way and not be guided by mere similarities" (6.3.1139^{b}19), we should not call anything a "science" unless it deals with eternal, entirely exceptionless facts about universals that are wholly necessary and do not at all admit of being otherwise (1139^{b}20–21). Since he is here explicitly (1139^{b}27) epitomizing his more detailed discussion of science in the *Posterior Analytics*, we should take the latter too as primarily a discussion of science in the exact sense, which it calls *epistêmê haplôs*—unconditional scientific knowledge. It follows that only the strictly theoretical sciences are sciences in this sense. It is on these that the others should be modeled to the extent that they can be: "it is the things that are always in the same state and never undergo change that we must make our basis when pursuing the truth, and this is the sort of thing that the heavenly bodies are" (*Met.* 11.6.1063^{a}13–15).

Having made this acknowledgment, we must also register the fact that Aristotle himself mostly does not speak in the exact way, but instead

1. See *Top.* 5.4.132^{b}10–11.

persistently refers to bodies of knowledge other than the strictly theoretical sciences as *epistêmai*. His division of the *epistêmai* into theoretical, practical, and productive is a dramatic case in point. But so too is his use of the term *epistêmê*, which we first encounter in the *Metaphysics* as a near synonym of *technê*, or craft knowledge, which is a productive science, not a theoretical one (1.1.981^{a}3).

Although an Aristotelian science is a state of the soul rather than a set of propositions in a textbook, it nonetheless does involve having a grasp on a set of true propositions (*NE* 6.3.1139^{b}14–16). Some of these propositions are indemonstrable starting-points (*archai*), which are or are expressed in definitions, and others are theorems demonstrable from these starting-points. We can have scientific knowledge only of the theorems, since—exactly speaking—only what is demonstrable can be scientifically known (6.6). Yet—in what is clearly another lapse from exact speaking—Aristotle characterizes "the most exact of the sciences," which is theoretical wisdom (*sophia*), as also involving a grasp by understanding (*nous*) of the truth where the starting-points themselves are concerned (6.7.1141^{a}16–18). He does the same thing in the *Metaphysics*, where theoretical wisdom is the *epistêmê* that provides "a theoretical grasp on the primary starting-points and causes"—among which are included "the good or the for-the-sake-of-which" (1.2.982^{b}7–10). It is for this reason that the primary god's grasp on himself through understanding is an exercise of scientific knowledge.

Now, each of these sciences, regardless of what group it falls into, must—for reasons having to do with the nature of definition and demonstration—be restricted in scope to a single genus of beings. Since being is not itself a genus (*APo.* 2.7.92^{b}14), as Aristotle goes out of his way not just to acknowledge but to prove (*Met.* 4.2), it apparently follows that there should be no such science as the science of being qua being—no such thing as theoretical wisdom. To prove that there is one thus takes some work.

It is a cliché of the history of philosophy that Aristotle is an empiricist and Plato a rationalist, and like all clichés there is some truth in it. In fact, Aristotle is not just an empiricist at the level of the sciences we call "empirical," he is an empiricist at all levels. To see what I mean, think of each of the special, genus-specific sciences—the *first-order* sciences—as giving us a picture of a piece of the world, a region of being. Then ask, What is the world like that these sciences collectively portray? What is the nature of reality as a whole—of being as a whole? If there is no answer besides the collection of special answers, the world is, as Aristotle puts it, episodic—like a bad tragedy (*Met.* 12.10.1076^{a}1). But if there is a unified answer, it should emerge from a meta-level, empirical investigation of the first-order sciences themselves. As each of these looks for universals (natural kinds) that stand in demonstrative causal relations to each other, so this meta-level investigation looks for higher-level universals that reveal the presence of common structures of explanation in diverse sciences:

> The causes and starting-points of distinct things are distinct in a way, but in a way—if we are to speak universally and analogically—they are the same for all. . . . For example, perhaps the elements of perceptible bodies are: as form, the hot and, in another way, the cold, which is the privation; and, as matter, what is potentially these directly and intrinsically. And both these and the things composed of them are substances, of which these are the starting-points, that is, anything that comes to be from the hot and the cold that is one [something-or-other], such as flesh or bone; for what comes to be from these must be distinct from them. These things, then, have the same elements and starting-points (although distinct things have distinct ones). But that all things have the same ones is not something we can say just like that, although by analogy they do.[2] That is, we might say that there are three starting-points—the form, the privation, and the matter. But each of these is distinct for each category—for example, in color they are white, black, and surface, or light, darkness, and air, out of which day and night come to be. (*Met.* 12.4.1070^{a}31–^{b}21)

The first-order sciences show the presence in the world of a variety of *different* explanatory structures. The trans-generic sciences, by finding commonalities between these structures, show the equally robust presence there of the *same* explanatory structure: form, privation of form, and matter.

The science to which form, privation, and matter belong is, in the first instance, trans-generic natural science. It is the one that would be the primary science were there no eternal immovable substances separable from the natural ones. But there is also a trans-generic—or universal—mathematical science (*Met.* 6.1.1026^{a}13–23). And the introduction of intelligible matter (7.10.1036^{a}11–12), as the matter of abstract mathematical objects, allows us to see a commonality in explanatory structure between the mathematical sciences and the natural ones. Between these two trans-generic sciences and the theological one (6.1.1026^{a}19), on the other hand,

2. (1) "Another way is to select by analogy. For it is impossible to take one identical thing that cuttlefish bone, fish spine, and animal bone must be called; but there will be things that follow these too, just as if there were some single nature of this sort" (*APo.* 2.4.91^{a}20–24). (2) "As for the underlying nature, it is scientifically knowable by analogy" (*Ph.* 1.7.191^{a}8–9).

the point of commonality lies not in matter, since the objects of theological science have no matter (12.6.1071[b]20–21), but rather in form. For what the objects of theology, divine substances (which includes human understanding or *nous*), have in common with those of mathematics and natural science is that they are forms, though—and this is the crucial point of difference—not forms in any sort of matter whatever. That form should be a focal topic of investigation for the science of being qua being is thus the result of an inductive or empirical investigation of the various first-order sciences, and then of the various trans-generic ones, which shows form to be the explanatory feature common to all their objects—to all beings.

It is this empirical fact that provides the science of being qua being with a genuine trans-generic object of study, thereby legitimating it as every bit as much a science as any generic-specific one. The science of being qua being is accordingly a science of form. The question now is, How can that science at the same time be theology, the science of divine substance? And to it Aristotle gives a succinct answer:

> We might raise a puzzle indeed as to whether the primary philosophy is universal or concerned with a particular genus and one particular nature; for it is not the same way even in the mathematical sciences but rather geometry and astronomy are concerned with a particular nature, whereas universal mathematics is common to all. If, then, there is no other substance beyond those composed by nature, natural science will be the primary science. But if there is some immovable substance, this [that is, theological philosophy] will be prior and will be primary philosophy, and it will be universal in this way, namely, because it is primary. And it will belong to it to get a theoretical grasp on being qua being, both what it is and the things that belong to it qua being. (*Met.* 5.1.1026[a]23–32)

So the primacy of theology, which is based on the fact that theology deals with substance that is eternal, immovable, and separable, is supposedly what justifies us in treating it as the universal science of being qua being.

To get a handle on what this primacy is, we need to turn to being and its structure. The first thing to grasp is that beings are divided into categories: substance, quality, quantity, relation, and so on. But of these, only beings in the category of substance are separable, so that they alone enjoy a sort of ontological priority that is both existential and explanatory (*Met.* 7.1.1028[a]31–[b]2). Other beings are affections of different sorts, which exist only by belonging to some substance. So if we want to explain what a quality is, for example, we have to say what sort of affection it is, and ultimately what in a substance is receptive of it. It is this fact that gives one sort of unity to beings: they are all either substances or affections of substances. Hence the famous claim which ends *Met.* 7.1:

> Indeed, the question that was asked long ago, is now, and always will be asked, and is always raising puzzles—namely, What is being?—is just the question, What is substance? . . . And that is why we too must most of all, primarily, and (one might almost say) exclusively get a theoretical grasp on what it is that is a being in this [substantial] way. (1028^{b}2–7)

The starting-points and causes of beings qua beings must, then, be substances. Thus while something is said to be in as many ways as there are categories, they are all so said "with reference to one thing and one nature" (*Met.* 4.2.1003^{a}33–34)—substance. It could still be the case, of course, that the cosmos is episodic like a bad tragedy, made up of lots of separate substances having little ontologically to do with one another, but the number of episodes has at least been systematically reduced.

Before turning to the next phase in being's unification, we need to look more closely at substance itself as it gets investigated and analyzed in *Metaphysics* 7–9. The analysis begins with a list of things that have a claim to being substance:

> Something is said to be substance, if not in more ways, at any rate, most of all in four; for the essence, the universal, and the genus seem to be the substance of each thing, and fourth of these, the underlying subject. (*Met.* 7.3.1028^{b}33–36)

But since "the primary underlying subject seems most of all to be substance" (7.3.1029^{a}1–2), because what is said or predicated of it depends on it, the investigation begins with this subject, quickly isolating three candidates: the matter, the compound of matter and form, and the form itself (1029^{a}2–3), which is identical to the essence (7.7.1032^{b}1–2). Almost as quickly (7.3.1029^{a}7–32), the first two candidates are at least provisionally excluded, leaving form alone as the most promising candidate for being substance. But form is "most puzzling" (1029^{a}33) and requires extraordinary ingenuity to explore.

Aristotle begins the investigation into it with the most familiar and widely recognized case, which is the form or essence present in the sublunary matter-form compounds that we see around us. This investigation is announced in *Metaphysics* 7.3.1029^{b}3–12, but not begun till some chapters later and not really completed till the end of 9.5. By then the various other candidates for being substance have been eliminated or reconceived, and actuality and potentiality have come to prominence. Hence in 9.6 it is with actuality or activity—*entelecheia* or *energeia*—that form, and so substance, is identified, and matter with potentiality.

Precisely because actuality and potentiality are the ultimate explanatory factors, however, they themselves cannot be given an explanatory definition in yet more basic terms. Instead, we must grasp them by means of an analogy:

> What we wish to say is clear from the particular cases by induction, and we must not look for a definition of everything, but be able to comprehend the analogy, namely, that as what is building is in relation to what is capable of building, and what is awake is in relation to what is asleep, and what is seeing is in relation to what has its eyes closed but has sight, and what has been shaped out of the matter is in relation to the matter, and what has been finished off is to the unfinished. Of the difference exemplified in this analogy let the activity be marked off by the first part, the potentiality by the second. (*Met.* 9.6.1048^{a}35–^{b}6)

What is common to matter-form compounds, mathematical objects, and divine substances, then, is actuality. In the case of matter-form compounds and numbers, the actuality is accompanied by potentiality—perceptual sublunary matter in the first case, intelligible matter in the second. In the case of divine substances and other such unmoved movers, it is not. They are "pure" activities or actualities, wholly actual at each moment. Matter-form compounds, by contrast, are never wholly actual—they are always in some way potential. You are actively reading this now, not actively swimming, but you could be swimming, since you have the presently un-activated capacity (or potentiality) to swim.

The science of being qua being can legitimately focus on form, or actuality, as the factor common to divine substances, matter-form compounds, and mathematical objects. But unless it can be shown that there is some explanatory connection between the forms in these different beings, the non-episodic nature of being itself will still not have been established, and the pictures given to us by the natural, mathematical, and theological sciences will, so to speak, be separate pictures, and the being they collectively portray will be divided.

The next stage in the unification of being and the legitimation of the science dealing with it qua being is effected by an argument that trades, unsurprisingly, on the identification of form and matter with actuality and potentiality. Part of the argument is given in *Metaphysics* 9.8–9, where the various sorts of priority requisite in a substance are argued to belong to actuality rather than to potentiality. But it is in *Metaphysics* 12.6 that the pertinent consequences are most decisively drawn:

> If there is something that is capable of moving things or acting on them, but that is not actively doing so, there will not [necessarily] be movement, since it is possible for what has a capacity not to activate it. There is no benefit, therefore, in positing eternal substances, as those who accept the Forms do, unless there is to be present in them some starting-point that is capable of causing change. Moreover, even this is not enough, and neither is another substance beyond the Forms. For if it will not be active, there will not be movement. Further, even if it will be active, it is not enough, if the substance of it is a capacity. For then there will not be *eternal* movement; for what is potentially may possibly not be. There must, therefore, be such a starting-point, the very substance of which is activity. Further, accordingly, these substances must be without matter; for they must be eternal, if indeed *anything* else is eternal. Therefore, they must be activity. (1071^{b}12–22)

Matter-form compounds are, as such, capable of movement and change. The canonical examples of them—perhaps the only genuine or fully fledged ones—are living metabolizing beings (*Met.* 7.17.1041^{b}29–30). But if these beings are to be actual, there must be substances whose very essence is activity—substances that do not need to be activated by something else.

With matter-form compounds shown to be dependent on substantial activities for their actual being, a further element of vertical unification is introduced into beings, since layer-wise the two sorts of substances belong together. Laterally, though, disunity continues to threaten. For as yet nothing has been done to exclude the possibility that each compound substance has a distinct substantial activity as its own unique activator. Being, in that case, would be a set of ordered pairs, the first member of which would be a substantial activity, the second a matter-form compound, with all its dependent affections.

In *Metaphysics* 12.8 Aristotle initially takes a step in the direction of such a bipartite picture. He asks how many substantial activities are required to explain astronomical phenomena, such as the movements of the stars and planets, and answers that there must be forty-nine of them (1074^{a}16). But these forty-nine are visibly coordinated with each other so as to form a system. And what enables them to do so, and constitute a single heaven, is that there is a single primary (or "prime") mover of all of them:

> That there is but one heaven is evident. For if there are many, as there are many humans, the starting-point for each will be one in form but in number many. But all things that are many in number have matter, for one and the same account applies to many, for example, humans, whereas Socrates is one. But the primary essence does not have matter; for it is an actuality. The primary immovable mover, therefore, is one both in account and in number. And so, therefore, is what is moved always and continuously. Therefore, there is only one heaven. (*Met.* 12.8.1074^{a}31–38)

The argument is puzzling, to be sure, since the immateriality that insures the uniqueness of the primary mover would seem to threaten the multiplicity of the forty-nine movers, since they are also immaterial; nonetheless, the point of it is clear enough: what accounts for the unity of the heaven is that the movements in it are traceable back to a single cause—the primary mover.

It is tempting to follow in Aristotle's footsteps at this point and discuss the nature of the primary mover—how he moves the primary heaven in the way, described by Dante, that an unmoved object of love or desire moves an animate being, so that the primary heaven, and the others as well, must all be animate beings in order to be so moved, and why it is that he must be a cosmic understanding that has understanding itself as its sole object. But it is better for present purposes to stick to our topic and look at the next phase in the unification of beings, in which the sublunary world is integrated with the already unified superlunary one studied by astronomy.

This takes place in *Metaphysics* 12.10, although elements of it have emerged earlier. One obvious indication of this unification is the dependence of the reproductive cycles of plants and animals on the seasons, and their dependence, in turn, on the movements of the sun and moon:

> The cause of a human is both his elements, fire and earth as matter and the special form [as form], and furthermore some other external thing, such as the father, and beyond these the sun and its movement in an inclined circle. (*Met.* 12.5.1071^{a}13–16)

And beyond even that there is the unity of the natural world itself, which is manifested in the ways in which its inhabitants are adapted to each other (*Met.* 12.10.1075^{a}16–25). Just how much unity all this results in—just what it means to speak of "the nature of the whole" (1075^{a}11) or of the universe as having "one ruler" (1076^{a}4)—is a matter of dispute. The fact remains, though, that the sublunary realm is sufficiently integrated with the superlunary one so that we can speak of them as jointly having a nature and a ruler and as being analogous not to Heraclitus' "heap of random sweepings," but to an army (1075^a13) and a household (1075^a22).

We may agree, then, that the divine substances in the superlunary realm and the compound substances in the sublunary one have prima facie been vertically integrated into a single explanatory system. When we look at the form of a sublunary matter-form compound, then, we will find in it the mark of a superlunary activator, just as we do in the case of the various heavenly bodies, and, as in the line of its efficient causes, we find "the sun and its movement in an inclined circle" (*Met.* 12.5.1071^a15–16). Still awaiting integration, though, are the mathematical objects, and their next of kin, Platonic Forms.

That there is mathematical structure present in the universe can seem to be especially clear in the case of the superlunary realm, just as mathematics itself, with its rigorous demonstrations and necessary and certain truths, can seem the very paradigm of scientific knowledge. So it is hardly surprising that some of Aristotle's predecessors, especially Pythagoreans and Platonists, thought that the primary causes and starting-points of beings are to be found in the part of reality that is mathematics friendly, or in some way mathematizable. For example, some Platonists (Plato among them, in Aristotle's much disputed view) held that for each kind of sublunary (or perceptible) thing there was an eternal intelligible Form to which it owed its being, and which owed its own being, in turn, to "the one," as its substance, and the so-called indefinite dyad of the great and the small, as its matter. So when we ask what makes a man a man, the answer will be because it participates in the Form of a man, which owes its being to the way it is constructed or generated from the indefinite dyad and the one. And because the Forms are so constructed, Aristotle says (anyway, on one reading of the text) that "the Forms are the numbers" (*Met.* 1.6.987^b20–22). Between these so-called Form numbers, in addition, are the numbers that are the objects of mathematics: the intermediates. This elaborate system of, as I put it, mathematics-friendly objects, then, are the substances—the ultimate starting-points and causes of beings qua beings.

Against these objects and the ontological role assigned to them, Aristotle launches a host of arguments (thirty-two or so in *Metaphysics* 1.9, twenty-four in 13.8–9, and many others elsewhere), proposing in their place an entirely different account of mathematical objects, which treats them not as substantial starting-points and causes but as abstractions from perceptible sublunary beings—dependent entities, in other words, rather than self-subsistent or intrinsic ones (*Met.* 13.2–3). This completes the vertical and horizontal unification of being: affections depend on substances, substantial matter-form compounds depend on substantial forms, or activities, and numbers depend on substances.

Beings are not said to be in accord with one thing, then, as they would be if they formed a single genus, but with reference to one thing—namely, a divine substance that is in essence an activity. And it is this more complex unity—compatible with generic diversity and a genuine multiplicity of distinct first-order sciences, but just as robust and well-grounded as the simpler genus-based sort of unity—that grounds and legitimates the science of being qua being as a single science dealing with a genuine object of study (*Met.* 4.2.1003^{b}11–16). The long argument that leads to this conclusion is thus a sort of existence proof of the science on which the *Metaphysics* focuses.

It is the priority of a divine substance, with that science as *its* science, that justifies each of the following descriptions of what the *Metaphysics* is about:

> If, then, there is no other substance beyond those composed by nature, natural science will be the primary science. But if there is some immovable substance, this [that is, theological philosophy] will be prior and will be primary philosophy, and it will be universal in this way, namely, because it is primary. And it will belong to it to get a theoretical grasp on being qua being, both what it is and the things that belong to it qua being. (*Met.* 6.1.1026^{a}27–32)

> Whether there is, beyond the matter of these sorts of substances, another sort of matter, and whether to look for another sort of substance, such as numbers or something of this sort, must be investigated later. For it is for the sake of this that we are trying to make some determinations about the perceptible substances, since in a certain way it is the function of natural science and secondary philosophy to have theoretical knowledge about the perceptible substances. (*Met.* 7.11.1037^{a}10–16)

> Since we have spoken about the capacity [or potentiality] that is said [of things] with reference to movement, let us make some distinctions concerning activity, both concerning what it is and what sort of thing it is. For the capable too will at the same time become clear as we make our determinations, because we do not say only of that which naturally moves something else, or is moved by something else, that it is capable, whether unconditionally or in a certain way, but also use the term in a different way, which is why in the course of our inquiry we went through the former. (*Met.* 9.6.1048^{a}25–30)

> Concerning the primary starting-points and the primary causes and elements, however, some of what is said by those who speak only about perceptible substance has been discussed in our works on nature, while some does not belong to the present methodical inquiry. But what is said by those who assert that there are other substances beyond the perceptible ones is something we need to get a theoretical grasp on next after what we have just discussed. (*Met.* 13.9.1086^{a}21–26)

The science of being qua being is a sort of theology, as *Metaphysics* 1.2 already told us it was, but it is a sort of theology only because of the special role of the primary god among beings.

Is the Investigation in the Metaphysics *a Scientific One?*

If we think of a science in the exact sense as consisting exclusively of what is demonstrable, as Aristotle himself sometimes does, as we saw, we will be right to conclude that a treatise without demonstrations cannot be scientific. But if, as he also does, we include knowledge of starting-points as part of science, we will not be right, since a treatise could contribute to a science not by demonstrating anything but by arguing to the starting-points themselves—an enterprise which couldn't without circularity consist of demonstrations *from* those starting-points. Arguments leading from starting-points and arguments leading to starting-points are different, we are invited not to forget (*NE* 1.4.1095^{a}30–32), just as we are told that because establishing starting-points is "more than half the whole" (1.7.1098^{b}7), we should "make very serious efforts to define them correctly" (1098^{b}5–6). We might reasonably infer, therefore, that the *Metaphysics* is a contribution to theology precisely because it contributes to the correct definition and secure grasp on starting-points without which no science can exist.

In our investigation of starting-points, "we must," Aristotle says, "start from things known *to us*" (*NE* 1.4.1095^{b}3–4). For the sake of clarity, let us call these *raw* starting-points. These are the ones we start from when we are arguing to *explanatory* starting-points. It is important not to confuse the two—especially when, as in the *Metaphysics*, the raw starting-points are in part the result of the sort of meta-level induction carried out on the various first-order sciences we looked at earlier and in part the result of a critical investigation of the views of other philosophers on the nature of the starting-points of such sciences (as, for example, in *Met.* 1.3–10).

In the case of the first-order sciences, the explanatory starting-points include, in particular, definitions that specify the genus and differentiae of the real (as opposed to nominal) universal essences of the beings with which the science deals (*APo.* 2.10.93^{b}29–94^{a}19). Since scientific definitions must be apt starting-points of demonstrations, this implies, Aristotle thinks, that the "extremes and the middle terms must come from the same genus" (1.7.75^{b}10–11). As a result a single canonical science must deal with a single genus (1.28.87^{a}38–39). To reach these definitions from raw starting-points, we first have to have the raw starting-points ready at hand. Aristotle is clear about this, as he is indeed about what is supposed to happen next:

> The method (*hodos*) is the same in all cases, in philosophy as well as in the crafts or any sort of learning whatever. For one must observe for both terms what belongs to them and what they belong to, and be supplied with as many of these terms as possible, and one must investigate them by means of the three terms [in a syllogism], in one way when refuting, in another way when establishing something. When it is in accord with truth, it must be from the terms that are cataloged as truly belonging, but in dialectical deductions it must be from premises that are in accord with [reputable] belief. . . . Most of the starting-points, however, are special to each science. That is why experience must provide us with the starting-points where each is concerned—I mean, for example, that experience in astronomy must do so in the case of astronomical science. For when the appearances had been adequately grasped, the demonstrations in astronomy were found in the way we described. And it is the same way where any other craft or science whatever is concerned. Hence if what belongs to each thing has been grasped, at that point we can readily exhibit the demonstrations. For if nothing that truly belongs to the relevant things has been omitted from the collection, then concerning everything, if a demonstration of it exists, we will be able to find it and give the demonstration, and if it is by nature indemonstrable, we will be able to make that evident. (*APr.* 1.30.46^{a}3–27)

Once we have a catalog of the *raw* starting-points, then, the demonstrative explanation of them from explanatory scientific starting-points is supposedly fairly routine. We should not, however, demand "the cause [or explanation] in all cases alike. Rather, in some it will be adequate if the fact that they are so has been correctly proved as it is indeed where starting-points are concerned" (*NE* 1.8.1098^{a}33–^{b}2). But what exactly is it to prove a starting-point correctly or adequately?

Aristotle describes theology as a branch of theoretical philosophy (*Met.* 6.1.1026^{a}18–19, 30–32) or theoretical science (11.7.1064^{b}1–3), and to the explanatory scientific starting-points of philosophical sciences, he claims, there is a unique route:

> Dialectic is useful in the philosophical sciences because the capacity to go through the puzzles on both sides of a question will make it easier to discern what is true and what is false in each. Furthermore, dialectic is useful in relation to the primary [starting-points] in each science. For it is impossible to say anything about these based on the starting-points properly belonging to the science in question, since these starting-points are, of all of them, the primary ones, and it is through reputable beliefs (*endoxa*) about each that it is necessary to discuss them. This, though, is a task special to, or most characteristic of, dialectic. For because of its ability to examine, it has a route toward the starting-points of all methodical inquiries. (*Top.* 1.2.101^{a}34–^{b}4)

Prima facie, then, the *Metaphysics* should correctly prove the explanatory starting-points of the science of being qua being by going through puzzles and solving these by appeal to reputable beliefs. But before we rush to the *Metaphysics* to see whether that is what we do find, we need to be clearer about what exactly we should be looking for.

Dialectic is recognizably a descendant of the Socratic elenchus, which famously begins with a question like this: What is (*ti esti*) piety? The respondent, sometimes after a bit of nudging, comes up with a universal definition: piety is what all the gods love, or whatever it might be. Socrates then puts this definition to the test by drawing attention to some things that seem true to the respondent himself but which conflict with his definition. The puzzle or *aporia* that results from this conflict then remains for the respondent to try to solve, usually by reformulating or rejecting his definition. Aristotle understood this process in terms that show its relationship to his own:

> Socrates, on the other hand, busied himself about the virtues of character, and in connection with them was the first to inquire about universal definition. . . . It was reasonable, though, that Socrates was inquiring into the what-it-is. For he was inquiring in order to deduce, and the what-it-is is a starting-point of deductions. For at that time there was not yet the strength in dialectic that enables people, even separately from the what-it-is, to investigate contraries, and whether the same science is a

> science of contraries; for there are two things that may be fairly ascribed to Socrates—inductive arguments and universal definition, both of which are concerned with a starting-point of scientific knowledge. (*Met.* 13.4.1078^{b}17–30; also 1.6.987^{b}1–4)

In Plato too dialectic is primarily concerned with scientific starting-points, such as those of mathematics, and seems to consist in some sort of elenchus-like process of reformulating definitions in the face of conflicting evidence so as to render them puzzle-free (*Republic* 532a–533d). Aristotle can reasonably be seen, then, as continuing a line of thought about dialectic, while contributing greatly to its exploration, systemization, and elaboration.

Consider now the respondent's first answer, his first definition: piety is what the gods love. Although it is soon shown to be incorrect, there is something quite remarkable about its very existence. Through experience shaped by acculturation and habituation involving the learning of a natural language, the respondent is confident that he can say what piety is. He has learned to apply the word "pious" to particular people, actions, and so on correctly enough to pass muster as knowing its meaning, knowing how to use it. From these particular cases he has reached a putative universal, something the particular cases have in common. But when he tries to define that universal in words, he gets it wrong, as Socrates shows. Here is Aristotle registering the significance of this:

> The things that are knowable and primary for particular groups of people are often only slightly knowable and have little or nothing of the being in them. Nonetheless, beginning from things that are poorly known but known to ourselves, we must try to know the ones that are wholly knowable, proceeding, as has just been said, through the former. (*Met.* 7.3.1029^{b}8–12)

The route by which the respondent reaches the universal that he is unable to define correctly is what Aristotle calls "induction (*epagôgê*)." This begins with (1) perception of particulars, which leads to (2) retention of perceptual contents in memory, and, when many such contents have been retained, to (3) an experience, so that for the first time "there is a universal in the soul" (*APo.* 2.19.100^{a}16). The universal reached at stage (3), which is the one the respondent reaches, is described as "indefinite" and "better known by perception" (*Ph.* 1.1.184^{a}22–25). It is the sort of universal, often quite complex, that constitutes a nominal essence corresponding to the nominal definition or meaning of a general term. Finally, (4) from experience come craft knowledge and scientific knowledge, when "from many intelligible objects belonging to experience, one universal supposition about similar things comes about" (*Met.* 1.1.981^{a}5–7).

The nominal (or analytic, meaning-based) definition of the general term "thunder," for example, might pick out the universal *loud noise in the clouds.* When science investigates the things that have this nominal essence, it may find that they also have a real essence or nature in terms of which their other features can be scientifically explained:

> Since a definition is said to be an account of what something is, it is evident that one sort will be an account of what its name, or some other name-like account, signifies—for example, what triangle signifies. . . . Another sort of definition is an account that makes clear why it exists. So the former sort signifies something but does not prove it, whereas the latter will evidently be like a demonstration of what it is, differing in arrangement from a demonstration. For there is a difference between saying why it thunders and saying what thunder is. In the first case you will say: because fire is being extinguished in the clouds. And what is thunder? The loud noise of fire being extinguished in the clouds. Hence the same account is given in different ways. In one way it is a continuous demonstration, in the other a definition. Further, a definition of thunder is a noise in the clouds, and this is a conclusion of the demonstration of what it is. The definition of an immediate item, though, is an indemonstrable positing (*thesis*) of what it is. (*APo.* 2.10.93^{b}29–94^{a}10)

A real (or synthetic, fact-based) definition that analyzes this real essence into its "elements and starting-points" (*Ph.* 1.1.184^{a}23), which will be definable but indemonstrable within the science, makes intrinsically clear what the nominal definition made clear to us only by enabling us to recognize instances of thunder in a fairly—but imperfectly—reliable way. As a result, thunder itself, now clearly a natural and not just a conventional kind, becomes better known not just to us but entirely or unconditionally. These analyzed universals, which are the sort reached at stage (4), are the ones suited to serve as starting-points of the sciences and crafts: "experienced people know the that but do not know the why, whereas craftsmen know the why, that is, the cause" (*Met.* 1.1.981^{a}28–30).

Socrates too, we see, wanted definitions that were not just empirically adequate but also explanatory: in telling Euthyphro what he wants in the case of piety, he says that he is seeking "the Form itself *in virtue of which* all the pieties are pieties" (Plato, *Euthyphro* 6d10–11). That is why he rejects the definition of piety as being what all the gods love. This definition is in one way correct, presumably, in that if something is pious it is necessarily loved by the gods and vice versa, but it isn't explanatory, since it doesn't tell us what it is about pious things that makes all the gods love them, and so does not identify the Form in virtue of which they are pious (9e–11b).

Let us go back. We wanted to know what was involved in proving a scientific starting-point. We were told how we could *not* do this, namely, by demonstrating it from scientific starting-points. Next we learned that dialectic had a route to it from reputable beliefs. At the same time, we were told that induction had a route to it as well—something the *Nicomachean Ethics* also tells us: "we get a theoretical grasp on some starting-points through induction, some through perception, some through some sort of habituation, and others through other means" (1.7.1098^{b}3–4). This suggests that induction and dialectic are in some way or other the same process.

What shows a Socratic respondent to be wrong is an example that his definition does not fit. The presentation of the example might be quite indirect, however. It might take quite a bit of stage setting, elicited by the asking of many questions, to bring out a puzzle. But if it does succeed in doing so, it shows that the universal grasped by the respondent and the definition of it produced by him are not entirely or unconditionally knowable and that his state is not one of clear-eyed understanding:

> A puzzle in thought makes manifest a knot in the subject matter. For insofar as thought is puzzled it is like people who are tied up, since in both cases it is impossible to move forward. That is why we must get a theoretical grasp on all the difficulties beforehand, both for these reasons and because those who inquire without first going through the puzzles are like people who do not know where they have to go. And, in addition, a person [who has not already grasped the puzzles] does not even know whether he has found what he is inquiring into. For to someone like that the end is not clear, whereas to a person who has already grasped the puzzles it is clear. (*Met.* 3.1.995^{a}30–^{b}2)

But lack of such clear-eyed understanding of a scientific starting-point has serious downstream consequences:

> Anyone who, on the other hand, is going to have scientific knowledge through demonstration must not only know the starting-points more and be more persuaded of them than of what is being proved, but also there must be nothing else more persuasive or more known to him among the opposites of the starting-points from which there will be a deduction of

> the contrary error, if indeed anyone who has unconditional scientific knowledge must be incapable of being persuaded out of it. (*APo.* 1.2.72^{a}37–^{b}4)

If dialectical examination brings to light a puzzle in a respondent's thought about a scientific starting-point, then he cannot have any unconditional scientific knowledge even of what he may well be able to demonstrate correctly from it. Contrariwise, if dialectical examination brings to light no such puzzle, he apparently does have clear-eyed understanding, and his route to what he can demonstrate is free of obstacles.

At the heart of dialectic, as Aristotle understands it, is the dialectical deduction (*dialektikos sullogismos*). This is the argument lying behind the questioner's questions, partly dictating their order and content and partly determining the strategy of his examination. In the following passage it is defined and contrasted with two relevant others:

> Dialectical arguments are those that deduce a contradiction from reputable beliefs; examinational ones are those that deduce one from things that seem so to the answerer and that it is necessary for the one who pretends to possess the relevant science to know (in what way has been determined elsewhere); contentious ones are those that deduce or appear to deduce one from what appear to be reputable beliefs, but are not. (*SE* 2.165^{b}3–8)

If we think of dialectical deductions in this way, a dialectician, in contrast to a contender, is an honest questioner, appealing to genuinely reputable beliefs and employing valid deductions. "The arguments of disputatious people and sophists are the same," Aristotle says, "but are not for the sake of the same things: rather, if it is for the sake of apparent victory, it is contentious, if for the sake of apparent wisdom, it is sophistical" (*SE* 11.171^{b}27–29). Nonetheless, Aristotle does also use the term *dialektikê* as the name for the craft that honest dialecticians and sophists both use:

> In dialectic a sophist is so called in virtue of his deliberate choice, and a dialectician is so called not in virtue of his deliberate choice, but in virtue of the capacity he has. (*Rh.* 1.1.1355^{b}20–21)

If dialectic is understood in this way, a dialectician who deliberately chooses to employ contentious arguments is a sophist (1.1.1355^{a}24–^{b}7). We need to be careful, therefore, to distinguish *honest* dialectic from what we may call *plain* dialectic, which—like all crafts—can be used for good or ill (*NE* 5.1.1129^{a}13–17).

The canonical occasion for the practice of the Socratic elenchus, obviously, is the examination of someone else. But there is nothing to prevent a person from practicing it on himself: "How could you think," Socrates asks Critias, "that I would refute you for any reason other than the one for which I would refute myself, fearing lest I might inadvertently think I know something when I don't know it?" (Plato, *Charmides* 166c–d). Dialectic is no different in this regard:

> The philosopher, who is investigating by himself, does not care whether, though the things through which his deduction proceeds are true and knowable, the answerer does not grant them (because they are close to what was proposed at the start, and he foresees what is going to result), but rather is presumably eager for his claims to be as knowable and as close to it as possible. For it is from things of this sort that scientific deductions proceed. (*Top.* 8.1.155^{b}10–16)

What we are to imagine, then, is that the philosopher surveys the raw scientific starting-points, constructing detailed catalogs of these. He then tries to formulate definitions of the various universals involved in them that seem to be candidate scientific starting-points, testing these against the raw scientific starting-points by trying to construct demonstrations from them. But these definitions will often be no more than partial: the philosopher is only on his way to complete definitional starting-points, just as the demonstrations will often be no more than proto- or nascent demonstrations. The often rudimentary demonstrations that we find in Aristotle's scientific treatises are surely parts of this process of arguing *to* not *from* starting-points. We argue to these in part by seeing whether or to what extent we could demonstrate from them.

So: First, we have the important distinction between dialectic proper, which includes the use of what appear to be deductions from what appear to be reputable beliefs, and honest dialectic, which uses only genuine deductions from genuine reputable beliefs. Second, we have the equally important distinction between the use of dialectic in examining a potentially hostile respondent and its use by the philosopher in a perhaps private pursuit of the truth. Third, we have an important contrast between honest dialectical premises and philosophical ones or scientific ones: honest dialectical premises are reputable beliefs, philosophical and scientific premises must be true and knowable. Fourth, we have two apparently equivalent routes to scientific starting-points: one inductive, which starts from *raw* starting-points, and the other dialectic, which starts from reputable beliefs.

According to the official definition, reputable beliefs are "things that are believed by everyone, by the majority, or by the wise—either by all of them, or by most, or by the most well known and most reputable" (*Top.* 1.1.100^{b}21–23). Just as the scientist should have a catalog of scientific truths ready to hand from which to select the premises of his demonstrations, so a dialectician ought also to select premises "from arguments that have been written down and produce catalogs of them concerning each kind of subject, putting them under separate headings—for example, 'Concerned with good,' 'Concerned with life'" (1.14.105^{b}12–15).

Clearly, then, there will be considerable overlap between the scientist's catalog of raw starting-points and the honest dialectician's catalog of reputable beliefs. For, first, things that are believed by reputably wise people are themselves reputable beliefs, and, second, any respondent would accept "the things believed by those who have investigated these crafts—for example, a doctor about issues in medicine, or a geometer about those in geometry, and similarly in other cases" (*Top.* 1.10.104^{a}8–37). The catalogs also differ, however, in that not all reputable beliefs need be true. If a proposition is a reputable belief, if it would be accepted by all or most people, it is everything an honest dialectician could ask for in a premise, since his goal is simply this: to show by honest deductions that a definition offered by any respondent whatever conflicts—if it does—with other beliefs the respondent has. That is why having a complete or fairly complete catalog of reputable beliefs is such an important resource for a dialectician. It is because dialectic deals with things only "in relation to belief," then, and not as philosophy and science do, "in relation to truth" (1.14.105^{b}30–31), that it needs nothing more than reputable *beliefs*.

Nonetheless, the fact that all or most people believe something leads us "to trust it as something in accord with experience" (*Div. Somn.* 1.462^{b}14–16), and—since human beings "are naturally adequate as regards the truth and for the most part happen upon it" (*Rh.* 1.1.1355^{a}15–17)—as containing some truth. That is why, having cataloged some of the things that people believe happiness to be, Aristotle writes:

> Some of these views are held by many and are of long standing, while others are held by a few reputable men. And it is not reasonable to suppose that either group is entirely wrong, but rather that they are right on one point at least or even on most of them. (*NE* 1.8.1098^{b}27–29)

Later he generalizes the claim: "things that seem to be so to everyone, these, we say, *are*" (*NE* 10.2.1172^{b}36–1173^{a}1). Raw starting-points are just that—raw. But when refined some shred of truth is likely to be found in them.

So likely, indeed, that if none is found, this will itself be a surprising fact needing to be explained: "when a reasonable explanation is given of why an untrue view appears true, this makes us more persuaded of the true view" (7.14.1154^{a}24–25). It is the grain of truth enclosed in a reputable belief that a philosopher or scientist is interested in, then, not in the general acceptability of the surrounding husk, much of which he may discard.

The process of refinement in the case of a candidate explanatory starting-point is that of testing a definition of it against reputable beliefs. This may result in the definition being accepted as it stands or in its being altered or modified. The same process applies to the reputable beliefs themselves, since they may conflict not only with the definition but also with each other. Again, this may result in their being modified, often by uncovering ambiguities within them or in the argument supporting them, or by drawing distinctions that uncover complexities in these, or they may be rejected entirely, provided that their appearance of truth is explained away.

The canonical occasion for the use of honest dialectic, as of the Socratic elenchus and plain dialectic, is the examination of a respondent. The relevant premises for the questioner to use, therefore, are the reputable beliefs in his catalog that his respondent will accept. Just how wide this set of beliefs is in a given case depends naturally on how accessible the subject matter on which he is being examined is to untrained respondents. We may all have some beliefs about thunder and other phenomena readily perceptible to everyone, which are—for that very reason—reputable. But about fundamental explanatory notions in an esoteric science we may have none at all.

When a scientist is investigating by himself, the class of premises he will select from is the catalog of *all* the raw starting-points of his science, despite a natural human inclination to do otherwise:

> [People] seem to inquire up to a certain point, but not as far as it is possible to take the puzzle. For it is customary for all of us to make our inquiry not with an eye to the thing at hand but with an eye to the person who says the contrary; for a person even inquires within himself up to the point at which he is no longer able to argue against himself. That is why a person who is going to inquire well must be capable of objecting by means of objections proper to the relevant genus, and this comes from having a theoretical grasp on all the differentiae. (*Cael.* 2.13.294^{b}6–13)

Hence a scientist will want to err on the side of excess, adding to his catalog any reputable belief that appears to have any relevance whatever. When he formulates definitions of candidate scientific starting-points from which he thinks he can demonstrate the raw ones, he must then examine himself to see whether he really does have the scientific knowledge of it that he thinks he does. If he is investigating together with fellow scientists, others may examine him: we all do better with the aid of co-workers (*NE* 10.7.1177^{a}34). What he is doing is using honest dialectic on himself or having it used on him. But this, we see, is little different from the final stage—stage (4)—of the induction we looked at earlier. Induction, as we might put it, is in its final stage (possibly self-directed) honest dialectic.

In a famous and much debated passage, Aristotle writes:

> We must, as in the other cases, set out the things that appear to be so, and first go through the puzzles, and, in that way, prove preferably all the reputable beliefs about these ways of being affected, or, if not all of them, then most of them and the ones with the most authority. For if the objections are resolved and the reputable beliefs are left standing, that would be an adequate proof. (*NE* 7.1.1145^{b}2–7)

The specific topic of the comment is "these ways of being affected," which are self-control and its lack as well as resilience and softness. Some people think that it applies only to this topic and should not be generalized, even though "as in the other cases" surely suggests a wider scope, as does this parallel text:

> We must try to make our investigation in such a way that the what-it-is is given an account of, so that the puzzles are resolved, the things that are believed to belong to place will in fact belong to it, and furthermore, so that the cause of the difficulty and of the puzzles concerning it will be evident, since this is the best way of proving each thing. (*Ph.* 4.4.211^{a}7–11)

In any case, as we can now see, that scope is in fact entirely general, since it describes the honest dialectical or inductive route to the starting-points of *all* the sciences and methods of inquiry, with *tithenai ta phainomena* ("setting out the things that appear to be so") describing the initial phase in which the raw starting-points are collected and cataloged.

Now that we know what it means for honest dialectic of the sort employed by the philosopher to provide a route to the explanatory starting-points of the philosophical sciences, we are in a position to see that it is precisely such a route that the *Metaphysics* takes to those of the science of being qua being. Since this route is the sort any science must take to prove its explanatory starting-points, the investigation undertaken in the

Metaphysics is a scientific one. It is not, to be sure, a demonstration from the starting-points of being qua being, but rather a proof of the starting-points themselves, which, if successful, allows us to achieve the sort of puzzle-free grasp on them that the primary god, without having to work through any of the puzzles that muddy our vision, has on the starting-point of everything—himself.

The scientific starting-points we have been discussing are those that, because they are special to a specific first-order science, are grounded in the first-order genus with which it deals. These are the ones that, because they are analogous to those of other first-order sciences, have more general higher-order versions grounded in higher-order genera, or categories. But there are other sorts of scientific starting-points, such as the principle of non-contradiction and other starting-points of demonstration, that all first-order sciences directly use, but that, precisely because they are not grounded in a first-order genus, none deals with (*Met.* 3.3.996^{b}26–997^{a}11). Similarly, there are the various affections that hold of all beings qua beings, rather than qua being members of a first-order genus, such as "prior and posterior, genus and species, whole and part, and others of this sort" (4.2.1005^{a}15–18). Each of these too must be defined in a way that resolves the puzzles to which they give rise. This work is largely of the sort that we would classify as conceptual. But this should not distract us from the fact that its results must be grounded, like those of mathematics, in empirical reality—in being itself considered qua being.

Aristotle's God and Ours

In many of the religions with which we are likely to be most familiar, a god (or if the religion is monotheistic—as I shall henceforth suppose it is—God) plays two roles, one cosmological and the other moral. God creates the world and judges people, rewarding the good and punishing the evil. The moral role, in turn, has consequences for what sorts of beings we are. If we are to be judged and either rewarded or punished, and this does not occur while we are alive here on earth, it must happen afterward, so that, unlike cats and dogs and other creatures, we must somehow survive our so-called death, now to be conceived as a sort of separation of our soul (the thing we most of all are) from our animal body. Moreover, the moral laws or standards in accord with which God will judge us stem either in whole or in part from him. Perhaps we could find out for ourselves why we should not lie, steal, or commit adultery, but that we should keep holy the sabbath day, and what doing so involves, or avoid certain foods or practices, is something we need to learn from God (see *Pol.* 7.12.1331^{a}24–30).

When we consider God's cosmological role, perhaps the main problems we confront are those of establishing his existence and how or why he creates a world like this one. Suppose, for example, we say that God created the world *ex nihilo*—out of nothing. Then we might wonder who or what created God. If some other being did, then the same question can be asked about that one. To stop this potentially infinite—and so non-explanatory—regress of creators, God must have a special ontological status: while the world only contingently exists, and so might not have existed, he must exist necessarily. He must be *causa sui*—a cause of himself.

Aristotle's primary god escapes this problem by—to put it this way—not needing to create anything, because the world or universe has no beginning in time. It is eternal both backward and forward, just as he himself is. He sustains the world by being, in the way we explored, the most primary of the primary substances, but he does not create anything either *ex nihilo* or in any other way.

Is the escape genuine, though, or simply posited? This is a hard question, but in most respects it seems to be an empirical one. If science tells us—as to some extent it does—that there could never not have been a physical universe of some sort, so that its existence is necessary and in need of no non-physical creator of the sort that God is conceived to be, our belief in that need stems from a false conception of the physical. In this respect, then, Aristotle would be closer to the truth about the world than creationism is. But if science leaves the question of the origin of the world open, so that, for all it has to tell us, it might have been created by God, although equally well it might have had some as yet unknown scientific explanation, then we should suspend judgment about its origin. Empirical questions require empirical answers. If we cannot find those answers, we are not simply free to import answers from some other source.

It might be responded that God's existence—indeed his necessary existence—can be established on strictly rational grounds, without any need for empirical support. The famous ontological argument of Saint Anselm of Canterbury (1033/4–1109 AD) might be taken to show as much. Anything that could be God must be omniscient, omnipotent, and omnibenevolent—all knowing, all powerful, and all good. He must be the best of all possible beings. That is just the definition of what it is to be a genuine god. Suppose that both A and B fit the definition, but that A exists while B does not. Then, B—the argument claims—cannot be God, since a god that does not exist is clearly a less perfect being than one that does exist. Therefore, A—as the most perfect being—*must* exist.

This argument has been much studied and reformulated, and indeed much reviled, but for present purposes, we have no need to reach any final conclusions as to its soundness. And the reason we do not stems from God's other role—his moral one. Here the major problems are threefold. The first is the so-called problem of evil. If a perfect God created the world, why is there so much evil in it? One might think to answer "because there are free human agents in the world, and they—the evil ones—are responsible for it." Again without wishing to settle matters in any final way, we might ask how human agents can possibly be responsible for natural disasters like earthquakes, volcanic eruptions, and destructive meteorites. We might also be puzzled as to why untrammeled freedom is so overwhelmingly valuable that a perfect God would endow us with it, knowing (since he is omniscient) the awful consequences. So even if a perfectly good god does exist, we are a long way short of having an explanation of why a world like ours does.

The second problem is that of the standards by which God will judge us. After all, there are many religions in the world, even many divergent denominations within what purports to be a single religion—within Christianity alone there are allegedly some 45,000 of these! Most of these religions represent God in ways that add to the thin conception of him at work in the ontological argument, and sometimes are positively inconsistent with it, making them in that regard idolatrous. So, again, even if a perfect God exists, that does not mean that our God—the God of our religion—is that one. But leaving the issue of idolatry aside we may focus instead on the important ways in which these religions, or denominations within a single religion, represent the laws—the moral principles—in accord with which God will judge us (if in the religion in question he is thought to do so). For example, Roman Catholicism regards male masturbation as a mortal sin; Anglicanism takes no view as to its sinfulness; and Methodism regards it as an important part of childhood and adolescent sexual development, not to be stigmatized. Even if we are confident that there is a god and that he will judge and reward or punish us, we might worry that the god we face may not be using the standard that we thought. The moral role of God, then, becomes more equivocal than—when looked at from within a particular religion—it might seem.

In this regard too, Aristotle's primary god might with some justification be thought to do better. For as we shall see—especially in Chapter 6—his role in our ethical lives is exactly like that of happiness, properly conceived. Indeed, he is, one might without much exaggeration say, true happiness personified. But that fact too is something that Aristotle thinks emerges from scientific study of the world and ourselves, and not from the revelations special to—and only accessible from within—a particular religion or denomination. Reason as embodied in empirical science leads us to Aristotle's god and explains his nature. He neither knows about nor keeps a record of our sins nor runs another world in which the good are rewarded and the evil punished. Virtue is its own reward, vice its own punishment. Happiness is something accessible in this world to those who seek it in the right way.

The third problem internal to the conception of God concerns the sorts of beings we are. Are we products of evolution, as Charles Darwin might be taken to have discovered we are, fated like other animals to die and be no more, or are we somehow eternal beings, souls, something more like God himself? How might we settle such a question? Are souls things that empirical science can investigate? Can we just see that we have one and that dogs do not? And even if we can somehow know that we have a soul, how can we know that our souls are immortal, and not things that themselves pass away and die? Are immortal souls also religious posits that vary from sect to sect, denomination to denomination? Rather than try to answer these large questions, let us instead notice that they diminish in significance if the god there actually is does not judge us, if virtue is its own reward, and if happiness is something we can have here. Aristotle's own complex view of the soul is explored in Chapter 4.

Our God is one to whom we can pray, not just in the sense of turning our minds and hearts toward him in worship and gratitude, but also in an intercessory way. We can ask God to help us, even to do what would otherwise be impossible by performing miracles on our behalf. Aristotle too sometimes speaks of prayer in something like this way, and in some of the texts included here tells us how to pray and what to pray for.[3] Since much can happen in Aristotle's world that is not necessitated by anything, but is a matter of luck or chance, or is determined by what we freely do, such prayers might amount to little more than wishes focused on such things, that are prayerful simply in that they acknowledge the reality of the divine order of things where necessity prevails. Perhaps their intercessory aura is no more than the unexorcised ghost of Greek popular religion with its pantheon of gods, ever ready to help or harm. In the absence of Aristotle's lost book *On Prayer*[4] (mentioned in F49), it is difficult to be entirely sure. But, in any case, in places where belief in God—or even in the Greek

3. *NE* 3.10.1118^{a}32–^{b}1, 5.1.1129^{b}1–6, *Pol.* 4.11.1295^{b}28–34 countenance intercessory prayer provided it is for the right sorts of things, none of which should be impossible (*Pol.* 7.4.1325^{b}35–1326^{a}5). In the fragment of his will, which ends our selection of texts, Aristotle tells us that he has prayed himself for the safety of Nicanor.

4. If indeed *Peri euchês*—and not *Peri eutuchês* (*On Good Luck*)—is its proper title.

pantheon, as traditionally conceived—is deeply entrenched, a knowledgeable politician or legislator, equipped with practical wisdom or political science, will have to know how best to accommodate that belief if he is to have any hope of success, just as he will have to know how best to work within an oligarchy or democracy, even if he himself does not agree with its goals and values.[5]

That point aside, the fact that in Aristotle's view we do live in a rationally ordered universe is, to put it this way, something to be grateful for, since it makes it possible for us to figure out how we might best live in harmony with the rational order of our larger world. For the understanding present in the primary god and the heavenly bodies exists in us as well, enabling us to discover and properly appreciate this order. Prayers can properly acknowledge that, and would be, strictly speaking, impious if—by ignorant intercession—they failed to do so.

The Audience for Theology

In the *Nicomachean Ethics*, Aristotle famously tells us that it is not a work for young or immature people, inexperienced in the practical matters with which it deals:

> But each person correctly judges the things he knows and is a good judge of these. Hence a person well educated in a given area is a good judge in that area, while a person well educated in all areas is an unconditionally good judge. That is why a young person is not a suitable audience for politics; for he has no experience of the actions of life, and the accounts are in accord with these and concerned with these. (*NE* 1.3.1094^{b}25–1095^{a}4)

It is less often recognized that he issues a similar warning in the *Metaphysics*, and that here, as in the *Nicomachean Ethics*, he makes being well educated a prerequisite:

5. Thus while someone who knows political science must know "what the best constitution is and what it would have to be like to be most of all in accord with our prayers, provided that no external impediments stand in its way," he must also know "which constitution is fitting for which cities. For achieving the best constitution is presumably impossible for many of them, and so neither the unconditionally best constitution nor the one that is best in the underlying circumstances should be neglected by the good legislator and true politician" (*Pol.* 4.1.1288^{b}23–27).

> That is why we should already have been well educated in what way to accept each argument, since it is absurd to look for scientific knowledge and for the way characteristic of scientific knowledge at the same time—and it is not easy to get hold of either. Accordingly, we should not demand the argumentative exactness of mathematics in all cases but only in the case of things that include no matter. (2.3.995^{a}12–16)

But whereas in the case of ethics and politics the relevant experience is practical, in theology—in the science of being qua being—it is theoretical. There we need experience in life. Here we need experience in the sciences. And in both we need the sort of training in honest dialectic, logic, and what we would call the "philosophy of science," for which the treatises in the so-called *Organon* (*Categories*, *De Interpretatione*, *Prior* and *Posterior Analytics*, *Topics*, and *Sophistical Refutations*) might serve—or might once have served—as a textbook.

There is much in these treatises, as in others, then, that readers of the *Metaphysics* are supposed to know already. When it is simply information or arguments that are at issue, notes can provide what we need. But there is more to being well educated than being well informed; we must also be the intellectual equivalent of morally virtuous.

When dialectic has done its testing of the opposing sides of a puzzle, we hear in the *Topics*, it "only remains to make a correct choice of one of them" (8.14.163^{b}11–12). And what enables us to make such a choice is the "naturally good disposition (*euphuia*)" that enables people to "discern correctly what is best by a correct love or hatred of what is set before them" (163^{b}15–16). The reference to "what is best" suggests that this disposition is the *euphuia* also referred to in the following passage:

> His seeking of the end in question is not self-chosen, rather, we must be born possessed of a sort of sight by which to discern correctly and choose what is truly good, and a person in whom this by nature operates correctly is naturally well disposed; for this is what is greatest and noblest and is not the sort of thing we can get from someone else or learn but the sort of thing whose condition at birth is the one in which it will later be possessed and, when it is naturally such as to be in a good and noble condition, will be the naturally good disposition (*euphuia*) in its complete and true form. (*NE* 3.5.1114^{b}5–12)

And that, in fact, is what the distinction between philosophy and sophistry, which uses all of plain dialectic's resources, might lead us to expect, since "philosophy differs from dialectic in the way its capacity is employed, and from sophistic in the life it deliberately chooses" (*Met.* 4.2.1004[b]23–25).

Now, a deliberate choice of how to live is at bottom a choice of an ultimate end or target for our life: "anyone capable of living in accord with his own deliberate choice should posit some target for living nobly, whether honor, reputation, wealth, or education, looking toward which he will do all his actions" (*EE* 1.2.1214[b]6–9). And what "teaches *correct* belief" about this end or target, thereby insuring that the deliberate choice of it is correct, is "natural or habituated virtue of character" (*NE* 7.8.1151[a]18–19). It is in this, we may infer, that the naturally good disposition under discussion consists. Hence if we possess it, and it has been properly developed by a good upbringing and education, when we hear from the *Nicomachean Ethics* that the starting-point it posits as the correct target for a human life is "activity of the soul in accord with virtue, and if there are more virtues than one, in accord with the best and most complete" (1.7.1098[a]16–18), we will accept it as true, and so strive to clear away the puzzles in such a way as to sustain its truth. If we do not possess it, we will reject this starting-point, so that in our choice between the conflicting sides of these puzzles, we will go for the wrong ones:

> The truth in practical matters must be judged from the works and the life; for these are what have the controlling vote. When we examine what has been previously said, then, it must be judged by bringing it to bear on the works and the life, and if it is in harmony with them, one must accept it, but if it clashes, one must suppose it mere words. (*NE* 10.8.1179[a]17–22)

In the *Rhetoric*, however, we learn of an apparently different sort of good natural disposition which might seem, from the company it keeps, to be an exclusively intellectual trait: "good natural disposition, good memory, readiness to learn, quick-wittedness . . . are all productive of good things" (1.6.1362[b]24–25). When it comes to solving dialectical problems bearing on "truth and knowledge," we might conclude, such an apparently intellectual good natural disposition is all we need, even if, when it comes to those bearing on "pursuit and avoidance" (*Top.* 1.11.104[b]1–2), we also need its apparently more ethical namesake. It would be a mistake, though, to rush to this conclusion. For the ultimate starting-point and cause that the *Metaphysics* finally uncovers, which is at once the active understanding of active understanding, the prime unmoved mover, and the primary god, is the ultimate starting-point and cause for beings qua beings—*all of them.* And that means that it is our ultimate starting-point and cause too.

When we look at our lives from the outside, so to speak, from the theoretical point of view, if the *Metaphysics* is right, we see something amazing, namely, that the heavenly bodies, those bright denizens of the starry heavens above, are living beings who, like us, are moved by a desire for the best good—for the primary god. When we view it from the inside, from that perspective from which "the truth in practical matters" can alone be discerned, the *Nicomachean Ethics* tells us that we will find that we are moved by the same thing—that as the good for the heavenly bodies consists in contemplating the primary god, so too does our happiness:

> The activity of a god, superior as it is in blessedness, will be contemplative. And the activity of humans, then, that is most akin to this would most bear the stamp of happiness. (*NE* 10.8.1178^{b}21–23)

But Aristotle's hand is tipped even within the *Metaphysics* itself:

> [Active understanding rather than receptive understanding] seems to be the divine thing that understanding possesses, and contemplation seems to be most pleasant and best. If, then, that good state [of activity], which we are sometimes in, the [primary] god is always in, that is a wondrous thing, and if to a higher degree, that is yet more wondrous. And this is his state. And life too certainly belongs to him; for the activity of understanding is life, his activity is that; and his intrinsic activity is life that is best and eternal. We say, then, that the god is a living being who is eternal and best, so that living and a continuous and everlasting eternity belong to the god, for this is the god. (12.7.1072^{b}22–30)

That is why "we should not, in accord with the makers of proverbs, 'think human things, since you are human' or 'think mortal things, since you are mortal' but rather we should as far as possible immortalize, and do everything to live in accord with the element in us that is most excellent" (*NE* 10.7.1177^{b}31–34), this being our understanding—our divine *nous*.

Aristotle arrives at this great synthesis of theory and practice, as we saw, on empirical grounds—by reflecting on, and drawing inductive conclusions from, the various sciences, theoretical, practical, and productive, as they existed in his day. He is not doing "armchair" metaphysics, or recording the tenets of a new religion to be accepted on faith, but drawing on his own vast knowledge of these sciences to reach a unified explanatory picture of being as such and our place in it as practical agents and theorizers.

If we followed in his footsteps, drawing on our sciences, from theoretical physics to engineering, economics, and ethics, what conclusions would we reach? If we are to be Aristotelians now it cannot be by parroting Aristotle's theories. Instead, it must be by taking him as a paradigm of how we might be philosophers and theologians ourselves—a "paradigm in the heavens," so to speak, "for anyone who wishes to look at it and to found himself on the basis of what he sees" (Plato, *Republic* 592b).

1. Early Intimations

De Interpretatione 4.17^{a}3–4

There is not truth or falsity in every sentence—for example, a prayer is a sentence but is neither true nor false.

De Interpretatione 13.23^{a}23–24

Some things are activities without potentialities—for example, the primary substances.[1]

Prior Analytics 1.36.48^{b}35–37

"The opportune time is not the time needed, for there is an opportune time for a god, but not a time needed, because nothing is needed for a god."[2]

Topics 1.11.105^{a}5–7

Those who puzzle over "whether one must honor the gods and love one's parents or not" need punishment, whereas those who puzzle over "whether snow is white or not" need perception.

---

1. See *Met.* 12.6.1071^{b}19–20.

2. A god has no needs, so he cannot be benefited by having his needs satisfied (compare *Top.* 2.2.109^{b}33–35 on harms). Not all good things, though, are good because they satisfy a need. What is opportune (*kairos*) is what is good in the category of time (*NE* 1.6.1096^{a}26–27). So the opportune time for a god to do something—e.g., rise at the natural time, in the case of Helios (the sun)—would be the good time to do so, since "what is in accord with nature is by nature in the noblest possible condition" (*NE* 1.9.1099^{b}21–22).

Topics 2.2.109b33–35

If the problem is whether it is possible to do injustice to a god, ask: "What is doing injustice?" For if it is to harm voluntarily, it is clear that it is not possible for a god to suffer injustice, since it is not possible to harm a god.

Topics 2.11.115b30–35

One will not say that it is noble to sacrifice one's father, but rather that for some people it is noble, whereas, one will say, with no addition, that to honor the gods is noble. So whatever, with no addition whatever, seems to be noble or shameful or anything else of that sort, will be said to be unconditionally so.

Topics 4.5.126a34–b1

Both a god and an excellent person are capable of doing base things, but are not of the sort to do them; for the base are all said to be such in accord with their deliberate choice. Further, every capacity is choiceworthy; for even the capacities for base things are worthy of choice, which is why we say that a god and an excellent person have them; for we say that they are capable of doing base things.

Topics 5.1.128b19–20

A god is an immortal animal.

Topics 5.4.132b10–11

"Living thing that shares in scientific knowledge" is true of the god.

Topics 5.6.136^{b}6–7

Since perceptible living thing is not a special affection of any of the other living things, intelligible living thing could not be a special affection of what is a god.

2. The Immovable Mover

Physics 8.1.251a8–252a5

We say, then, that movement is the activation of the movable, insofar as it is moveable. For each sort of movement, therefore, |a10| there must exist things that are capable of it. In fact, even apart from the definition of movement, everyone would agree that for each sort of movement it must be what is capable of the movement that is in the movement—for example, it is what is alterable that is altered and what is changeable with respect to place that is in spatial movement. So there must be a burnable before there is |a15| a being burnt, and a capable of burning something before there is a burning. Accordingly, these things too, having not existed, must come to be at some time, or they must always exist.

Accordingly, if each of the movable things came to be, then before the movement in question there must have been another change and movement in which the thing capable of being moved or of moving something came to be. But if such things always preexisted |a20| without there being any movement, it is evidently absurd when we first stop to think about it, and must become still more so as we go on doing so. For if some things are movable while others are capable of moving things, then if there is a time when there is a first mover and a first moved, and another time when there is no such thing, but it is at rest, it must change |a25| previously; for there was some cause of its being at rest; for rest is a privation of movement. So prior to the first change there will be a previous change.

For some things move things in only one way, while others do so with contrary movements—for example, fire heats but does not cool, whereas the science of contraries seems to be one science. |a30| Now, there appears to be something similar occurring even in the former case (for cold heats in a way by turning aside or retiring, just as the person with scientific knowledge errs voluntarily when he uses his scientific knowledge in the reverse way), |251b1| but things, at any rate, that are capable of affecting or being affected, or of moving something or being moved, are not capable of it under all conditions, but only if they are in a certain condition and are near each other. So when one thing has approached another, it moves it, and the other is moved, that is, when one was such that it was capable of moving the other and the other of being moved. If, accordingly, the movement was not always going on, it is clear that they were not |b5| in a condition such that the one was capable of being moved and the other capable of moving it, but rather one of them had to change; for in things that are related it is necessary for this to happen—for example, if one thing was not double another but is double it now, one of the two, if not both, must have changed. Therefore, there will be a change previous to the first change.

In addition to these considerations, how will there be a before |^{b}10| and after if time does not exist?[1] Or how will there be time if movement does not exist? If time is really a number of movement or a sort of movement, if indeed there is always time, movement too must be eternal. . . .

The same argument also applies to movement's not being capable of passing away; for just as the coming to be of movement implied the existence of a change previous to the first, |^{b}30| in the same way here it implies the existence of one later than the last; for a thing does not cease being in movement and being movable at the same time, for example, being burned and being burnable (for it is possible for something to be burnable that is not burning), and neither do being capable of moving something and moving it. And what is capable of causing something to pass away will have to pass away after it has caused it |252^{a}1| to pass away, and what is capable of causing this to pass away will in turn have to pass away later; for passing away is also a sort of change. If, then, these things are impossible, it is clear that there is eternal movement, not movement at one time, rest at another. In fact, to say such things seems more a matter of fabricating stories.

Physics 8.4.255^{b}31–256^{a}3

If, then, all things that are in movement are moved either by nature or contrary to nature and by force, and if things moved by force and contrary to nature are all moved by something, and something other than themselves, and if, in turn, things moved by nature are moved by something, both those moved by themselves and those not moved by themselves (for example, the light and the heavy—|^{b}35| for they are moved either by what caused them to come to be and made them light or heavy,[2] |256^{a}1| or by what removed the thing that was impeding or preventing), then all things that are in movement are moved by something.

1. Compare *Met.* 12.6.1071^{b}7–9.

2. I.e., the hot material that made a potentially hot thing actually hot, or the cold material that did the same to a potentially cold thing. See *Ph.* 8.4.255^{a}22–23, ^{b}8–11.

Physics 8.5.256a4–258b9

And this will happen in one of two ways. Either it is not through itself[3] that the mover moves the thing, but rather it is through something else that the mover moves it, or it is through itself, and this latter mover will act either first |a5| after the last movement or through several intermediates[4]—for example, the stick moves the stone, which is moved by the hand, which is moved by the human being, who is no longer moved by anything else.

We say, of course, that both things cause movement, both the last and the first mover, but more so the first; for it moves the last, |a10| but the last does not move the first, and without the first the last will not move anything, whereas the first will do so without the last—for example, the stick will not move anything if it is not moved by the human.

If, then, everything that is in movement must be moved by something, and either by something moved by something else or not, and if it is moved by something else, there must be some |a15| first mover that is not moved by anything else, whereas if the first mover is of the latter sort, there is no necessity for the other sort (for it is impossible for a series of movers that are moved by something else to go on without limit; for of unlimited series there is no first member)—if, then, everything that is in movement is moved by something, and the first mover is moved, but not by anything else, |a20| it must be moved by itself.

Further, it is also possible to go through the same argument in the following way. For every mover moves something by means of something. For the mover moves either by means of itself or by means of something else—for example, a human being moves something either by means of himself or by means of a stick, and the wind knocked something down either by means of itself or by means of a stone driven by it. But it is impossible for a mover to move something without moving by means of itself |a25| that by means of which it moves the thing. But if it moves it by means of itself, there is no necessity for there to be anything else by means of which it does the moving, whereas if there is something else by means of which it does the moving, there must be something that causes movement not by means of something [else] but by means of itself, or the series will go on without limit. If, then, a moved thing moves something, it is necessary for the series to stop and not go on without limit; for if the stick causes movement by being moved by the hand, the |a30| hand moves the stick, whereas

3. Reading δι᾽αὐτὸ.

4. Starting from the thing X whose movement is the last one, work back through the chain of X's movers—we either come first to what moves it through itself or do so after going through several intermediate movers.

if something else causes movement by means of the hand, then something else is the mover of the hand as well. Whenever, then, movement by means of something is at each stage caused by something else, there must be some prior thing that causes movement by means of itself. If, then, this thing is moved, but nothing else is the mover of it, it must move itself. So according to this argument too, either what is moved is immediately moved |256b1| by something that moves itself or at some time the series arrives at such a thing.

And if, in addition to the things we have just said, we investigate in this third way, these same conclusions will result. For if everything that is in movement is moved by something that is in movement, either this being in movement belongs to the movers coincidentally, |b5| so that each of them causes movement, but not because it is itself in movement, or it does not belong coincidentally but intrinsically. In the first case, if the mover is moved coincidentally, it is not necessary for it to be moved. But if this is so, clearly it is possible that at some time no being is in movement; for what is coincidental is not necessary, but admits of not being. |b10| If, then, we posit what is possible, nothing impossible will result, but presumably a falsehood may. But for there to be no movement is impossible; for it was proved previously[5] that there must always be movement.

Also, this result is reasonable. For there must be three things: the mover, the moved, and that by means of which the mover moves. Now, the moved |b15| must be in movement, but it is not necessary for it to move anything, whereas that by which the mover moves must both move something and be in movement; for it changes together with, at the same time as, and in the same respect as the moved. This is clear in the case of things that cause movement with respect to place; for the movers and the moveds must be making contact with each other up to a certain point. But what moves in such a way as not to be that by which it moves is immovable. And since |b20| we see the last thing, namely, what is capable of being moved but does not have a starting-point of movement, and also see what is moved by another and not by itself,[6] it is reasonable, not to say necessary, to suppose that there is also a third thing that causes movement while being immovable. That is why Anaxagoras speaks correctly when he says that the [divine] understanding is unaffectable and unmixed, |b25| since, at any rate, he makes it the starting-point of movement; for only in this way could it cause movement while being itself immovable, and only by being unmixed have supreme control.

5. In *Ph.* 7.1.

6. Reading ὑπ᾽ ἄλλου δὲ ἀλλ᾽ οὐχ ὑφ᾽ αὑτοῦ.

But then if the mover is moved not coincidentally but necessarily, and if it were not moved, would not move anything, it is necessary for the mover, insofar as it is moved, to be moved so that[7] it is in accord with the same species |b30| of movement as the moved, or in accord with a distinct one. I mean, for example, either that what is heating something is itself being heated, what is making something healthy is becoming healthy, and what is carrying something is being carried, or that what is making something healthy is being carried and what is carrying something is being increased in size. But it is evident that the latter is impossible; for one must speak [of the movements by] dividing as far as the atomic [species]—for example, one must say that if someone is teaching some topic in geometry, |257a1| he is being taught this same topic, and that if he is throwing something, he is being thrown in the same manner of throwing. Or it may not be this way, but one genus may derive from another—for example, what is causing spatial movement is increasing in size, and what is causing this increase is being altered by something else, and what |a5| is causing this alteration is being moved with another sort of movement. But this series must stop; for the sorts of movements are limited. And to say that the series bends back again, and that what is causing the alteration is spatially moving is to do the same as if one said immediately that what is causing spatial movement is spatially moving, and the one who is teaching is being taught (for it is clear that everything that is moved is also moved by |a10| the mover that is higher up in the series, and more so by the prior of two movers). But this, of course, is impossible; for it follows that the one who is teaching is the one who is learning—although the one must have, and the other not have, scientific knowledge.

Further, what is still more unreasonable is that it follows that everything that is capable of moving something is capable of being moved, if indeed everything |a15| that is moved is moved by something that is moved; for it will then be capable of being moved. It is just as if someone said that everything that is capable of making something healthy is capable of being made healthy, and that everything capable of building is capable of being built, either immediately or through several intermediaries. I mean, for example, if everything that is capable of moving something is capable of being moved by something else, but not with the same sort of movement with which it moves its |a20| neighbor, but with another sort (for example, what is capable of making something healthy is capable of learning), and, by going up through the series, we at some time arrive at the same species

7. Reading ὥστε.

of change, as we said earlier.[8] Well, the first alternative is impossible, and the second is fabricated; for it is absurd that what is capable of altering something must be capable of being increased. It is not necessary, therefore, for what is moved always to be moved by something else |a25| that is itself moved. Therefore, the series will stop. So either what is first moved will be moved by something at rest, or it will move itself.

But then if there were in fact any need to investigate whether what moves itself or what is moved by something else is cause and starting-point of movement, everyone would take it to be the former; for what is itself intrinsically a cause is always prior as a cause[9] |a30| to what is itself a cause in virtue of something else. So we must investigate this by making a fresh start: if something moves itself, how and in what manner does it cause movement?

It is necessary, of course, for everything that is in movement to be divisible into parts that are always divisible; for it was proved previously[10] in our universal discussions about nature that everything that is intrinsically moved is continuous. |257b1| It is impossible, then, for what moves itself to move itself in its entirety; for it would be spatially moved as a whole, and it would spatially move itself with the same spatial movement, while being one and indivisible in species, and it would be altered and alter itself, so that it would be teaching and learning at the same time, and making healthy and being made healthy with the |b5| same health. Further, it was determined[11] that it is the movable that is moved; but it is in movement potentially, not actually. But what is potentially proceeds to actuality, and movement is the incomplete actualization of what is moveable. The mover, on the other hand, is already in activity—for example, what is hot heats, and, in general, what has the form begets [something that has] it. So [if a thing can move itself as a whole,] the same thing |b10| will be hot and not hot at the same time in the same respect, and likewise in each of the other cases in which the mover and the moved must be synonymous. Therefore, one part of what moves itself is the mover and another part is the moved.

But that it is not self-moving in this way, namely, that each of the two parts is moved by the other, is evident from the following considerations. For, first, there will be no first mover, |b15| if each part does move the other (for the prior mover is more of a cause of the movement than what comes next in the series, and more of a mover; for we saw that there are two ways

8. At *Ph.* 8.5.257a7–12.

9. Reading αἴτιον ἀεὶ πρότερον.

10. At *Ph.* 6.4.234b10–20.

11. At *Ph.* 8.1.251a9–16.

to move things, namely, by being moved by something else and by being self-moved; and what is further from the last thing that is moved is closer to the starting-point of movement than what is intermediate). Further, it is not necessary for the part that is the mover to be moved except |b20| by itself. It is coincidental, therefore, if the other part moves it in return. We may take it, therefore, that it is possible for it not to move it. One part is moved, therefore, whereas the other is an immovable mover. Further, it is not necessary for the mover to be moved in return. On the contrary, either it must move something while being immovable or it must be moved by itself, if indeed there must always be movement. Further, |b25| a thing would be moved with the movement it causes, so that what heats would be heated.

But then no primary thing that moves itself has one or more parts each of which moves itself. For if the whole is moved by itself, it will either be moved by one of its parts or the whole will be moved by the whole. If, then, it is moved by some part being moved by |b30| itself, this part would be the primary self-mover (for separated it will move itself, whereas the whole will no longer do so). If, on the other hand, the whole is moved by the whole, it would be coincidental that the parts moved themselves. So, if it is not necessary that they do so, the case in which they are not moved by themselves may be taken. Of the whole [cause], therefore, one part will cause movement while being immovable, while the other |258a1| will be moved; for only in this way will it be possible for something to be self-moved.

Further, if indeed the whole moves itself, part will cause movement and part will be moved. AB will be moved, therefore, both by itself and by A alone. And since what causes movement may either be moved by something else or be immovable, |a5| and what is moved may either move something or move nothing, the self-mover must be composed of a part that is immovable but causes movement, and further of a part that is moved but does not necessarily move anything, but may or may not do so. For let A be the part that causes movement but is immovable, and B the part that is moved by A and moves C, which is moved by |a10| B but moves nothing else; for even if C is in fact reached through several intermediates, let us suppose it is reached through only one. The whole ABC, then, moves itself. But if I take away C, AB will move itself, A causing movement and B being moved, whereas C will not move itself, or be moved at all. But then neither |a15| will BC move itself without A; for B causes movement by being moved by something else, not by being moved by any part of itself. Therefore, AB alone moves itself. It is necessary, therefore, for what moves itself to have a part that causes movement but is immovable and a part that is moved but does not necessarily move anything, with either both parts making contact with each other, or one of the two |a20| with the other. If, then, the mover is continuous (for what is moved must, of course, be continuous), each part will make contact with the other. It is clear, then, that the whole moves itself not by a part being such as to move itself, but instead it moves itself as a whole, being moved and causing movement by part of it being the mover and part the moved. For it does not |a25| cause movement as a whole nor is it moved as a whole, but instead it is A that causes movement and B alone that is moved.

A puzzle arises, however, if one takes something away either from A (if the immovable mover is continuous) or from B, the part which is moved: Will what remains of A cause movement or what remains of B be moved? For if so, AB would not be the primary thing |a30| that is moved by itself; for when something is taken away from AB, what remains of AB will still move itself. Or is it rather that nothing prevents either both parts or, at any rate, one part—the moved one—from being potentially divisible |258b1| but actually undivided, if when divided it no longer has the same nature? In that case, nothing prevents the primary self-mover from being in what is potentially divisible.

It is evident from these considerations, therefore, that the primary mover is immovable; for whether the series stops at once, because |b5| what is moved, but moved by something, is moved by the first immovable mover, or whether it is moved by something that moves itself and stops itself, in either case the primary mover of all moved things is immovable.

Physics 8.6.258b10–260a19

Since there must always be movement without intermission, |b10| there must be something eternal, whether one or more than one, that first causes movement. And what is a first mover must be immovable. Now, whether each of the immovable movers is eternal is not relevant to the present argument, but that there must be something that is immovable and outside all change, both unconditionally and coincidentally, but which is capable of moving |b15| something else, will be clear if we investigate in the following way.

Let it be granted, then, if you wish, that in the case of certain things, it is possible for them at times to be and at times not to be, without any process of coming to be or passing away (for perhaps it is necessary, if something without parts at one time is and another time is not, that anything of that sort should, without undergoing any process of change,[12] at one time be and another time not be). And of the starting-points that are |b20| unmoving but can cause movement, let it also be possible for some of them to be at one time and not be at another. Even so, this is not possible for all of them; for it is clear that there is some cause of the self-movers being at one time and not being at another. For everything that moves itself must have magnitude,[13] if nothing without parts is in movement, but for the |b25| mover to have it is not at all necessary, given what we have said.

That some things, then, come to be and some pass away, and that this happens continuously, of this no unmoving thing that is not eternal could be the cause, nor, again, could one that moves some things, while others move others.[14] For of the eternity and continuity neither each of them nor all can be the cause; for this state of things exists |b30| eternally and of necessity, whereas, though the sum of all those movers is unlimited, they do not all exist at the same time. It is clear, therefore, that even if some of the immovable movers and many of the self-movers |259a1| pass away countless times, and others succeed them, and even if one thing that is immovable moves one thing while another moves another, nonetheless there is something that encompasses them all, and this, which is beyond each of them, is the cause of some things existing and others not, and of the continuous process of change. And this |a5| causes the movement of these other movers, while they cause the movement of the others.

If indeed, then, movement is eternal, the first mover will also be eternal, if there is just one. But if there are several, there will be several eternal movers. But we must believe that there is one rather than many, and a limited rather than an unlimited number; for when the consequences are the same,

12. Aristotle thinks that nows (*Met.* 3.5.1002b6–7), points (8.5.1044b22), and essences or forms (3.1043b14–18) are like this, as are the various activities or actualities, such as hearing or perceiving (*Sens.* 6.446b2–4).

13. Begin by granting that some things T can come to be and pass away without undergoing any process of change that requires an antecedent cause (*Ph.* 8.6.258b16–20). Then grant that some of the starting-points S available as immovable movers to cause eternal movement can be at one time and not at another (258b20–22). Then ask: Is it possible for all the elements of S to be at one time and not be at another? Answer: it is not possible for all of them. Why? Consider the self-movers. Since they are moved movers they must have magnitude (6.4), and thus parts, and so are not in T. Hence they must have antecedent causes in S of their being at one time and not being at another. So these causes cannot themselves be at one time and not at another, which their status as immovable (and so as not needing to have parts) allows.

14. Reading οὐδ' αὖ τῶν ἀεὶ μὲν ταδί κινούντων, τῶν δ' ἕτερα.

we must always take the limited number, since in |a10| things that are by nature, what is limited and better must, if it is possible, be present to a higher degree.[15] And in fact one is enough, namely, the first of the immovable movers, which, being eternal, will be the starting-point of movement for the others.

It is also evident from the following considerations that the first mover must be something that is one and eternal. For it has been proved that there must always be movement. |a15| But if it always is, it must be continuous; for in fact what always exists is continuous, whereas what is successive is not continuous. But then if it is continuous, it is one. And it is one if the mover is one and what it moves is also one; for if the movement were to be caused by one thing, then by another, the whole movement would not be continuous but successive.

On the basis of these considerations, then, one may be persuaded that |a20| there is some first immovable mover, and also by looking again at the starting-points [of the argument]. It is evident, accordingly, that there are some beings that are at times in movement and at times at rest. And because of this it has become clear that it is not the case either that all things are in movement or that all are at rest or that some things are always at rest and the others always in movement; for things that play a double game |a25| and have the capacity to be in movement and to be at rest prove the truth about these alternatives. And since the existence of such things is clear to all, we wished to prove the nature of the other two sorts of things, and prove that there are some things that are always immovable and some things that are always in movement. Proceeding toward this end, and having established[16] that everything that is moved is moved by something, |a30| and that this thing is either immovable or moved, and that, if it is moved, it is moved either by itself or by another at each stage, we advanced[17] to the point of grasping that the starting-point of the movement of things that are in movement is, among moving things, the self-mover, but among all things, the immovable mover. But we see that beings |259b1| that move themselves are evidently of this sort—for example, the animate ones and the genus of animals. And these in fact yielded the belief that perhaps it is possible for movement to come about without having existed previously at all, because we see this happening in these things (for at one time they are unmoving and then they are in movement |b5| once again, so it seems).

15. I.e., to a higher degree than their opposites (because nature does nothing pointlessly).

16. In *Ph.* 8.4.

17. In *Ph.* 8.5.

But[18] we must grasp the fact that animals move themselves with only one sort of movement,[19] and that they do not in the strict sense cause it; for the cause does not derive from the animal itself, but rather there are other natural movements inherent in animals with which they do not move due to themselves, such as increase, decrease, and respiration, which each animal has while it is at rest and not moving with |b10| the movement that is due to itself. The cause of this is what encompasses the animal and many of the things that enter into it—for example, in some cases nourishment; for when nourishment is being concocted, animals sleep, and when it is being distributed [to the various parts] they wake up and move themselves, the first starting-point of movement being from the outside, which is why they are not always in continuous movement due to themselves; for the mover is something else,[20] which is itself moving and changing |b15| in relation to each thing that moves itself. In all these, however, the first mover and the cause of their self-movement[21] is itself moved by itself, but coincidentally[22]; for the body changes its place, so that what is in the body does so as well, and moves itself by means of leverage.

On the basis of these considerations, then, one should be persuaded that if something |b20| belongs among the things that are [intrinsically] immovable but are themselves moved[23] coincidentally, it is incapable of causing continuous movement. So if indeed there must be continuous movement, there must be a primary mover that is not moved even coincidentally, if there is to be, as we have said, an unceasing and undying |b25| movement among the beings, and if being itself is to remain in itself and in the same[24]; for if the starting-point remains as it is, the universe must also remain as it is, since it is in continuous relation to the starting-point. (But to be moved coincidentally by itself is not the same as to be moved coincidentally by something else; for to be moved coincidentally by [1] something else belongs even to some starting-points in the heaven, namely, [2] those |b30|

18. Reading δὲ.

19. Namely, spatial movement, or movement with respect to place.

20. I.e., something in what encompasses the animal, such as food.

21. I.e., the soul, with its perceptual, imaginative, understanding, and desiring parts.

22. The soul moves from place to place by moving the body from place to place.

23. Reading αὐτῶν κινουμένων.

24. I.e., within the same limits.

that are spatially moving with several spatial movements, whereas [3] to be moved coincidentally by itself belongs only to things that pass away.[25])

Moreover, if there is in fact something that is always of this sort, namely, moving something while itself remaining immovable and eternal, then the first thing that is moved by it must be eternal as well. Indeed, this is clear also from the fact that |260ª1| there would not be any coming to be, passing away, or change with respect to other things unless something that is in movement causes the movement; for the immovable mover will always move things in the same way and with one movement, seeing that it itself does not change at all in relation to what it moves. But what is moved |ª5| by something that, though it is moved, is moved directly by what is immovable, because it is related to things now in one way now in another, will not be the cause of the same movement, but instead, because of being in contrary places or forms,[26] it will produce contrary movements in each of the other things that it moves and cause it at one time to be at rest and at another time in movement. |ª10|

It has become evident, then, from what we have said, what the resolution is of the puzzle we raised at the start[27] as to why it is that all things are not either in movement or at rest, or why some are not always in movement and the others always at rest, but instead some are sometimes in movement and sometimes not. For the cause of this is now clear, namely, that some things are moved by an eternal immovable mover, which is why they are always in movement, whereas some things |ª15| are moved by a moved and changing mover, so that they too must change. But the immovable mover, as we said, seeing that it remains simple, selfsame, and in the same, will move things with a movement that is one and simple.

---

25. The reference in [2] is to the sun, moon, and planets, which have complex orbits, in contrast to those of the so-called fixed stars. The reference in [1] is to the celestial spheres in the surface of which these heavenly bodies are set. These spheres are members of a set of spheres, each member of which has its poles set in the surface of the next sphere outside it. Since these spheres, like the others in the system, are animate beings, possessed of souls (*Cael.* 2.12.292ª14–22), these souls are spatially moved coincidentally by the other spheres in the set and their souls. The contrast in [3] is with mortal terrestrial animals like us whose souls are coincidentally moved when the bodies they themselves animate are spatially moved.

26. Since the heavenly bodies undergo only one sort of change, namely, change with respect to place (or spatial movement), they cannot change their form, species, or any of their intrinsic affections. The reference, therefore, must be to such things as the changing inclination of the sun.

27. At *Ph.* 8.3.253ª22–24.

Physics 8.7.260^{a}20–261^{b}26

This will also be made more evident, however, if we make a new start |^{a}20| where these issues are concerned. For we must investigate[28] whether it is possible for any sort of movement to be continuous or not and, if it is possible, what sort it is, and which sort of movement is primary; for if indeed there must always be movement, and if a particular sort is primary and continuous, it is clear that the primary mover causes this sort of movement, which must |^{a}25| be one and the same, continuous, and primary.

Since, though, there are three sorts of movement: that with respect to magnitude, that with respect to affection, and that with respect to place, it is this last, which we call "spatial movement," that must be primary. For it is impossible for there to be increase without previous alteration; for what increases is in one way increased by what is like itself, |^{a}30| but in another way by what is unlike itself; for contrary is said to nourish contrary. But everything gets added by becoming like to like. It is necessary, then, for this change to a contrary[29] to be an alteration. But if there is in fact alteration, there must be something causing the alteration and |260^{b}1| making the actively hot from the potentially hot.[30] It is clear, then, that the mover is not always in the same situation, but sometimes closer, sometimes further away, from what is altered. But without spatial movement this cannot happen. If, therefore, there must always be movement, |^{b}5| there must also always be spatial movement as the primary sort of movement; and if there is a primary sort and a posterior sort of spatial movement, there must always be the primary sort.

Further, the starting-point of all affections is condensation and rarefaction; for in fact heavy and light, soft and hard, hot and cold, seem to be sorts of density or rarity. |^{b}10| And condensation and rarefaction are aggregation and disaggregation, in virtue of which substances are said to come to be and pass away. And things that aggregate and disaggregate must change with respect to place. But then the magnitude of what increases and decreases also changes with respect to place.

Further, it will be evident also from the following investigation that |^{b}15| spatial movement is primary. For, as in the case of other things, so too in the case of movements, they are said to be primary in many ways. And what is said to be prior is that without which the other things will not

28. See *Ph.* 8.8.261^{a}27–265^{a}12.

29. The change in the nourishment from being unlike what it nourishes (non-concocted, undigested) to being like what it nourishes (concocted, digested).

30. As is required for the concoction of nourishment.

exist, whereas it can exist without them, and there is also priority in time and with respect to substance. So, since there must be movement continuously, and it would exist continuously either |b20| if it were continuous or if it were successive, but more so if it were continuous, and since it would be better for it to be continuous than successive, and we always suppose the better to exist in nature, if it is possible, and it is possible for movement to be continuous (this will be proved later[31]; for now let us assume it), and since no other movement can be continuous except spatial movement, |b25| spatial movement must be primary. For there is no necessity for what spatially moves either to increase or to alter, nor of course to come to be or pass away. But none of these other movements can exist without the existence of the continuous movement that the primary mover causes.

Further, spatial movement is primary in time; for this is the only sort of movement possible for eternal things. [It might be objected,] however, that for each particular thing |b30| that comes to be, spatial movement must be the last of its movements; for after a thing comes to be, first alteration and increase occur, whereas spatial movement is a movement that belongs to things that are already completed. But prior to this there must be something else that is in movement with a spatial movement, which |261a1| will be the cause even of the coming to be of the things that come to be, though not itself coming to be (for example, what begets is the cause of what is begotten[32]), although it might seem that coming to be is the primary sort of movement, because the thing must first come to be. But though this is so in the case of any particular thing that comes to be, |a5| nonetheless there must be something in movement that is prior to the things that come to be, which does not itself come to be, and something else prior to this. And since coming to be cannot be primary (for then all things in movement would admit of passing away), it is clear that none of the movements that are next in order can be prior to spatial movement. By "the ones next in order" I mean increase, then alteration, decrease, |a10| and passing away; for all these are posterior to coming to be, so that if not even coming to be is prior to spatial movement, none of the other changes is either.

In general, it appears that what comes to be is incomplete and proceeds to a starting-point, so that what is posterior in order of coming to be is prior in nature. And spatial movement is the last sort to belong to all the things that are coming to be. That is why, |a15| due to a lack of the [requisite]

---

31. *Ph.* 8.8.

32. I.e., what antecedently has the completed form (and so is not coming to be as something that has it) begets what will have it. See *Ph.* 8.5.257b10.

instrumental part,[33] some living things are entirely without movement, such as plants and many genera of animals, while movement belongs to others when they are becoming complete. So if spatial movement belongs more to the things that have more fully achieved their due nature, this sort of movement would also be prior to the others with respect to substance—both because of the foregoing considerations and because what is moved in a spatial movement departs less from its substance than in any other sort of movement; |a20| for it alone does not at all change what it is, whereas what is altered changes its quality, and what increases and decreases changes its quantity. Above all it is clear that this movement—movement with respect to place—is the movement that what moves itself most of all causes in the strict sense. And yet it is this—what moves itself—that we say is the starting-point of things that are moved and of things that are movers |a25| and is primary among things moved.

It is evident from these considerations, therefore, that spatial movement is the primary sort of movement. But we must now prove what sort of spatial movement is primary. At the same time, though, the truth of the assumption we made both just now and previously[34]—namely, that it is possible for there to be a movement that is continuous and eternal—will be evident from this same methodical inquiry. |a30|

Now, that none of the other sorts of movement can be continuous is evident from what follows. For all movements and changes are from opposites to opposites—for example, of coming to be and passing away, being and not being are the defining marks; of alteration, they are the contrary affections; and of increase and decrease, they are greatness and |a35| smallness, or complete and incomplete magnitude. And the movements to contraries are contrary ones. But what is not always in movement with a certain movement, |261b1| though it existed previously, must previously have been at rest. It is evident, then, that what changes will be at rest in the contrary. It is likewise too in the case of changes[35]; for passing away and coming to be, whether unconditional or a particular sort in relation to a particular sort, are opposites.[36] So, if it is impossible |b5| for something to be changing in opposite ways at the same time, change will not be continuous, but there will be an interval of time between these opposed changes. For it makes no difference whether contradictory changes are contrary or not (for this

33. Reading τοῦ ὀργάνου.

34. At *Ph.* 8.7.260b23 ("just now") and 3.253a29 ("previously").

35. At 8.7.261b1–3 Aristotle deals with movements, which are from contrary to contrary. He now switches to consider changes (coming to be, passing away) that are not movements, and are from contradictory to contradictory. See 5.1.225a34–b9.

36. See *Ph.* 1.7.190a31–b10, 5.1.225a13–20.

is not being used in the argument), as long as they cannot be present in the same thing at the same time. Nor does it make a difference if it is not necessary for the thing to be at rest |b10| in the contradictory state, or if change is contrary to rest (for presumably a non-being cannot be at rest, and passing away is change to non-being), but only whether there is a time interval between the opposed changes; for that way the change is not continuous; for even in the previous cases the contrariety [of the states] was not the useful thing; instead, the impossibility of their belonging at the same time was.

Nor need |b15| one be troubled by the fact that the same thing will have more than one contrary—for example, that movement is contrary to rest and to movement to the contrary. We have to grasp only this: that in a way movement is opposed both to the contrary movement and to rest, just as the equal and the moderate are opposed both to what exceeds it and what is exceeded by it, and that it is not possible |b20| for opposites, whether movements or changes, to be present at the same time. Further, in the case of coming to be and passing away it would seem to be entirely absurd if what had come to be must pass away immediately without remaining for any interval of time. So on the basis of these changes one should be persuaded with respect to the others, since it is natural for what is similar to hold |b25| in all cases.

Physics 8.8.261b26–265a12

We are now in a position to state that it is possible for there to be an unlimited movement that is one and continuous, and that this is movement in a circle. For everything that is in spatial movement moves either in a circle, in a straight line, or in a mixture of the two, so that if one of the former two is not continuous, the combination of both |b30| cannot be continuous either. Now, it is clear that what is in spatial movement in a limited straight line is not in continuous spatial movement[37]; for it turns back, and what turns back in a straight line is moved with contrary movements; for with respect to place, up is contrary to down, forward to backward, and left to |b35| right; for these are the contrarieties of place. But we have previously determined[38] what the one and continuous movement is, namely, that it is

37. Unlimited movement in a straight line is impossible because no magnitude is actually unlimited. See *Ph.* 3.5, 8.

38. In *Ph.* 5.4.

the movement of one thing, in one |262a1| interval of time, and in something undifferentiated with respect to species (for we saw[39] that there were three things: the thing in movement, for example, a human or a god; when it moves, that is, the time; and third, what it is in, and this is place, affection, species, or size). But contraries differ in species and are not one; |a5| the differentiae of place being those we mentioned. And a sign that movement from A to B is contrary to movement from B to A is the fact that they stop or pause each other if they occur at the same time. And likewise in the case of a circle—for example, movement from A clockwise to B is contrary to movement from A counterclockwise to C (for they stop each other, even if they are continuous and do not |a10| turn back, because contraries destroy and prevent each other), whereas lateral movement is not contrary to upward movement.[40]

It is most of all evident, however, that movement in a straight line cannot be continuous from the fact that what turns back must stop, not only if it is moving in a straight line, but even if it is spatially moving in a circle. For spatially moving in a circle |a15| is not the same as circular movement; for at one time what moves in a circle is in connected movement, whereas at another time it turns back again to the same point from which it began. One may be persuaded that such movement must come to a stop not only on the basis of perception but also on the basis of argument.[41] We may start with this. For when there are three things, starting-point, mid-point, and end-point, the mid-point is both end-point and starting-point in relation to the other two, |a20| and is one in number, but two in account.[42] Further, potentially is distinct from actively. So any point between the extremes of a straight line is potentially a mid-point, but not actively so, unless what is in movement divides the line there by coming to a standstill and starting to move again. In this way the mid-point becomes starting-point and end-point—|a25| a starting-point of the later part, and an end-point of the first part (I mean, for example, if in its spatial movement A comes to a standstill at B and then travels again to C). But when its spatial movement is continuous, A cannot either have arrived at or have departed from point B, but can only be there in a now, and not in any interval of time except the one in which that now marks a division, |a30| namely, the whole time.

39. At *Ph.* 5.4.227b21–228a6.

40. Since they do not destroy or prevent each other.

41. Aristotle often conjoins an appeal to perception (here, appearances) with an appeal to argument, or to things that are in accord with argument (*kata ton logon*) or in accord with reason.

42. The mid-point is one point in number, but relative to the starting-point it is an end-point, and relative to the end-point it is a starting-point, and so it is two in account.

But if someone were to grant that it has arrived and has departed, A will always be at a stop when it is in spatial movement; for it is impossible for A to have arrived at and to have departed from B at the same time. |262b1| It will do so, therefore, at distinct points of time. Therefore, there will be a time interval between them. So A will be at rest at B, and similarly at the other points; for the same argument will apply to each. But[43] whenever the thing in spatial movement A uses the mid-point B as both end-point |b5| and starting-point, it must be at a standstill, because of making it be both, just as one might also do by understanding it that way. But A is the point it has departed from as a starting-point, and C is the one it arrives at when it reaches the end-point and comes to a standstill.[44]

That is why we must also state this in response to the following puzzle. For if line E is equal to line F, and A is in continuous spatial movement |b10| from the extremity E to C, and A is at point B at the same time as D is in spatial movement from the extremity F to the other extremity G in a uniform way and with the same speed as A, D will arrive at G before A arrives at C [Fig. 1].

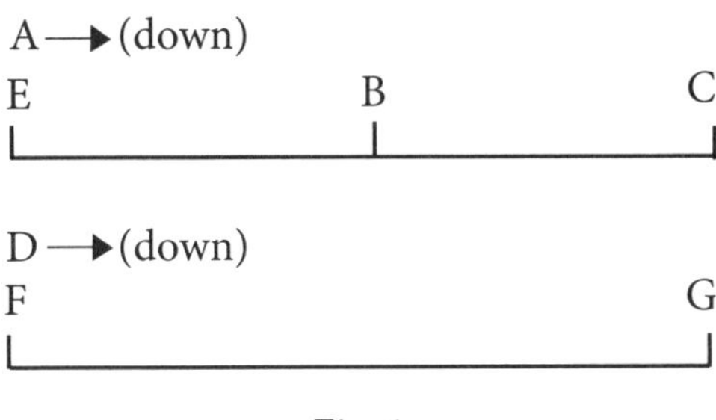

Fig. 1

For what started and departed earlier must arrive earlier. Therefore[45] A has not arrived at |b15| and departed from B at the same time, and that is why it lags behind. For if it does so at the same time, it will not lag behind; on the contrary, to lag behind it must come to a standstill. We must not grant, therefore, that at the time A arrived at B, D was at the same time in movement from F (for if A has arrived at B, its departure will also have occurred, and not at the same time), but it was there in a temporal instant |b20| and not in a temporal interval.

43. Reading δὲ.

44. Aristotle uses A, and later D and G, to refer both to points and to the objects that begin or end their spatial movements at them.

45. Reading ἄρα.

In this case, then, where movement is continuous, it is impossible to speak this way. In the case of something that turns back, however, it is necessary to speak this way. For if G spatially moves to D and, turning back, spatially moves back down again, it has used the extremity D as both an end-point and a starting-point, one point as two. That is why |ᵇ25| it must be at a standstill, and has not arrived at and departed from D at the same time; for then it would be there and not there in the same now. But then we surely cannot state the same resolution over again; for it is not possible to state that G is at D in an instant, and that it has not arrived at or departed from it. For it must |ᵇ30| arrive at an actual end-point, not a potential one. For points in the middle are potential, whereas this one is actual, and an end-point from below, a starting-point from above—related to the movements [of D], therefore, in the same ways. |263ᵃ1| What turns back along a straight line must, therefore, come to a standstill. Therefore, it is not possible for continuous movement in a straight line to be eternal.

One must reply in the same way to those who pose Zeno's argument and ask whether one must always traverse the half, |ᵃ5| but these halves are unlimited in number, and it is impossible to traverse what is unlimited. Or to those who pose the same argument in another way and require that during the movement we count the half movement before the whole as we come to each halfway point, so that in traversing the whole it comes about that we have counted an unlimited number. And this is admittedly |ᵃ10| impossible.

Now, in our first accounts concerned with movement[46] we resolved [this puzzle] due to time having unlimited parts within itself; for nothing absurd follows if in an unlimited time one traverses unlimited parts. And the unlimited is present as much in the time as in the length. But though this resolution is adequate relative to the questioner |ᵃ15| (for the question is whether in a limited time it is possible to traverse or count unlimited things), relative to the thing and the truth it is not adequate; for if someone sets aside the issue of length and the question of whether in a limited time one can traverse an unlimited number of things and inquires about the time itself |ᵃ20| (for the time is divisible without limit), this resolution will no longer be adequate. But it is the truth that must be stated, namely, precisely the one that we stated in our accounts just now.[47] For if someone divides a continuous line into two halves, he treats one point as two; for he makes it both a starting-point and an end-point. And both counting and |ᵃ25| dividing in half make it this way. And if one divides in this way, neither

46. In *Ph.* 6.2.233ᵃ21–31, ᵇ9.

47. At *Ph.* 8.8.262ᵃ19–ᵇ21.

the line nor the movement will be continuous; for continuous movement is over a continuum, and in a continuum there is an unlimited number of halves, not in actuality, however, but in potentiality. But if one makes them actual, one will not make the movement continuous, but rather come to a standstill, which is evidently precisely what happens |a30| when one counts the halves; for one must count one point twice; for the end-point of one half |263b1| will be the starting-point of the other, if one does not count the continuous line as one, but as two halves. So one must reply to the question of whether it is possible to traverse unlimited things either in time or in length that in one way it is and in another way it is not. For in the case of actually unlimited things it is not possible, |b5| but in the case of potentially unlimited ones it is possible; for a thing moving continuously has coincidentally traversed unlimited things, whereas unconditionally it has not; for a line is coincidentally an unlimited number of halves, but its substance—that is, its being—is something else.

It is also clear that unless one posits that the point of time that divides earlier from later always belongs to the later, |b10| so far as the thing is concerned, the same thing will both be and not be at the same time, and when it has come to be it will not be. The point, though, is common to both—that is, to both the earlier and the later—and is the same and one in number, though not the same in account (for it is end-point of one and starting-point of the other). But so far as the thing is concerned, it always belongs to the later affection. Let the time be ACB, |b15| and the thing D, which is white in time A and not white in time B. In time C, therefore, it is white and not white. For it is true to say that it is white in any time in A, if it was white in all this time, and in B that it is not white. But C is in both times. Therefore, we must not grant that it is white in all of A, but rather at all times except the last now, which is |b20| C; and this already belongs to the later period.[48] And if not white was coming to be and white passing away in all of A, not white has come to be and white has passed away at C. So this is the first time at which it is true to say that the thing is white or that it is not white.[49] Otherwise, at the time it has come to be, the white will not exist and at the time it has passed away, it will exist. Alternatively, it must be white and not white at the same time, and, in general, must be and not be. |b25|

But if whatever exists without having previously existed must come to be, and if when it is coming to be, it does not exist, time cannot be divisible

48. Reading τὸ ὕστερον.

49. Up to now Aristotle has been describing a case of change from white to not white (passing away). This disjunctive formulation generalizes his discussion to cases of change from not white to white (coming to be).

into indivisible times. For if D was coming to be white in time A, and has at once come to be white and is white in another indivisible but contiguous time B (if D was coming to be white in A, it was not white, |b30| but it is white in B), there must be an intermediate coming to be, so that there must also be a time in which D was still coming to be white. The same argument does not apply, though, to those |264a1| who say that there are no indivisible times, but that D has come to be and is white at the extreme point, with which nothing is contiguous or successive. But indivisible times are successive.[50] And it is evident that if D was coming to be white in the whole time A, there is no time in which |a5| it has come to be white and was coming to be white that is greater than the whole time in which it only was coming to be white.[51]

By these and other such arguments, which properly belong to the subject, one may be persuaded. But the result would seem to be the same if we investigate the issue logico-linguistically as follows. For everything that is in movement continuously, if it is not knocked aside by anything else, then precisely the point it arrived at by |a10| its spatial movement is the one it was previously spatially moving toward—for example, if something arrived at B, it was spatially moving toward B, and not merely when it was in the neighborhood of B, but as soon as it started to move; for why would it be doing so now rather than previously? And similarly in the case of the other [sorts of movement and change]. Suppose, then, that what is in spatial movement away from A, when it arrives at C, will again return to A with a |a15| continuous movement. At the time, therefore, that it is spatially moving from A toward C, it is also spatially moving to A with a movement that is from C, so that it will have contrary movements at the same time; for movements in contrary directions along a straight line are contraries. At the same time, it will also be changing from what it is not at [, namely, C]. If, then, this is impossible, it must come to a standstill at C. Its movement, therefore, is not one movement; for a movement that is interrupted |a20| by a stop is not one movement.

Further, this is also evident, as a more universal point about all sorts of movement, from the following considerations. For if everything that is

50. See *Ph.* 5.3.226b34–227a12.

51. On the view under analysis there are no indivisible times, and so no nows or temporal points, as Aristotle understands them. But D, he says, is and comes to be white at precisely such a temporal point, namely, the extreme point of A—call it t_e. His argument now is that A + t_e cannot be a greater period of time than A, as it would have to be if there were no temporal points, but only divisible temporal intervals. Considered as a point, of course, t_e belongs "as far as the thing is concerned" to the later interval it defines (*Ph.* 8.8.263b10–11), but considered as an interval it does not.

in movement is moved with one of the sorts of movement already mentioned and is at rest with the opposite sort of rest (for we saw[52] that there are no others beyond these), what does not always move with this sort of movement (I mean the ones that are distinct in |^{a}25| species, not if some part of the whole is[53]) must previously have been at rest in the opposite state of rest. If, then, movements in contrary directions along a straight line are contraries and it is not possible to be in contrary movements at the same time, what is in spatial movement from A to C would not at the same time be in spatial movement from C to |^{a}30| A. And since it is not in both spatial movements at the same time, but will move with the latter movement, it must be at rest at C; for this is the sort of rest that is opposite to the movement from C. It is clear, therefore, from these considerations that the movement will not be continuous.

Further, there is also |264^{b}1| this argument, which more properly belongs to the topic than the aforementioned ones. For suppose that the not white has passed away at the same time as the white has come to be. If, then, the alteration to white and from white is continuous and the white does not remain white for some time, at the same time as the not white has passed away the white has come to be |^{b}5| and the not white has come to be; for the time of the three will be the same.

Further, if time is continuous, it does not follow that movement is continuous, but that it is successive. And how could the extreme point of contraries—for example, of whiteness and blackness—be the same?[54]

A circular movement, on the other hand, will be one and continuous; for nothing impossible follows; for what is moving from A will at the same time |^{b}10| be moving to A with the same proposed end (for what it will arrive at is what it is moving to), but without having contrary or opposite movements at the same time; for not every movement to A is contrary or opposite to a movement from A, but rather they are contrary only if they

---

52. In *Ph.* 5.2.

53. The contrast is between a case in which X was not always in movement with a movement of species S, and a case in which though X was not always in such movement one of its parts was always in movement of some sort. So if X is an animal, its heart may always be beating, but it need not always be in movement with respect to place. So if it is in movement with respect to place now, it must have been at rest with respect to place previously, though not necessarily in other species of rest.

54. For the change from being white to being black to be continuous, the extreme or last point of being white, P, would have to be the same as the first point of being black (*Ph.* 5.2.227^{a}10–12). But then the thing undergoing the change would have to be both black and white at P, which is impossible, since white and black are contraries.

are along a straight line[55] (for it has contraries with respect to place,[56] such as the extremities of a diameter, |b15| since they are farthest apart), and opposite if they are along the same line.[57] So there is nothing to prevent the movement from being continuous and without temporal intermission; for circular movement is movement from a point to itself, whereas movement along a straight line is from one point to another.

Also, circular movement is never in the same things, whereas rectilinear movement is repeatedly |b20| in the same things.[58] Now, it is possible for what repeatedly comes to be now in one thing now in another to move continuously, but it is not possible for what always comes to be in the same things; for then it would of necessity have contrary movements at the same time. So it is not possible for a thing to move continuously in a semicircle or in any other arc; |b25| for it would of necessity make the same movement repeatedly and change to contrary changes; for the starting-point and limit are not united. But in circular movement they are, and it alone is complete.[59]

It is evident from this division that none of the other sorts of movements can be continuous either; for in all the others we find the same things |b30| being traversed repeatedly—for example, in alteration there are the

55. Contrariety is "a sort of greatest difference"—for example, where "the distance between the extremes is greatest" (*Met.* 10.4.1055a3–9). Thus on a straight line AB, A is contrary to B, since the distance between them is greatest (*Ph.* 5.3.226b32–33), and so movement from A to B is contrary to movement from B to A. Contrariety is thus a sort of opposition (*Met.* 10.4.1055b1).

56. See *Ph.* 8.8.261b34–36.

57. Suppose AB is the arc of a circle greater than a semicircle. Then movement from A to B is opposite to movement from B to A, but since the distance between A and B is not the greatest one, the movements are not contrary.

58. The things in question must, it seems, be the starting-point and end-point (or limit) of the movements, since it is the fact that these are united in the case of circular but not rectilinear movement that makes the former continuous and the latter not (*Ph.* 8.8.264b27–28). To say that a movement is *in* these, however, is not to say that it is between them, but that it has its coming to be in them (264b21–22). Thus what makes circular movement continuous is that its starting-point now comes to be in one thing (one point on the circumference) now in another, and that this is also its end-point (since the two are united), so that these movements are never contraries or opposites. In the case of rectilinear movement, on the other hand, the starting-point and end-point are repeatedly the same and are repeatedly the contraries of the starting-point and end-point of the next movement in the sequence. At each stage, therefore, a movement changes to its contrary movement or change (264b25–27). As a result, the sequence of movements cannot constitute one continuous movement.

59. "If indeed by complete we mean a thing outside which nothing can be found . . . , and if something can always be added to a straight line but never to a circle, it is evident that the line that encompasses a circle is complete" (*Cael.* 2.4.286b18–22).

intermediate stages, in quantitative change the intermediate magnitudes, and in coming to be and passing away it is the same way; for it makes no difference whether we make the stages in the change few or many, or whether we add or subtract a stage in between, |265a1| in either case we find the same things being traversed repeatedly.

It is clear, then, from these considerations that those physicists who claim that all perceptible things are always in movement do not speak well; for things must move with one of these sorts of movement, and especially, according to them, alteration; |a5| for things are always in flux, they say,[60] and in decay, and furthermore they speak even of coming to be and passing away as alteration. The present argument, by contrast, states universally that it is not possible to move continuously with any sort of movement except in a circle, so that nothing can do so either with alteration or with increase.

Let so much be said by us, then, to prove that there is neither unlimited |a10| nor continuous change except for circular spatial movement.

Physics 8.9.265a13–266a9

And it is clear that circular spatial movement is the primary sort of spatial movement. For every spatial movement, as we said earlier,[61] is either circular, rectilinear, or a mixture of the two. And the first two must be prior to the last; |a15| for it is composed of them. And the circular is prior to the rectilinear; for it is simpler and more complete. For a straight line that is unlimited cannot be traversed (for such an unlimited straight line does not exist[62]; and even if it did, nothing would traverse it; for the impossible does not happen, and it is impossible to traverse an unlimited line). But in the case of movement along a limited line, |a20| if it turns back, it is composed of two movements, while if it does not turn back, it is incomplete and capable of passing away. And the complete is prior to the incomplete,

60. Aristotle describes Plato as being familiar from youth with "Cratylus and the Heraclitean beliefs that all perceptibles are always flowing" (*Met.* 1.6.986a32–34).

61. At *Ph.* 8.8.261b29.

62. See *Ph.* 3.5, 8.

in nature, in account, and in time, and what is incapable of passing away to what is capable of passing away.[63]

Further, what can be eternal is prior to what cannot be eternal. But in fact circular movement can be eternal, |^{a}25| but none of the other sorts, whether of spatial movement or of any other sort whatever, can be so; for rest must occur, and if rest occurs, the movement has passed away.

And it is reasonable that circular movement should be one and continuous, and that rectilinear movement should not; for of movement along a straight line there is a definite starting-point, end-point, and mid-point, which are all contained in it in such a way that there is a point from which |^{a}30| what is in movement will start and a point at which it will end (for everything is at rest at the limits, whether the one from which it moves or the one to which), but of movement along a circular line they are indefinite; for why should any point on the line be a limit more than any other? For each point is alike a starting-point, a mid-point, and an end-point, so that what is in movement is always at the starting-point and at the end-point and also never at them. This is why |265^{b}1| a revolving sphere is in a way both in movement and at rest; for it occupies the same place. The cause of this is that all these features belong to the center-point; for in fact it is starting-point, mid-point, and end-point of the magnitude.[64] So, because this point is outside the circumference, there is nowhere for the spatially moving [sphere] to rest as |^{b}5| if it has traversed its course (for it

63. "Eternal things are prior in substance to things that pass away, and nothing eternal exists potentially. Here is the reason. Every capacity [or potentiality] is at the same time for something and for the contradictory. For while what is incapable of belonging cannot belong to anything, everything that is capable admits of not being active. So what is capable of being admits both of being and of not being. So the same thing is capable both of being and of not being. But what is capable of not being admits of not being. And what admits of not being can pass away, either unconditionally or in that way in which it is said to admit of not being, namely, with respect to place, or to quantity, or to quality—'unconditionally' is 'with respect to substance.' So none of the things that cannot unconditionally pass away are unconditionally potential (although nothing prevents one from being so in a certain respect—for example, with respect to quality or place). So all of them are actively [what they are]. Nor are any of the necessary beings potential ones (and yet these are primary things, since if they were not, nothing would be). Nor, then, is movement potential, if some movement is eternal" (*Met.* 9.8.1050^{b}6–20).

64. The idea is perhaps this. If a sphere is defined as the locus of points equidistant from an internal fixed point (the center), then the center is a starting-point, in the sense that it is the starting-point of (the construction of) the sphere, as of course is the circumference, since its distance from the center is also definitive of the sphere, as Aristotle recognizes at *Ph.* 8.10.267^{b}6–7. Since the radii converge at the center it is also the point to which the sphere contracts, and is in that sense its end-point. It is a mid-point, since it is in the middle of the sphere.

is always spatially moving around a mid-point but not to an extreme one), and because of this, the whole is in a way always at rest and remains,[65] and is also always in continuous movement. And there is this reciprocal relation; for in fact because the revolution is also the measure of movements,[66] it must be primary (for everything is measured by what is primary[67]), and because it is primary, |b10| it is the measure of the other sorts of movement.

Further, only circular movement can be regular; for things in rectilinear movement move spatially in an irregular way from the starting-point and to the end-point; for the further everything removes itself from its resting point, the faster is its spatial movement. Circular movement, on the other hand, alone has neither starting-point nor end-point naturally within itself, but rather has them |b15| outside.[68]

The fact that spatial movement with respect to place is the primary sort of movement is attested by all those thinkers who have made mention of movement; for they all assign the starting-points of movement to things that cause movement of this sort. For aggregation and disaggregation are movements with respect to place, and it is in this way |b20| that love and strife move things; for strife disaggregates and love aggregates them.[69] And the [divine] understanding, Anaxagoras says, disaggregates things as the first cause of movement.[70] The same is true of those[71] who mention no cause of this sort but say that things are in movement because of the void. For they too say that nature is moved with movement with respect to place |b25| (for movement because of the void is spatial movement and, as it were, in place[72]), and they think that none of the other movements

65. Reading διὰ τὸ τοῦτο μένειν.

66. See *Ph.* 4.14.223b18–23.

67. "The being for one is . . . most of all the being for a first measure of each genus, and, in the fullest way, of that of quantity. For it is from this that it has been extended to the other kinds. For a measure is that by which quantity is known, and a quantity insofar as it is a quantity is known either by a one [or a unit] or by a number, and all number by a one, so that all quantity insofar as it is quantity is known by the one, and what quantities are primarily known by, this is itself one. That is why the one is the starting-point of number insofar as it is number. And, by extension from this, so too in the other genera what is said to be a measure is the primary thing by which each is known, and the measure of each thing is a one [or a unit], in length, in breadth, in depth, in weight, in speed" (*Met.* 10.1.1052b16–27).

68. I.e., at the center (*Ph.* 8.9.265b4).

69. The reference is to Empedocles. See *Ph.* 8.1.250b26.

70. See *Ph.* 1.4.187a21, 8.1.250b24.

71. The reference is to the atomists Leucippus and Democritus. See *Ph.* 4.6.213b2–22.

72. Movement in a void is only with respect to place, because an Aristotelian place must be encompassed by body, not void. See 4.4.212a5–6.

belongs to the primary things,[73] but only to their compounds; for they also say that increase and decrease and alteration result from the aggregation and disaggregation of the indivisible bodies. It is the same way too with those who make condensation and rarefaction the cause |^{b}30| of coming to be and passing away; for in fact they regulate these by aggregation and disaggregation.[74]

Further, beyond these there are those who make soul the cause of movement[75]; for they say that what moves itself is the starting-point of all things that are in movement, and an animal and every animate thing moves itself with movement with respect to place.[76]

Also, |266^{a}1| we say that only what is in movement with respect to place is in movement in the strict sense; if it remains at rest in the same place, but increases or decreases or happens to alter, it is in movement in a way, but we do not say that it is in movement unconditionally. |^{a}5|

It has been stated, then, that there always was and always will be movement throughout all time; what the starting-point of eternal movement is; further, what the primary movement is; what sort of movement can alone be eternal; and that the primary mover is immovable.

Physics 8.10.266^{a}10–267^{b}26

Let us now say that this mover must be without parts and without magnitude, |^{a}10| after first determining some prior issues concerning it. And one of these is that no limited thing can cause movement for an unlimited time. For there are three things: the mover, the moved, and third, that in which, namely, time. And these are either all unlimited, all limited, or some are limited—that is, two or one. Let, then, |^{a}15| A be the mover, B the moved, and C the unlimited time. Then let D move some part E of B. Not, then, in a time equal to C; for the greater movement takes more time. So F, the time of the movement, is not unlimited. Now, by adding to D I shall use up A, and by adding to E I shall use up B. But I shall not use up the time by always taking a corresponding amount from it; |^{a}20| for it is unlimited. So all of A

73. I.e., atoms or "indivisible bodies" (*Ph.* 8.9.265^{b}29).

74. See *Ph.* 1.4.187^{a}12–16.

75. I.e., Plato and the Platonists.

76. "Now, that for which the name is 'soul,' what is the account of it? Do we have another besides what was just now stated, 'the movement capable of moving itself'?" (Plato, *Laws* 895e–896a).

will move the whole of B in a limited time period of C. It is not possible, therefore, for an unlimited movement to be due to a limited mover.

It is evident, then, that a limited magnitude cannot cause movement for an unlimited time. And that, in general, an unlimited capacity cannot be present in a limited magnitude |266ᵃ25| will become clear from the following considerations. For let the greater capacity be the one that always produces an equal effect in a shorter time, as in the case of heating, sweetening, or throwing—in fact, of causing movement in general. What is affected, therefore, must undergo some effect due to the limited magnitude that has an unlimited capacity, and an effect greater than one due to any other; for the unlimited one is greater than any other. |ᵃ30| But then this cannot take any time at all. For if A is the time in which an unlimited strength heated or pushed something, whereas in time AB some limited one did so, by continually adding to this strength a greater limited one I shall eventually |266ᵇ1| have caused the movement in question in time A; for by continually adding a limited quantity I shall exceed every definite quantity, and by subtracting, fall short of any definite one in like manner. The limited capacity, therefore, will cause a movement in a time equal to that taken by the unlimited one. But this is impossible. No limited thing, therefore, can |ᵇ5| have an unlimited capacity.

Neither, moreover, can a limited capacity be present in an unlimited magnitude. And yet it is possible for a greater capacity to be present in a lesser magnitude. True, but a still greater capacity can be present in a greater magnitude. Let AC, then, be an unlimited magnitude. Then [a part of it] BC has a certain capacity, which in a certain time caused D to move—namely, in time t_1t_3. If, then, |ᵇ10| I take twice BC, it will cause the movement in half the time (assuming this to be the proportion), so that it will cause [D] to move in half the time,[77] namely, t_2t_3. Therefore, by always taking in this way I shall never exhaust AC, whereas I shall always be taking a smaller part of the given time. The capacity, therefore, will be unlimited; for it exceeds every limited capacity, if, at any rate, |ᵇ15| every limited capacity must also take a limited time to do what it does (for if such-and-such capacity takes such-and-such time, a greater capacity will cause the movement in a shorter but still definite time that is inversely proportional to the capacity). But a capacity must always be unlimited—just as a number or a magnitude is—if it exceeds every definite one. |ᵇ20| This may also be proved in the following way; for if we take a certain capacity, the same in genus as the one in the unlimited magnitude, but this one being in a

77. Reading κινήσει χρόνῳ.

limited magnitude, it will be commensurable with the limited capacity in the unlimited magnitude.

It is clear from these considerations, then, that it is not possible for an unlimited capacity |b25| to be present in a limited magnitude, nor for a limited capacity to be present in an unlimited one. But where spatial movements are concerned it will be well to go through a puzzle first. For if everything in movement is moved by something (that is, the ones that do not move themselves), how is it that some will move continuously even when they are not in contact with their mover—for example, projectiles? And if |b30| the mover at the same time moves something else, such as the air, which causes movement by being moved, it is likewise impossible for it to be in movement when the first mover is not in contact with it and moving it—on the contrary, all the things will be in movement at the same time and will stop whenever the first mover stops, even if, |267a1| like a magnet, it makes what it has moved capable of causing movement.

We must, then, say this: that the first mover makes the air, water, or whatever naturally moves or is moved, capable of causing movement. However, this does not at the same time stop moving and stop being moved, but rather |a5| it stops being moved at the same time as its mover stops moving it, but it still causes movement, which is why it moves something else contiguous to it, and the same account applies to the latter. But it begins to stop whenever the capacity to cause movement becomes less in each contiguous thing. And it finally stops when the previous one no longer makes the next one a mover, but only something moved. And these things, |a10| the mover, on the one hand, the moved, on the other, must stop at the same time, as must the whole movement. Now, this movement comes to be in things that admit of being at one time in movement and at another time at rest, and it is not continuous, though it appears to be; for it occurs either in successive things or in things making contact; for there is not one mover, but movers contiguous to each other. That is why in air |a15| and in water this sort of movement occurs—the sort that some people call "reciprocal replacement." But it is impossible to resolve the puzzles raised in any other way than the aforementioned one. In reciprocal replacement, by contrast, everything would at the same time produce movement and be in movement, and so also stop at the same time. But as things stand it is evident that there is one thing in continuous movement. What, then, is it due to? For it is not due to the same thing [that started it moving]. |a20|

Since among the beings there must be continuous movement, and this is one movement, it must be a certain magnitude's one movement (for what is without magnitude does not move)—it must be of one thing and due to one thing (for otherwise it will not be continuous, but rather a series of movements contiguous to each other and divided).[78] The mover, then, if it is one mover, will cause movement either by being moved or by being immovable. If, then, it is |^{a}25| moved, it will itself have to follow along and undergo change, and at the same time be moved by something, so that the series will stop when it will arrive at a movement |267^{b}1| that is due to something immovable. For this of necessity does not undergo change along with the others, but will always be capable of causing movement (for to cause movement in this way involves no labor[79]), and this movement is regular, either alone or more so than any other; for the mover is never subject to any change. And neither must what is moved be subject to any change |^{b}5| in relation to the mover, if its movement is to remain the same. It is necessary, then, for the mover to be either at the center or on the circumference of a circle; for these are its starting-points.[80] But the things closest to the mover move fastest. And such is the movement of the circumference. That, therefore, is where the mover is.

There is a puzzle, though, as to whether it is possible for anything in movement to cause movement continuously, but not like something that pushes |^{b}10| again and again, where [the movement caused is] continuous by being successive[81]; for such a mover must either always push or pull or both, or another thing must receive one from another and again another mover, as was mentioned a moment ago in the case of projectiles, if the air, being divisible, causes movement by one part always being moved after another. In either case there cannot be one movement, but a contiguous series.[82] |^{b}15| The only continuous movement, therefore, is that which the immovable mover causes; for it always remains in the same state and so will continuously stand in the same relation to what it moves.

Now that these points are determined, it is evident that it is impossible for the first and immovable mover to have any magnitude. For if it has magnitude, this must be either limited or unlimited. But that there cannot be an unlimited |^{b}20| magnitude was proved previously in the *Physics*,[83]

---

78. See 8.1–2.

79. "That is why the sun, the stars, and the whole heaven are always active, and there is no fear that they may sometime stand still, which is what those concerned with nature fear, nor do they get tired doing this. For movement is not for them connected with a capacity for the contradictory, as it is for things that can pass away, so that the continuity of the movement is laborious, since the substance that is matter and potentiality, and not activity, is what causes this" (*Met.* 9.8.1050^{b}22–28).

80. See *Ph.* 8.8.265^{b}2–3n.

81. Reading συνεχής.

82. At *Ph.* 8.10.266^{b}28–267^{a}8.

83. *Ph.* 3.5.

and it has been proved just now[84] that a limited magnitude cannot have an unlimited capacity, and that something cannot be moved for an unlimited time by a limited magnitude. But the primary mover causes eternal movement for an unlimited time. It is evident, therefore, that it is indivisible |^{b}25| and without parts, and has no magnitude.

84. *Ph.* 8.10.266^{a}12–^{b}6.

3. The Heaven*

De Caelo 1.2.268ᵇ11–269ᵇ17

Where the nature of the All is concerned, whether it is unlimited in magnitude or its total mass[1] is limited must be investigated later.[2] Now, though, we shall speak about the parts of it with respect to form,[3] having made the following our starting-point:

For we say that all natural bodies and magnitudes are intrinsically capable of moving with respect to |ᵇ15| place; for nature, we say, is the starting-point of movement for them. Now, all movement with respect to place—which we call "spatial movement"—is either rectilinear or circular or a mixture of these[4]; for these are the only simple movements. And the cause of this is that these magnitudes are the only simple ones, namely, the straight line and the circumference. Circular movement is movement around the |ᵇ20| center, rectilinear is movement up and down. By "up" I mean away from the center, by "down," toward the center. So it is necessary for all simple spatial movement to be away from the center, toward the center, or around the center. And this seems to follow in accord with the account at the start[5]; for as body |ᵇ25| found its completion in [the number] three, its movement does too.

Since of bodies some are simple and others composed of these (by "simple" I mean those that in accord with nature have a starting-point of movement—for example, fire and earth, the species of these,[6] and things of the same kind as these), it is necessary that their movements too are in some cases simple and in others some sort of mixture—|ᵇ30| simple in the case of the simple bodies, mixed in the case of the composite ones,

---

* Simp. = Simplicius, *In Aristotelis De Caelo Commentaria* (Berlin, 1893).

1. *Ogkon*: An *ogkos* is generally a bulky body of some sort.

2. At *Cael.* 1.5–7.

3. I.e., about the forms or kinds of elements in the All.

4. See *Ph.* 8.8.261ᵇ28–29.

5. At *Cael.* 1.1.268ᵃ6–ᵇ10.

6. "For there is not only one species of fire; for glowing ember, flame, and light are distinct in species, though each of them is fire" (*Top.* 5.5.134ᵇ28–30). The species of earth are "sandy, stony, earthy, black, white" (Simp. 16.19–20). Compare, "Salt water is heavy and sweet water is light" (†*Pr.* 13.20.933ᵇ28–29).

but in their case movement is in accord with the predominant component.[7]

If indeed, then, there is simple movement, and circular movement is simple, and simple movement is movement of a simple body (for if the body is composite, its movement will be in accord with the mastering component), it is necessary for there to be some simple body that, in accord with its own nature, naturally moves spatially in a circle; for by force it is possible for it to be that of another, distinct body, but in accord with nature it is impossible, if indeed the movement of each of the simple bodies that is in accord with nature is one movement.

Further, if movement contrary to nature is contrary to movement in accord with nature, and if one thing has one contrary, then, it is necessary, since circular movement is simple, if it is not going to be in accord with the nature of the spatially moving body, that it is contrary to its nature. If, then, fire or something else of this sort is the thing spatially moving in a circle, its spatial movement in accord with nature will be contrary to the circular. But one thing has one contrary, and up and down are contrary to each other. If, on the other hand, it is some distinct body that is the one spatially moving in a circle contrary to nature, there will be some other movement that is in accord with nature. But this is impossible; for if it is up, it will be fire or air, and if it is down, water or earth.

But then too it is necessary for the spatial movement in question to be primary. For the complete is prior in nature to the incomplete, and the circle is one of the complete things, whereas no straight line is; for an unlimited one is not complete (for [to be complete (*teleion*)] it would have to have a limit, that is, an end [*telos*]) and neither is any of the limited ones (for all limited ones have something outside them; for any of them can be extended). So if indeed a movement that is prior is movement of a body that is prior in nature, and circular movement is prior to rectilinear, and rectilinear movement is movement of the simple bodies (for example, fire spatially moves in a straight line upward and earthy bodies in a straight line toward the center), it is necessary for circular movement to be the movement of some simple body; for the spatial movement of mixed bodies, we have said,[8] is in accord with the simple body that is the mastering one in the mixture.

On the basis of these considerations, then, it is evident that there is some natural corporeal substance beyond the ones composed here, more divine and prior to all these. And, further, if one were to assume that all

7. I.e., the simple body that there is most of in the mixture. See *Cael.* 1.2.269a29–30.

8. At *Cael.* 1.2.269a1–2.

movement is either in accord with nature or contrary to nature, and that what is contrary to nature for one thing is in accord with nature for another (for example, as is the case with upward and downward movements, which are contrary to nature and in accord with nature for earth and fire, respectively), |269a35| it would necessarily follow that circular movement too, since it is |269b1| contrary to nature for these, is in accord with nature for something else.

In addition, if circular spatial movement is in accord with nature for anything, it would clearly be some simple and primary body which in accord with nature spatially moves naturally in a circle, as fire does upward and earth downward. |b5| If, on the other hand, the things that spatially move in a circle perform the all-around spatial movement contrary to nature, it would be a wondrous and altogether unreasonable thing for this movement alone to be continuous and eternal, since it is contrary to nature[9]; for it is evident in other cases that the ones contrary to nature pass away fastest. So if indeed the thing spatially moving [in a circle] is fire, |b10| as some people say,[10] this movement will be no less contrary to nature for it than movement downward; for we see that the movement of fire is the rectilinear one away from the center.

This is why a person who makes his deductions on the basis of all these considerations would be persuaded that there is some body beyond the ones around us here, separate from them, |b15| and having a nature that is more estimable to the extent that it stands further off from those here.

De Caelo 1.3.269b18–270b31

Since some of the things that have been said are being assumed while others have been demonstrated, it is evident that not all body has lightness or heaviness. But we must set down what we mean by "the light" and "the |b20| heavy"—now in a way that is sufficient for our present needs, though later in a more exact one,[11] when we investigate their substance. Heavy, then, is what naturally moves spatially toward the center, light, away from the

9. And hence forced.

10. See Thales DK A17a = TEGP 26; Anaximander DK A21 = TEGP 22, TEGP 29; Anaximenes DK A7, A12 = TEGP 12, 16; Heraclitus DK B30 = TEGP 47; Parmenides DK B12 = TEGP 26.F12; Anaxagoras DK A84 = TEGP 50; Plato, *Timaeus* 40a, *Epinomis* 982a–b.

11. At *Cael.* 4.1–4.

center; heaviest, what sinks below all the downward-moving bodies, lightest, what rises above all |b25| the upward-moving ones.

It is necessary, then, for everything that moves down or up to have lightness, heaviness, or both—though not in relation to the same thing; for things are heavy and light in relation to each other—for example, air is light in relation to water, whereas water is so in relation to earth. The body, though, that spatially moves in a circle cannot possibly have heaviness or lightness; |b30| for neither in accord with nature nor contrary to nature does it admit of moving toward the center or away from the center. For in accord with nature, rectilinear spatial movement does not pertain to it; for the movement of each of the simple bodies is, as we saw,[12] one movement, so that the body that spatially moves in a circle will be the same as one of the bodies spatially moving in this way. On the other hand, if it is moved contrary to nature, then if downward movement |b35| is contrary to nature, upward will be in accord with nature, and if upward is contrary to |270a1| nature, downward will be in accord with nature; for we posited[13] that, of contrary movements, if one is contrary to nature for something, the other is in accord with nature.

Since, however, the whole and the part—for example, all of earth and a small clod—spatially move in accord with nature to the same place, it follows, first, |a5| that it[14] has neither lightness nor heaviness (for otherwise it would be capable of spatially moving either toward the center or away from the center in accord with its own nature). Next, it follows that it cannot be moved with respect to place by being hauled either up or down; for it does not admit of moving, either in accord with nature or contrary to nature, |a10| with a movement other than its own, either itself or any of its parts; for the same argument applies to whole and part.

It is equally reasonable to suppose about this body that it is incapable of coming to be and passing away, incapable of increase, and incapable of alteration, because everything that comes to be comes to be from its contrary and from an underlying subject, and passes away |a15| similarly, namely, from an underlying subject, because of a contrary, and to a contrary, as was said in our first accounts.[15] Also, contrary spatial movements are of contraries. If, then, this body can have no contrary, because there cannot in fact be a movement contrary to spatial movement in a circle, nature seems to have correctly |a20| removed from

12. At *Cael.* 1.2.269a8–9.

13. At *Cael.* 1.2.269a32–34.

14. I.e., the part.

15. *Ph.* 1.7–9

among the contraries the body that was going to be incapable of coming to be and passing away. For coming to be and passing away belong in the realm of contraries.

But then too everything that increases, increases because of something of the same kind being added to it and dissolving into its matter. But there is none from which this body has come to be.[16]

But if it is not capable of either increase |a25| or passing away, the same thinking leads us to suppose that it is not capable of alteration either. For alteration is movement with respect to quality, and qualitative states and dispositions—for example, health and disease—do not come about without change with respect to the affections. But all natural bodies that change with respect to an affection |a30| we see are subject both to increase and decrease—for example, the bodies of animals and plants and their parts, and also those of the elements. So if indeed the body in circular movement does not admit of either increase or decrease, it is reasonable for it to be unalterable as well. |270a35|

Why, then, the primary body is eternal and not subject to increase or decrease, |270b1| but rather incapable of aging, incapable of alteration, and unaffectable, is—provided our assumptions are persuasive—evident from what has been said.

It seems too that the argument attests to the things that appear to be so, and the things that appear to be so attest to the argument; for all |b5| human beings have a supposition about the gods, and all—both barbarians and Greeks, as many as acknowledge gods at all—assign the highest place to the gods, on the assumption, clearly, that immortal is closely linked with immortal; for any other way is impossible. If indeed, then, there is something divine, as indeed there is, the things just now said |b10| about the substance that is primary among the bodies were correctly said.

But this result also follows sufficiently enough through perception, at any rate, for (one might almost say) merely human conviction; for in all of past time, according to the record people have handed down one to another, nothing appears to have changed either in the whole of the outermost heaven[17] |b15| or in the parts proper to it.[18]

16. Coming to be requires matter as an underlying subject (*Cael.* 1.3.269a15). Since the body in circular movement does not come to be, it does not have such matter, and so has none to be added to in the way required for growth.

17. The outermost (or, looking inward, the first) heaven is the sphere of the fixed stars.

18. I.e., the sphere of the fixed stars and the constellations they form.

And it seems that the name too has been handed down even to the present time by the ancients, who conceived of it in the very way we ourselves speak of it; for one must acknowledge that the same beliefs return to us not once or twice but an unlimited number of times.[19] That is why, on the supposition that |^{b}20| the primary body was something distinct, beyond earth, fire, air, and water, they gave the name *aithêr* ("ether") to the uppermost place,[20] positing a name for it from the fact that, throughout eternal time, it is running always (*thein aei*).[21] Anaxagoras, on the other hand, does not use this name correctly; for he uses *aithêr* in place of "fire."[22] |^{b}25|

It is also evident from what has been said why the number of what are called "simple bodies" cannot be greater; for it is necessary for the movement of a simple body to be simple, and we say that the following are the only simple movements: circular and rectilinear, the latter having two parts, one |270^{b}30| away from the center, the other toward the center.[23]

De Caelo 1.4.271^{a}33

The god and nature, however, make nothing pointlessly.

De Caelo 1.8.276^{a}18–277^{b}26

Let us now say why there cannot be several heavens either, for we said[24] that this must be investigated, in case someone thinks that it has not been proved universally about all bodies that it is impossible for any of them at

19. See *Met.* 12.8.1074^{a}38–^{b}14.

20. I.e., the place is the outermost or first heaven, which is eternally revolving.

21. "As for *aithêr*, I'd explain it as follows: it is right to call it *aithêr*, because it is always running and flowing (*aei thei rheôn*)" (Plato, *Cratylus* 410b).

22. See DK B2 = TEGP F2; also *Cael.* 3.3.302^{b}4, *Mete.* 1.3.339^{b}22–25, 2.9.369^{b}14–15. However, Anaxagoras is probably on better etymological grounds than Aristotle in connecting (if he did) *aithêr* to fire, since it seems in fact to derive from the verb *aithô* ("kindle," "light up"; passive: "burn").

23. See *Cael.* 1.2.168^{b}14–26.

24. At *Cael.* 1.7.274^{a}24–28.

all to exist outside |^{a}20| the cosmos, but that the argument[25] applies only to those with no definite position.

For all things both remain at rest and move both in accord with nature and by force, and, where they remain at rest not by force, they also spatially move to in accord with nature, and where they spatially move to [in accord with nature], they also remain at rest in [not by force]; on the other hand, where they remain at rest by force, they also spatially move to by force, and where they spatially move to by force, |^{a}25| they also remain at rest by force. Further, if this spatial movement is by force, its contrary is in accord with nature. If, then, earth will spatially move by force from there to the center here, it will spatially move in accord with nature from here to there; and if earth from there remains at rest here not by force, it will spatially move here in accord with nature too. But[26] the spatial movement that is in accord with nature is a single one.

Further, it is necessary for all the cosmoses, |^{a}30| being admittedly similar in nature, to be composed of the same bodies.[27] But then it is necessary for each body to have the same capacity—I mean, for example, fire and earth and the ones intermediate between |276^{b}1| them[28]; for if these are homonyms and are not said of things there in accord with the same form as of those among us, then the universe too would be said to be a cosmos homonymously. It is clear, therefore, that one of them must spatially move naturally away from the center, while another does so toward the center, if indeed all |^{b}5| fire is the same in form as other fire (and also each of the others), just as the parts of fire are in this cosmos.

That this is of necessity so is evident from our hypotheses about movement; for the movements are limited, and each of the elements is said to be what it is with reference to one of the movements. So if indeed movements are in fact the same, |^{b}10| it is necessary for the elements too to be everywhere the same.

25. The argument referred to is that of *Cael.* 1.7.275^{b}5–11: "[1] Moreover, whatever bodies are in a place, at any rate, are also perceptible. [2] Therefore, there is no unlimited body outside the heaven. Nor yet is there one up to a certain magnitude. Therefore, there is no body at all outside the heaven. [3] For if it is intelligible, it will be in a place. For 'outside' and 'inside' signify place. So it will be perceptible. But nothing perceptible is not in a place." The potential objector worries, then, that in [1] and [3], "place" means "definite place" (that is, the spatial envelope of a definite body). But, for example, the Platonic Forms (intelligible objects) might be thought to be "outside" the heaven, without being in some definite place.

26. Reading μία δ᾽.

27. See *Cael.* 1.6.275^{b}32–276^{a}1.

28. I.e., air and water.

Therefore, the parts of earth in another cosmos will be naturally such as to spatially move toward the center of this one, and fire there toward the extremity of this one. But this is impossible; for if this happens, it is necessary for earth in its own cosmos to spatially move upward, and fire toward the center. |b15| Similarly, the earth here will move in accord with nature away from the center in moving toward the center there, because of the way the cosmoses are positioned in relation to each other. For either we must not posit that the simple bodies have the same nature in the several heavens, or in saying that they do, it is necessary to make a unique center and a unique extremity. |b20| But if this is so, there cannot be more than one cosmos.

But to think that the nature of the simple bodies is then different the more or less distant they are from their proper places is unreasonable; for what difference will it make to say that they are this distant or that distant? They will differ in proportion to the distance, but their form will remain the same. |b25|

Moreover, it is necessary for the simple bodies to have some movement; for that they do move is evident. Are we to say, then, that all their movements are by force, even contrary ones? But what does not naturally move at all cannot be moved by force. If, therefore, some movement in accord with nature belongs to them, it is necessary for the movement of particular ones that are the same in form to be |b30| toward a place that is one in number—for example, toward this center and this extremity. But if they are toward places that are the same in form, but many (because as particulars they are in fact many, but in form |277a1| each is undifferentiated [from the others]), then there will not be such [a place] for one but not for another of the parts, but for all alike; for all are alike undifferentiated in form, although any one is distinct in number from any other. What I mean is this: if the parts here behave in a similar way both toward each other and toward the ones in another |a5| cosmos, then one taken from here will not behave differently toward the ones in another cosmos than toward those in its own, but in a similar way. So either it is necessary for these assumptions to be altered, or it is necessary for there to be a unique center and a unique extremity. But if this is so, then, |a10| by the same proofs and the same necessities, there must also be only one heaven and not several.

That there is a certain place that it is natural for earth to spatially move toward, and also one for fire, is clear from other [sorts of change]. For, in general, what moves changes from something to something, and these—the from which and the to which—differ in form. And all |a15| change is limited—for example, what becomes healthy changes from sickness to health, and what increases changes from smallness to largeness. So too for what spatially moves; for it too comes to be somewhere from somewhere. Therefore, what it naturally moves from and to must differ in form, just as what becomes healthy [does not change to] some random destination, nor to whichever one the mover wishes.[29] |^{a}20|

Therefore, fire—and earth too—spatially moves not without limit but toward opposite points. But with respect to place up is opposed to down, so that these will be the limits of spatial movement. (Since even spatial movement in a circle has in a way opposite points, namely, the end-points of its diameter, though to the whole movement nothing is contrary, so even for these[30] the movement is in a certain way toward opposite and |^{a}25| limited points.) Therefore, it is necessary for it to have some end and not spatially move without limit.

A proof of there being no spatial movement without limit is that earth, the closer it gets to the center the faster it spatially moves, while fire does so the closer it gets to the upper place. But if the spatial movement were without limit, its speed would be unlimited too, and if the speed were, so too would be the heaviness |^{a}30| and the lightness involved; for just as[31] a thing that is lower than another because of its speed is fast because of its heaviness, so if the increase in heaviness were unlimited, the increase in speed would be unlimited as well.

But |277^{b}1| then neither could they be moved upward and downward by something else, nor by force or squeezing out, as some people say.[32] For then more fire would move more slowly upward and more earth more slowly downward. As things stand, however, the contrary always happens:

29. What becomes healthy must change precisely to being healthy (otherwise healthy would not be what it was becoming), and this is so even if the mover (that is, the doctor) is trying (ineptly or criminally) to make him something other than healthy.

30. I.e., things that spatially move in a circle, the pertinent ones being the celestial bodies.

31. Rejecting the addition of εἰ.

32. "For [Democritus] the shapes and atoms are unlimited and those that are spherical he says are fire and soul—which are like the so-called motes in the air that appear in the sunbeams that come through our windows. The aggregate of such seeds, he says (and likewise Leucippus), are the elements of the whole of nature, while those of them that are spherical are the soul, because being of such a shape they are especially capable of moving through everything and—being themselves moving—of moving the rest, on the supposition that the soul is what imparts movement to animals. That is why too they make breathing the defining mark of being alive. For when the surrounding air compresses their bodies, it squeezes out (*ekthlibontos*) those atomic shapes which, because they are never at rest themselves, impart movement to animals. Then aid comes from outside by the entry of other similar atoms in breathing. For these prevent the squeezing out of those that are already inside, helping to counteract what is doing the compressing and solidifying. And life continues just so long as they are capable of doing this" (*DA* 1.2.404^{a}1–16). *Mete.* 2.9.369^{a}23–24 uses squeezing out the pit of a fruit as an illustration.

more fire, or more earth, spatially moves faster to its own place. Nor would it spatially move faster toward the end |^{b}5| if it were by force and squeezing out; for everything spatially moves more slowly the further it gets from what did the forcing, and what it spatially moves from by force, it spatially moves to not by force. So by getting a theoretical grasp on these points it is possible to get adequately persuaded about what is being said.

Further, [that there is a unique heaven] might also be proved by means of the arguments from primary philosophy, and from |^{b}10| movement in a circle,[33] which is necessarily eternal both here and in other cosmoses as well.

It should also be clear to those who investigate in the following way that it is necessary for there to be a unique heaven. For since there are three corporeal elements, the places of the elements will also be three, one around the |^{b}15| center for the body that sinks, another for the body that spatially moves in a circle, which is the extremity, and a third intermediate between them for the middle body.[34] For it is necessary for what rises above to be in this one. For if it is not in this one, it will be outside. But it is impossible for it to be outside. For one is without heaviness, the other has heaviness, and the lower place is that of the body that has heaviness (if indeed |^{b}20| that of what is heavy is toward the center). Moreover, it could not be so, contrary to nature; for then it will be in accord with nature for another one; but there is, as we saw, no other one. Therefore, it is necessary for it to be in the intermediate place. What the differentiae of this place are, we shall say later.[35]

Concerning the bodily elements, then, what sort they are and how many, and what the place of each is, and further, in general, how many |^{b}25| in number the places are, is clear to us from what has been said.

---

33. That only movement in a circle can be eternal is argued in *Ph.* 8.8, but no argument exists connecting this to the uniqueness of the heaven. But *Cael.* 1.8.276^{b}26–277^{a}12 shows how one might be constructed.

34. Aristotle has so far distinguished only three proper places: up, down, and center. So he has made correlative room for only three bodily elements: the one that sinks (earth); the one that moves in a circle (ether); and what he here refers to simply as "the middle body," whose place must be intermediate between the other two. Later, as he says at 1.8.277^{b}23–24, this place will be differentiated into a place for water (above earth) and for fire (above water). But for present purposes these differentiations are unneeded.

35. At *Cael.* 4.4.

De Caelo 1.9.277b27–279b3

That the heaven is not only unique, but that there cannot come to be more and, further, that it is eternal, being incapable of coming to be and of passing away, we should now state, first of all going through the puzzles about this.[36]

For it might seem to those who investigate in the following way that there cannot be one, unique heaven; |b30| for in everything that is constituted and has come to be by nature or by craft, the shape [or form] taken intrinsically and the shape mixed together with the matter are distinct. For example, the form of the sphere and the gold or bronze sphere are distinct; and, again, the |278a1| shape of the circle and a brazen or wooden circle are distinct; for in stating the essence for sphere or for circle, we do not mention bronze or gold in the account, on the supposition that these are not [parts] of its substance; whereas if we are speaking of the brazen or golden one, we do mention it, also if we cannot |a5| understand or grasp any other, beyond the particular one. For sometimes nothing prevents this from happening—for example, if only one circle were grasped[37]; for the being for circle will be no less distinct from the being for this circle, and the one is the form, whereas the other is the form in the matter, that is, one of the particulars.

Since, then, the heaven is perceptible, |a10| it will be one of the particulars; for everything perceptible is in matter. But if it is one of the particulars, the being for this heaven and the being for heaven unconditionally will be distinct. Therefore, this heaven and heaven unconditionally will be distinct, and the latter as being form and shape, the former as being mixed with matter. But of what there is a certain shape or form of, there either is or can |a15| come to be many particular instances. For if there are Forms, as some say,[38] it is necessary for this to result—and no less so if nothing of this

36. Reading οὐρανός.

37. A form (shape) is a universal, which is reached by induction from particulars. If the inductive basis consists of just one particular, the universal may be difficult to distinguish from it, nonetheless the being for (essence of) the particular is distinct from that of the universal: "In the case of things that evidently come to be in different kinds (*eidos*) [of materials], as circle does in bronze and stone and wood, it seems clear that these, for example, the bronze or the wood, do in no way belong to the substance of the circle, because of being separate from them. But in the case of things that are not seen being separate, nothing prevents the situation from being similar, just as if all the circles were seen to be of bronze. For nonetheless the bronze would still not belong to the form, but it would be difficult to subtract it in thought" (*Met.* 7.11.1036a31–b3).

38. I.e., Plato and his followers.

sort[39] is separable; for we see in all cases in which the substance [= essence] is in matter that things of the same form are several, indeed unlimited in number. So either there are or can be several heavens. |a20|

On the basis of these considerations, then, one might suppose either that there are or that there can be several heavens. We must go back, however, and investigate which of these is correctly stated and which incorrectly.

That the account of the shape [or form] without the matter and of the one in the matter are distinct is correctly stated, and let it be true. But nonetheless |a25| there is no necessity, because of this, for there to be several cosmoses, nor even that several can come to be, if indeed this one is composed of the totality of matter, as in fact it is.

What is being said will perhaps be clearer put in the following way. For if aquilinity is curvature in a nose, or in other words, in flesh, and if flesh is matter for aquilinity,[40] then if of the totality of flesh one [parcel of] |a30| flesh were to come to be composed, and the aquiline belonged to it, nothing else either would or could be aquiline. Similarly, if fleshes and bones are matter for what is human, if of the totality of flesh and of all the bones a human were to come to be composed in a way incapable of dissolution, it would be impossible for another human being to come to be. |a35| And similarly in other cases; for in general, nothing whose substance is in |278b1| some underlying matter can come to be without there being some matter.

The heaven is certainly one of the particulars and one of the things composed of matter. But if it is composed not of a part of matter but of the totality of it, the being for the heaven itself and for this |b5| heaven are distinct, yet it is not the case either that there is another one or even that several could come to be, because this one includes the totality of the matter. It remains, therefore, to prove this: that the heaven is composed of the totality of natural and perceptible body.

---

39. I.e., no universal.

40. I.e., flesh is the hypothetically necessary matter for aquilinity—the only matter in which it can be realized—in the way that iron is for a saw: "Why is a saw such as it is? So that *this* may be, and for the sake of *this*. But in fact it is impossible that this thing that the saw is for the sake of should come to be unless it is made of iron. It is necessary, therefore, for it to be made of iron, if there is to be a saw with its function. The necessity, then, is hypothetical, but not [necessary] as an end. For the necessity lies in the matter, whereas the for-the-sake-of-which lies in the account" (*Ph.* 2.9.200a10–15). Notice "proper matter" at *Cael.* 1.9.279a8. Here aquilinity substitutes for the more common snubness to make the same point. See *Met.* 6.1.1025b28–1026a6.

Let us first state what we say it is to be a heaven and in how many ways,[41] in order that |b10| what we are inquiring into will become clearer to us.

In one way, then, we say that the substance belonging to the outermost revolution of the universe is heaven, or the natural body that is on the outermost circumference of the universe; for more than anything else it is the last upper region that we usually call "heaven," the one in which we say that everything divine also has its seat. |b15|

In another way, it is the body that is continuous with outermost circumference of the universe, in which we find the moon, the sun, and some of the stars; for we say that these bodies too are in the heaven.

Further, we say that the body that is encompassed by the outermost circumference is heaven; for we are accustomed to say that |b20| the whole and the universe is heaven.

Heaven is said, then, in three ways. The whole encompassed by the outermost circumference is of necessity composed of the totality of natural perceptible body, because there neither is nor can be any body outside the heaven.

For if there is a natural body outside the outermost circumference, |b25| it is necessary for it to be either one of the simple ones or one of the composite ones, and for it to be there either in accord with nature or contrary to nature. But it could not be one of the simple ones. For it has been proved[42] that the one that spatially moves in a circle cannot change its own place. But neither can it then be the one that moves from the center nor the one that sinks. |b30| For they could not be there in accord with nature (for other places are proper for them), while if indeed they are there contrary to nature, the place outside will be natural for some other body; for what is contrary to nature for it is of necessity in accord with nature for something else. But there is, we saw,[43] no other body beyond these. Therefore, it is not possible for any of the simple bodies to be outside |b35| the heaven. But if none of the simple ones can be, neither can any of the mixed ones; |279a1| for where a mixed one is, it is necessary for simple ones to be as well.

Moreover, neither can a body come to be there; for it will do so either in accord with nature or contrary to nature, and it will be either simple or mixed, so that, again, the same argument will apply; for it makes no difference to investigate if it is, or if it can come to be. |a5|

41. "If we know in how many ways something is said of things, we shall not be trapped by a false deduction ourselves, but rather will know if the questioner should fail to produce his argument related to the same thing [as we asked about]" (*Top.* 1.18.108a26–29).

42. In *Cael.* 1.2–3.

43. Also in *Cael.* 1.2–3.

It is evident, therefore, from what has been said that no corporeal mass either is or can come to be outside [the heaven]. Therefore, the total cosmos is composed of the totality of its proper matter; for its matter is natural perceptible body.[44] So neither are there now several heavens, nor have there been, nor can there come to be. On the contrary, |a10| this heaven is one, unique, and complete.

At the same time it is clear that there is neither place, nor void, nor time outside the heaven. For in every place body can exist; and void, they say, is that in which body does not exist, but in which it can; and time is a number of movement,[45] and there is no movement without natural body. |a15| But it has been proved[46] that outside the heaven there neither is nor can be body. Therefore, it is evident that there is neither place nor void outside it.

That is why things that are there are naturally such as not to be in place, nor does time age them, nor is there any change for any of the things that are stationed above the outermost spatial movement[47]; instead, |a20| unalterable and unaffectable, having the best and most self-sufficient life, they are attaining their end throughout all eternity (*aiôn*). (For in fact this name *aiôn* was given utterance by the ancients in a divinely inspired way. For the end that encompasses the time of a given thing's life, outside of which nothing exists in accord with nature, is called the *aiôn* ["lifetime"] of it. And by the same argument, the |a25| end of the entire heaven too, that is, the end that encompasses all of time and the unlimited, is *aiôn* ["eternity"], immortal and divine, deriving its name from its always being [*aiei einai*].) From it too the being and life for other things derive, for some in a more exact way, for others in a more obscure one.

---

44. See *Cael.* 1.9.278^{b}22–23.

45. "Time is the measure of movement" (*Ph.* 4.12.221^{b}7).

46. At *Cael.* 1.9.278^{b}21–279^{a}9.

47. (1) One of the things so stationed is the primary god, an intelligible substance, a divine self-understanding, that is at once an "active understanding [that] is active understanding of active understanding" (*Met.* 12.9.1074^{b}34–35), and the unmoved mover of the primary or outermost heaven, and so of all else (7.1072^{b}13–30). (2) In *Met.* 12.8, however, Aristotle raises the question of "whether we should posit one substance of this sort or several, and, if several, how many" (1073^{a}14–15). He concludes that there are forty-seven, which is a miscalculation, the number actually yielded by his account is forty-nine. Thus, including the primary god, there are at least fifty things that are "stationed above the outermost spatial movement."

And in fact, just as in the philosophical works in circulation[48] |a30| about things divine, it is often brought to light in the arguments that whatever is divine, whatever is primary and highest, is necessarily unchangeable. The fact that this is so attests to what has been said. For neither is there anything else greater[49] that will move it (for then that thing would be more divine[50]), nor has it any defect, nor does it lack any of the noble things proper to it. That it is moved with an unceasing movement is also reasonable; for everything |279b1| ceases moving when it arrives at its proper place, but, in the case of the body that moves in a circle, the place it starts from and at which it ends are the same.

De Caelo 1.12.281a28–283b22

Having made these determinations, what comes next must be discussed. [1] If, accordingly, some things are capable of being and of not being, [2] it is necessary that there be some greatest time determined both for their being and for their not being; I mean, during which the thing at issue is capable |a30| of being and of not being, [3] with respect to any category—for example, [being or not being] human, white, three-cubits

48. The reference, apparently, is to works written by Aristotle himself, or by someone else, and "in circulation" (*NE* 1.5.1096a3) outside the Lyceum. Whatever the precise reference here, it must be to accounts with which the audience of *De Caelo* was familiar. *Exôterikoi logoi* ("external accounts"), which seem to be the same sort of things, are also mentioned at *Ph.* 4.10.217b30, *Met.* 13.1.1076a28–29, *NE* 1.13.1102a26, 6.4.1140a2, *EE* 1.8.1217b20, 2.1.1218b32, *Pol.* 3.6.1278b30, 7.1.1323a21, and "the common accounts" at *DA* 1.4.407b29.

49. *Kreittôn* comes from *kratus* ("strong"), but is also used as the comparative of *agathos* ("good"). Thus, at *NE* 10.7.1177b34–1178a2, the activity of the *kratiston* (superlative of *kratus*) divine element (1177b28) in us (= the understanding) is that of the element that exceeds everything "in its capacity and esteem (*dunamei kai timiotêti*)." *Kreittôn*, therefore, should be understood both as greater in capacity and greater in esteem.

50. See *Met.* 12.9.1074b15–35.

long, or anything else of this sort.[51] For if there will not be a certain quantity [of time], but always a longer one than any proposed and none than which it is shorter, the thing will be capable of being for an unlimited time, and of not being for another |281b1| unlimited time—but this is impossible.

Let our starting-point be the following: Impossible and false do not signify the same thing. However, there is an impossible and possible, a false and a true, that are based on a hypothesis (I mean, for example, it is impossible for a triangle |b5| to contain two right angles and it is possible for the diameter to be commensurable, if these things hold). But there are also things that are possible and impossible, false and true, unconditionally. It is not the same thing, then, for something to be unconditionally false and to be unconditionally impossible. For to say, when you are not standing, that you are standing is false, but not impossible. Similarly, to say that a person playing the lyre, |b10| but not singing, is singing is false, but not impossible. But for someone to be standing and sitting at the same time, and for the diagonal to be commensurable, it is not only false, but also impossible. It is not the same thing, then, to assume something false and something impossible. And the impossible results from the impossible.

A person does of course |b15| at the same time have the capacity for sitting and for standing, because when he has the one, he also has the

51. (i) Start with [3] and notice that it shows that the sense of "being" employed in [1] is predicative being, so that the claim is that some things are capable of being F and of not being F—where F is drawn from one of the categories. (ii) Notice, second, the difference between [2a] being for a maximum time capable of being F and of not being F, and [2b] being capable of being F for a maximal time and of not being F for a maximal time. That [2b] is the intended sense is clear from *Cael.* 1.12.282b12–14: "For it is capable of being and of not being for a definite time (I mean of being for a quantity of time and of not being [for a quantity of time])." (iii) Notice, third, that Aristotle is not claiming that if something is capable of being F and of not being F, then there is some time at which it must be F and some time at which it must be not F. He is explicit that a thing can be capable of something that it never at any time actually does: "this cloak is capable of being cut up, but it will not be cut up but will wear out first" (*Int.* 19.19a12–14). His thought is rather that if something is capable of being F and of not being F, there must be a time at which *it is possible* for it to be F and a time at which *it is possible* for it to be not F—which is just what is ruled out in the case of an eternally existing being, since there cannot be two eternities, one in which it is F and another in which it is not F. That there be a *greatest* time in which a thing that is capable of being F can actually be F is probably a consequence of the idea that beings have definite lifetimes (see *Cael.* 1.9.279a23–25). (iv) Notice, finally, that [1] is not true of finitely existing beings. For if, for example, the greatest time determined for their being alive is some finite time, then there is no greatest one fixed for their being not alive, since that time is unlimited. The net result of (i)–(iv) is that "some things (*enia*)" in [1] must be taken to refer to the eternally existing things whose ordering results in a cosmos.

other—not so as to be sitting and standing at the same time, though, but rather at distinct times. But if something has a capacity for several things for an unlimited time, it cannot be [to do them] at distinct times, but at the same time.

So if for an unlimited time something is capable of passing away, it would have the capacity |b20| for not being. If, then, it has it for an unlimited time, let what it is capable of doing be realized. At the same time, therefore, it will actively be and not be at the same time. A falsehood would result, then, because a falsehood was assumed. But if what was assumed was not impossible, the result would not actually be impossible. Therefore, everything that always is, is unconditionally incapable of passing away.

Similarly, |b25| it is also incapable of coming to be; for if it is capable of coming to be, it will be capable of not being at some time—for while a thing capable of passing away is one that is previously, but now is not or can not be at some later time, a one capable of coming to be is one that can previously not be. But there is no time in which what always is, is capable of not being, whether for an unlimited or for a limited one; |b30| for it is also capable of being in a limited time, if indeed it is in fact capable of being in an unlimited one. Therefore, one and the same thing cannot be capable of being always and of not being always. Moreover, the negation is not possible either, I mean, not always being. Therefore, it is also impossible for something to always be and to be capable of passing away. Neither, similarly, is it capable of coming to be; for of two terms, if it is impossible |282a1| for the posterior one to hold [of something] without the prior one, and if it is impossible for the prior one to hold, it is also impossible for the posterior one to hold. So if what always is cannot at some time not be, it also cannot be capable of coming to be.

And since the negation of what is always capable of being is what is not always capable of being, |a5| while its contrary is what is always capable of not being, the negation of which is what is not always capable of not being, it is necessary for the negations of both to belong to the same thing, and that it be intermediate between what always is and what always is not, capable of being and of not being; for the negation of each will belong to it at some time, if not always. So if |a10| what not always is not will be at some time and not be at some time, clearly what is capable of not always being but is at some time will as well, so that it too will not be. Therefore, the same thing will be capable of being and of not being, and it is intermediate between the two.

The universal argument is this: Let A and B be incapable of belonging to the same thing, and let A or |a15| C and B or D belong to everything [Fig. 1]. It is necessary then that C and D belong to everything that is neither A nor B. Then let E be intermediate between A and B (for what is neither of two contraries is intermediate). It is necessary, then, for both C and D to belong to it. For A or C belongs to everything, so that one of them will also belong to E. Since, then, it is impossible that A belong to it, |a20| C will belong to it. The same argument also applies to D.

Neither what always is, then, nor what always is not is either capable of coming to be or capable of passing away. But it is clear too that if something is capable of coming to be or capable of passing away, it is not eternal. For it will at the same time be capable of always being and capable of not always being; but that this is impossible was proved previously.[52] |a25|

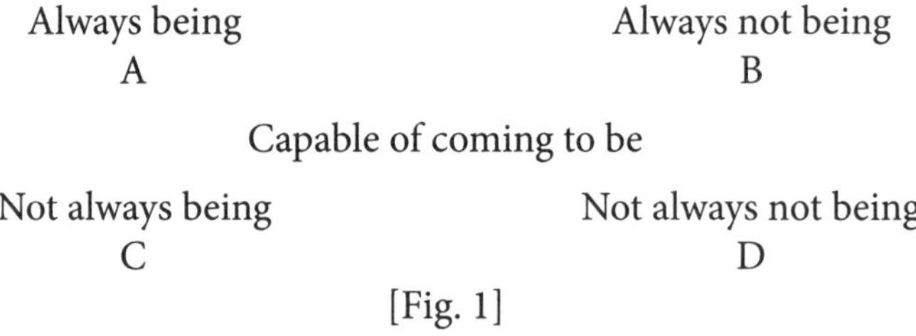

[Fig. 1]

If, then, something is incapable of coming to be, but is, is it necessary for it to be eternal, and likewise if something is incapable of passing away, but is? (I mean incapable of coming to be and incapable of passing away strictly speaking: something incapable of coming to be is now and previously it was not true to say that it is not; something incapable of passing away is now and it will not be true to say later that it is not.) |a30|

Or, rather, if these things follow along with each other, and what is incapable of coming to be is incapable of passing away and what is incapable of passing away is incapable of coming to be, then it is necessary for eternality to follow along with each of them, and whether something is incapable of coming to be or incapable of passing away, it is eternal. This is also clear from the |282b1| definition of them; for necessarily, in fact, if something is capable of passing away, it is capable of coming to be. For it is either incapable of coming to be or capable of coming to be. But if it is incapable of coming to be, it has been established[53] that it is incapable of passing away. And if it is capable of coming to be, then it is necessarily capable of passing away; for either it is capable of passing away or incapable of passing away. But if it is incapable of passing away, it has been established[54] that it is incapable of coming to be. If, on the other hand, |b5| incapable of passing away

52. At *Cael.* 1.12.281b20–25.

53. At *Cael.* 1.12.281b25–33.

54. At *Cael.* 1.12.281b33–282a1.

and incapable of coming to be do not follow along with each other, it is not necessary for either what is incapable of coming to be or what is incapable of passing away to be eternal.

But that it is necessary for them to follow along is evident from the following considerations. For capable of coming to be and capable of passing away follow along with each other. This too is clear from the previous [arguments]; for intermediate between what always is and what always is not |b10| is what follows along with neither of them, and it is what is capable of coming to be and capable of passing away. For it is capable of being and of not being for a definite time (I mean of being for a quantity of time and of not being [for a quantity of time]).

If, therefore, something is capable of coming to be or capable of passing away, it is necessary for it to be intermediate. For let A be what always is, |b15| B what always is not, C what is capable of coming to be, and D what is capable of passing away [Fig. 2]. It is necessary, then, for C to be intermediate between A and B. For there is no time in the direction of either limit in which either A was not or B was. But for what is capable of coming to be, it is necessary that there be such a time either actively or potentially, and for A and B there is not one in either way. Therefore, it [= C] will be, and again not be, for some definite quantity |b20| of time. And likewise too in the case of D. Therefore, each of the two is capable of coming to be and capable of passing away. Therefore, capable of coming to be and capable of passing away follow along with each other.

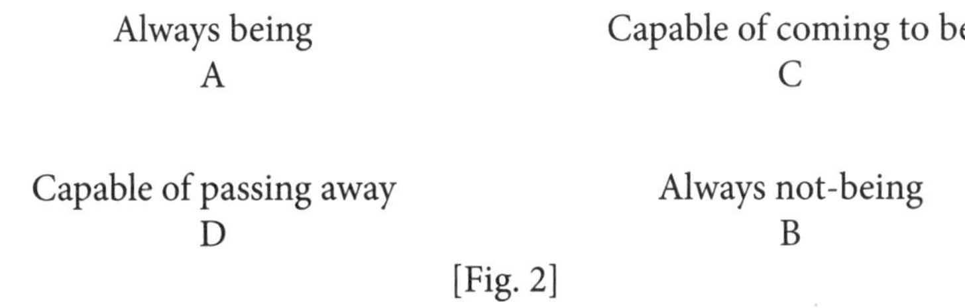

[Fig. 2]

Now, let E be incapable of coming to be, F be capable of coming to be, G be incapable of passing away, and H be capable of passing away. As for F and H, |b25| it has been proved[55] that they follow along with each other. But whenever things are established to be related as these are, such that F and H follow along with each other, and E and F never belong to the same thing, but one or the other belongs to everything, and likewise for G and H, then it is also

55. The reference is probably to *Cael.* 1.12.281b18–25 but could be to 282a4–14.

necessary that E and G follow along with each other. For let E not follow along with G. Therefore, F will follow along with |b30| G; for E or F belongs to everything. But then H also belongs to whatever F belongs to. Therefore, H will follow along with G. But it has been established that this is impossible. The same argument proves too that G follows along with E. |283a1|

Moreover, the same relation holds between what is incapable of coming to be, E, and what is capable of coming to be, F, as between the incapable of passing away, G, and what is capable of passing away, H [Fig. 3].

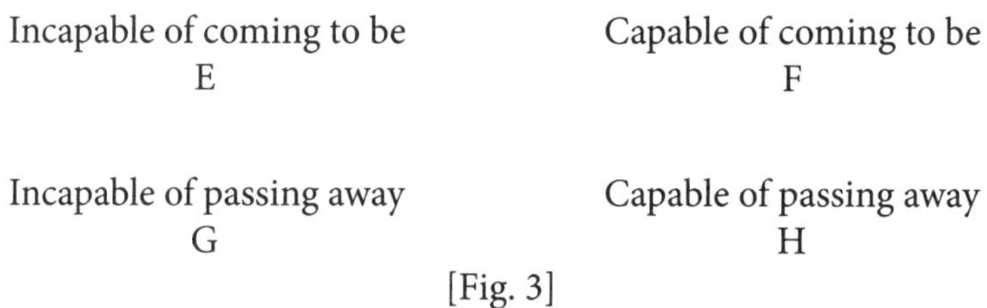

[Fig. 3]

To say that nothing prevents something that comes to be from being capable of passing away, and something incapable of coming to be from having passed away, if in the one case coming to be |a5| and in the other the passing away occurs only once, is to do away with one of the things that have been granted. For all things are capable either of affecting or of being affected, of being or of not being, for either an unlimited or for some definite quantity of time (and an unlimited one [simply] because of this, namely, because the unlimited is in a way definite, being what nothing is greater than). What is unlimited in some way, then, is neither unlimited nor definite. |a10|

Further, what more [cause] did what previously always was have to pass away, or what previously always was not to come to be, at this point [in time than any other]? For if there was no more, and the points are unlimited [in number], it is clear that for an unlimited time something was capable of coming to be and capable of passing away. Therefore, it was capable of not being for an unlimited time. Therefore[56] it will at the same time have a capacity for not being and for being—beforehand, |a15| if it is capable of passing away, afterward if it is capable of coming to be. So if we suppose the things it is capable of to be realized, contraries will belong to it at the same time.

Further, these things will belong to it alike at every point in time, so that for an unlimited time it will have a capacity for not being and for being; but it has been proved[57] that this is impossible. |a20|

56. Reading ἄρ'.

57. At *Cael.* 1.12.181b20–25.

Further, if the capacity belongs to it prior to its activation, it will belong to it for the entirety of time, even when it had not come to be and was not—the unlimited time in which it is capable of coming to be.[58] At the same time, then, it was not and had a capacity for being, both for being then and later on—therefore for an unlimited time.

It is also evident in another way that [the unlimited is incapable of passing away, because it is evident that] it is impossible for what is capable of passing away not to have passed away at some time. For it will always be at the same time |a25| both capable of passing away and not actually passed away. So at the same time it will be capable of always being and of not always being. Therefore, what is capable of passing away passes away at some time. And if it is capable of coming to be, it has come to be [at some time]; for it was capable of having come to be, and therefore of not always being.

It can also be seen in the following way that it is impossible either for what has come to be at some time to persist, incapable of passing away, or for what is incapable of coming to be |a30| and previously always was to pass away. For nothing can be by chance either incapable of passing away or incapable of coming to be. For what is by chance or by luck is beyond what always or for the most part either is or comes to be. But what is for an unlimited time, whether unconditionally |283b1| or from a certain point, belongs either always or for the most part. Therefore, it is necessarily by nature that things of this sort are at some times and not at others. And in things of this sort the same capacity is for what is contradictory, and the matter is the cause of their being and not being. So it is necessary for opposites to belong |b5| actively too at the same time.[59]

Moreover, it is not true to say of anything now that it is last year, or of something last year that it is now. Therefore, it is impossible for what is not at some time to be eternal at a later one; for later it will also have the capacity for not being—except not one for not-being-at-the-time-when-it-is (for then actively being will belong to it), but for not being last year or in time past. |b10| Let, then, what it is a capacity for belong to it actively. It will, therefore, be true to say of it now that it is not last year. But this is impossible; for there is no capacity for having come to be, but [only] for being now or being in the future. Likewise, if previously it is eternal and later will not be; for it will have a capacity for something that actively is not. So if we suppose |b15| what it is capable of to be realized, it will be true to say now that it is last year and, in general, in time past.

58. Reading γίγνεσθαι δυνάμενον.

59. Reading καὶ ἅμα.

And if we investigate in a natural scientific way, and not in universal terms, it will be impossible either for something that previously eternally is to pass away later, or for what previously is not to be eternal later on. For things that are capable of coming to be and capable of passing away are all alterable as well. But they are altered by their contraries, and the things from which natural beings are composed are also the same ones by which they are caused to pass away.

De Caelo 2.1.283^{b}26–284^{b}5

It is possible to obtain the conviction that the entire heaven has neither come to be nor is it possible for it to pass away, as some people say it is, but is one and eternal, having neither starting-point nor end of its entire eternity, on the basis of what has been said, and by means of the doctrine of those who speak otherwise by having it come to be; for if it is possible for things to be as we say, but not possible for them to be in the way described by those who say it comes to be, this should add great weight to the conviction about its being immortal and eternal.

That is why it is well to convince oneself that the ancient accounts, especially those of our forefathers, are true, namely, that there is something immortal and divine among the things that have movement, having movement of such a sort that there is no limit to it, but rather it is the limit of the others; for the limit belongs to what encompasses, and this movement, being complete, encompasses the incomplete movements, which have a limit and a cessation, while itself has neither a start nor an end, but rather is unceasing throughout unlimited time, and is the cause of the start of the others,[60] and receives their cessation.

The ancients assigned the heaven, that is, the upper place to the gods on the supposition that it alone is immortal. And the present account testifies to its being incapable of passing away and incapable of coming to be, and, further, to its being unaffectable by all mortal difficulty, and, in addition to these, it is unlabored,[61] because it needs no additional necessary force which restrains it, preventing it from spatially moving in another way that is natural to it; for everything of that sort is laborious, the more so the more eternal it is, and without a share of the best disposition.[62]

60. I.e., of the others that in fact have a start and a cessation.

61. See *Ph.* 8.10.267^{b}3n.

62. See *Cael.* 1.9.279^{a}18–22.

That is why one must not suppose it to be in accord with the myth of the ancients,[63] who say that the heaven needs the addition of some Atlas[64] for its preservation; for it seems that |^{a}20| the people who composed this account had the same supposition as the later ones; for on the supposition that all bodies have weight and are earthy, they supported the heaven in mythical fashion with an animate necessity.

One must not, then, suppose it to be this way, nor that, because of its whirling's having a spatial movement that is faster than its own balance-weight,[65] |^{a}25| the heaven has been preserved [from falling to the earth] for all this time, as Empedocles says.[66]

But neither is it reasonable that the heaven remains eternal because a soul necessitates it; for it is not possible for this sort of life to be painless and blessedly happy for a soul; for it necessarily, with respect to its movement,[67] involves force—if indeed it moves the primary body |^{a}30| in another way than with its natural spatial movement, and moves it continuously—and being unleisured and deprived of all thought-involving ease, if indeed it does not have, as does the soul of mortal animals, the relaxation of the body that comes about in sleep. Instead, it is necessary that a fate of some Ixion,[68] eternal and indefatigable, restrain it.

If, then, as we said, |^{a}35| it is possible for the primary spatial movement to be the way we have stated, |284^{b}1| not only is it more refined to think this

63. E.g., Hesiod, *Theogony*, 517.

64. See Hesiod, *Theogony*, 517. "What hinders a thing from moving or acting in accord with its own impulse is said to hold it—for example, the pillars hold the weight lying on them, and, as the poets say, 'Atlas holds up the heaven,' on the supposition that it would fall to the earth otherwise, as some of the physicists also say" (*Met.* 5.23.1023^{a}17–21).

65. "We see that the things that have a greater balance-weight (*rhopên*) of heaviness or lightness, other things being equal, spatially move across equal distances faster, and in accord with the ratio that their magnitudes bear to each other" (*Ph.* 4.8.216^{a}13–16). A's heaviness is its non-comparative tendency to move downward; its lightness, its non-comparative tendency to move upward: "By 'unconditionally light,' then, we mean that which spatially moves upward or to the extremity, and by 'unconditionally heavy' that which spatially moves downward or to the center. By 'light in relation to something else,' or 'lighter,' we mean that, of two bodies possessed of weight and of equal volume, the lighter one is the one that is exceeded by the other in the speed of its by nature downward movement" (*Cael.* 4.1.308^{a}29–33). A's balance-weight is its weight or lightness in comparison to B's, when A is in one pan of a (fair) balance or weighing-scale and B is in the other. If the A pan moves downward, A has a greater balance-weight of heaviness than B, and a smaller balance-weight of lightness. On the claim about whirling, see *Cael.* 2.13.295^{a}14–^{b}9.

66. At DK B35 = TEGP 51.F28.

67. Reading κατὰ τὴν κίνησιν.

68. A Thessalian king who attempted to rape Hera, the wife of Zeus; Zeus punished him by chaining him to a fiery wheel on which he was condemned to revolve forever.

way about its eternity, but also this is the only way to provide harmonious accounts that are in agreement with the prophecy about the god.[69] But let this be enough about these sorts of accounts for now. |^{b}5|

---

69. *Tê[i] manteia[i] peri ton theon*: The noun *manteia* occurs three times in Aristotle: here, at *HA* 8.18.601^{b}2 (referring to a text of Hesiod), and in F10. The latter, which is alone salient, suggests that *tê[i] manteia[i] peri ton theon* is referring to (1) prophetic experience of the sort that human beings allegedly have in sleep. Another possibility is (2) that floated by Simplicius: "Only if we say that [the heaven's] activity is not forced but in accord with nature can we provide indisputably harmonious accounts. He calls this the common conception (*koinên ennoian*) we have of the freedom from labor and blessed happiness of the divine and oracle because it inheres more strongly that what is demonstrated and is most steadfast and unchangeable. And the oracles that are in accord with divine knowledge are of this sort, beyond all demonstration and of unchangeable persuasiveness" (Simp. 382.26–32). A third option takes the reference to be to (3) the view of the ancients described at *Cael.* 2.1.284^{a}11–18, which, stemming as it does from myths and so on, has a genuinely inspirational character of the sort F10 attests to. See *Met.* 12.8.1074^{a}38–^{b}14 (noting *theiôs* at 1074^{b}9). But then these myths, however inspired they may seem to us, are at the same time the decayed remnants of past scientific theories every bit as sophisticated as our own. Notice the reference to prophets at *Cael.* 2.2.285^{a}3–4.

All of which brings us to the question of why we have (a) *peri* + the accusative *ton theon*, rather than (b) *peri* + genitive *tou theou.* With the genitive, *peri* means "about" in the sense of "concerning" or "dealing with," so that *tê[i] manteia[i] peri ton theon* is the prophecy dealing with the god. But this poses a problem: *manteia* is about the future. Hence the pseudo-Platonic definition of *manteia* as "scientific knowledge foreshowing an action without a demonstrative argument" (*Definitions* 414b) and the joke at *Rh.* 3.17.1418^{a}23–24 that the past is "scientifically knowable—'even to prophets (*mantesin*),' as Epimenides the Cretan said." *Peri* + the accusative, on the other hand, gives "around" a spatial sense of "around and about," or "surrounding," so that *tê[i] manteia[i] peri ton theon* refers to prophetic activity around (and so dependent on) the god, with no implication as to content, and so no requirement of futurity.

Next step: At *NE* 10.8.1179^{a}24–30 Aristotle writes: "if the gods exercise a sort of supervision over human affairs, as indeed they seem to, it would also be reasonable both that they should enjoy what is best and most akin to themselves (and this would be the understanding) and that they should reward those who most like and honor it for taking care of what they themselves love and for acting correctly and nobly. But that all these qualities belong most of all to the wise person is not unclear. Therefore, he is most loved by the gods." At the same time, however, he is explicit that the gods in question live exclusively contemplative lives (10.8.1178^{b}8–23), so that whatever supervision they exercise over human affairs must be of a somewhat special sort. Aristotle does not tell us what it is, but his identification of these gods with the heavenly spheres (*Met.* 12.8.1074^{a}38–^{b}14) suggests an answer. For the orderly revolutions of these spheres govern the seasons as well as the cycles of fertility and infertility of land and animals (*GA* 4.10.778^{a}4–9). Hence they confer benefits on all beings, but especially on those wise people who, through astronomical contemplation of the heavens, learn about these cycles, and adjust their lives accordingly. We might think of the case of Thales who "apprehended from his astronomy that a good olive harvest was coming" (*Pol.* 1.11.1259^{a}10–11).

Putting everything together, then, we should take *tê[i] manteia[i] peri ton theon* as referring to prophetic activity based on scientific knowledge of the movements of the primary heaven and other celestial phenomena, whose order and unforced movement is dependent on the soul (Aristotle's primary god) that is the basis in fact of the myth of Atlas.

De Caelo 2.2.284^{b}10–285^{b}8

First of all, if right and left do belong [to the heaven], one must suppose that prior starting-points belong to it in a prior way. These things have been determined in our works on the movement of animals, because they properly belong to the nature of animals[70]; for evidently in some animals it is evident that |^{b}15| all parts of this sort belong (I mean, for example, right and left), in others [only] some, while in plants only up and down belong.[71] If, however, one must ascribe some parts of this sort to the heaven as well, it is reasonable that the first one, as we said,[72] that belongs in animals belongs in it too; for there are three [pairs], each of which is a starting-point |^{b}20| of a sort. The three I mean are: up and down, front and its opposite, and right and left; for it is reasonable that all these dimensions belong to complete bodies. Up, though, is a starting-point of length, right of breadth, and front of depth. Further, |^{b}25| [they are starting-points] in another way, in accord with movements; for I mean by "starting-points" these things from which the movements first start for the things that have them. Growth, though, starts from the up, movement with respect to place from things right, and perception from the front; for by "front" I mean what perceptions are directed toward.[73]

That is why one must not look for up |^{b}30| and down, right and left, and front and back in every body, but only in those that, being animate, have a starting-point of movement within them; for in inanimate ones we do not see the starting-point from which the movement derives; for some things

---

70. In particular, *IA* 4–5.

71. See *Cael.* 2.2.284^{b}27–29n.

72. At *Cael.* 2.2.284^{b}11–14.

73. In the case of all sublunary living things, up and down are not just spatially or relationally distinguished but functionally and absolutely so: "The part from which the distribution of nourishment and growth derives in each living thing is the up, while the last part it reaches is the down. The former is a sort of starting-point, the other a limit" (*IA* 2.705^{a}32–^{b}2). That is why a plant, whose roots are down below, not as in animals up above, is a sort of upside-down animal: "Up and down are not the same for all things as they are for the universe, but as the head is of animals, so the roots are of plants—if we are to speak of instrumental parts as distinct or the same by appeal to their functions" (*DA* 2.4.416^{a}2–5; see also *PA* 4.10.686^{a}25–687^{a}2). Similarly, in animals the front is a starting-point, because it is what perception is directed toward (*IA* 4.705^{b}10–13). Even in earthworms, where right and left are more difficult to distinguish perceptually, the functional difference between them still exists: "the starting-point from which movement derives is the same in all [animals], and by nature has its position in the same place; and [the] right is that from which movement derives" (5.706^{a}10–13). Thus human beings put their left foot forward, unless they accidentally do the opposite, since "they move not by the leg they put forward, but by the leg with which they step off" (706^{a}8–9).

do not move at all, whereas others, though they do move, do not do so in every direction alike—for example, fire moves upward only |ᵇ35| and earth toward the center. But in things of this sort we speak of |285ᵃ1| up and down and right and left with reference to ourselves; for we speak of them either with reference to our own right, as prophets do,[74] or with reference to what is similar to our right, as with the sides of a statue, or of what has its position in the contrary way, speaking of right with reference to |ᵃ5| our left, and left with reference to our right, and of back with reference to our front. In these things themselves, on the other hand, we do not see any differences; for if they are turned around, we call their contraries "right," "left," "up," "down," "front," and "back."

. . .[75]

Since we have determined previously[76] that capacities of this sort belong in things that have a starting-point of movement, and the heaven is animate,[77] that is, has a starting-point of movement, it is clear that it also has both up and |ᵃ30| down and right and left.

For there is no need to be puzzled, because the shape of the universe is spherical, as to how there can be a right and a left of it when all its parts are similar and all the time moving. Instead, |285ᵇ1| we should understand that it is as if it were a thing in which there is a difference between right and left, even in their shapes, around which someone has placed a sphere; for it will then have the capacity corresponding to the difference, but would seem not to because of the uniformity of its shape. It is the same way with the starting-point |ᵇ5| of movement; for even if it never began moving, nonetheless it is necessary for it to have a starting-point from which it would have begun if it had begun moving, and, if it were to come to a stop, from which it would start moving again.

74. "We say that a bird that is on our right is a bird from the right and call it a right [= good] omen (*sumbolon*) in this way" (Simp. 383.38–384.2).

75. Omitting 285ᵃ7–27, which criticizes the Pythagoreans.

76. *IA* 4–5.

77. The heaven has not previously been characterized as animate, so its possession of a soul amounts here simply to its having a starting-point of movement, although there will later turn out to be more to it than that. See *Cael.* 2.12.292ᵃ18–21.

De Caelo 2.3.286^{a}7–12

The cause of [there being several spatial movements] must be grasped from the following. Each thing of which there is a function is for the sake of the function. The activity of a god is immortality, and this is eternal living. So it is necessary that eternal movement belongs to the god.[78] And since the heaven is such (for it is a certain divine body),[79] because of this it has a circular body, which by nature always moves in a circle.

78. This seems to conflict with the fact that Aristotle's primary god is "immovable and eternal" (*Ph.* 8.6.259^{b}32–33). (a) One way to remove the apparent conflict is to suppose that the claim belongs to an earlier phase in Aristotle's thought in which the unmoved mover played no part. But another is available that is more attractive, since it involves no otherwise unsupported appeals to chronology. (b) The primary heaven (or outermost sphere of the fixed stars) is a corporeal (though ethereal) sphere which, as animate, has a soul of its own (*Met.* 12.8), which soul, in the case of the primary heaven, is the immovable wholly intelligible self-contemplator that is the (primary) god. But just as "human" can refer to the animate body, the compound of body and soul, or to the understanding, which is the divine element in the human soul, so *theos* ("god") can refer either to the animate sphere or to the immovable understanding that moves it. We see this clearly in Plato: "Because we have not seen a god or adequately grasped one with our understanding," he says, "we imagine a kind of immortal living creature that has both a soul and a body, combined for all time" (*Phaedrus* 246c–d). But really it is the souls of these immortal creatures that are alone gods: "Consider the stars and the moon, the years, months, and all the seasons: what other account can we give except this same one? Since a soul or souls are evidently the causes of all these things, and good souls possessed of every virtue, we shall declare these souls to be gods" (*Laws* 899b). The next sentence in our text (*Cael.* 2.3.286^{a}10–12) involves essentially the same ambiguity (see next note). So "the god" in our text should therefore be taken to refer to the animate sphere, whose movement is quite consistent with the immovability of the understanding (which *is* the god) that moves it.

79. "Such (*toioutos*)" is probably best understood as referring to the previous sentence (*Cael.* 2.3.286^{a}10) and so as meaning "such as to have eternal movement belonging to it." The parenthetical clause is then genuinely explanatory. For knowing that the god (286^{a}10) is an unmoved mover (previous note), Aristotle knows he must explain how eternal movement can belong to it. Answer: considered as an animate sphere it is "a certain divine body," which is divine for just the reason that a human being's body is human, and as such can (coincidentally) move (see *DA* 1.3). Thus, as a human being is an animate body and so has a body, so the god, as an animate sphere, has a spherical body. But the god that has it—the being that is alone strictly speaking the god (previous note)—is the immovable self-contemplator, already in the picture in *Ph.* 8 and properly discussed in *Met.* 12.7–10.

De Caelo 2.5.287^{b}22–288^{a}12

There are two ways of moving in a circle[80] . . . ; that these movements are not contraries has been said previously.[81] But if nothing that is by luck or by chance can possibly be among the eternal things, |^{b}25| and the heaven is eternal, as its spatial movement in a circle, due to what cause does it spatially move in one direction and not in the other? For it is necessary for this either to be a starting-point or that there be a starting-point of it.[82]

Now, to try to prove all things, omitting nothing, in the same way as one does certain things, would perhaps seem to be a sign of great |^{b}30| naivety or of great audaciousness.[83] But it is not just, at any rate, to censure in the same way all [who do try]. Instead, one must look to see what the cause is of their saying what they say, and furthermore in what way they have hold of their conviction, whether in a merely human way or something stronger.[84] Indeed, when someone hits on necessities that are more exact, then one must show gratitude to the discoverers, for now, though, |288^{a}1| we must state what appears to be so.[85]

For if nature always produces the best of the things that are possible, and if, just as in the case of rectilinear spatial movements, that toward the upper place is more estimable (for the upper place is more divine than the lower), and in the same way too forward |^{a}5| spatial movement is more estimable than backward, and[86] if indeed [the heaven] has a right and a left, as was said previously[87] (and the puzzle just stated testifies that it does), it has a priority and a posteriority[88]; for this cause resolves the puzzle. For if things are in the best state possible, |^{a}10| this would in fact be the cause of what was stated; for it is best to be moved with a simple, unceasing movement, and for this to be in a direction that is more estimable.

80. Clockwise and counterclockwise.

81. At *Cael.* 1.4.271^{a}19–22.

82. I.e., the directionality of the heaven's rotation is either a starting-point, and so not open to demonstration, or something that can be demonstrated from a starting-point.

83. Compare: "Now some people do demand that we demonstrate even this [the principle of non-contradiction], but this is due to lack of educatedness. For it is lack of educatedness not to know what things we should look for a demonstration of and what things we should not. For it is in general impossible to demonstrate everything (for it would go on without limit, so that even then there would be no demonstration). But if there are things we should not look for a demonstration of, these people would not be able say what starting-point they think has more of a claim to be such" (*Met.* 4.4.1006^{a}5–11).

84. See *Cael.* 1.3.270^{b}11–13.

85. Compare *Met.* 12.8.1073^{b}8–17.

86. Reading ἔχει δέ.

87. At *Cael.* 2.2.285^{a}31.

88. I.e., a front (facing the direction in which it moves) and a back.

De Caelo 2.7.289a11–35

We should next speak about what are called "stars," what they are composed of, in what sorts of shapes, and what their movements are.

It is most reasonable, then, and follows from what we have said, to make each of the stars be composed of the body in which it has its spatial movement, since we said[89] that there is something |a15| that is of a nature to spatially move in a circle; for just as those who declare that the stars are fiery do so because they say that the upper body is fire, and that it is reasonable for each to be composed of what it is in, so we too are speaking in a similar way.[90]

The heat and light from the stars comes about when air is chafed by |a20| their spatial movement.[91] For movement is of a nature to ignite even

89. See *Cael.* 1.2–3. That the stars move in a circle is due to their matter (ether), but their movement in the most estimable direction (*Cael.* 2.5.288a10–12) is explained by the immovable mover (*Met.* 12.7.1072a19–30).

90. See *Cael.* 1.2.269b10–11.

91. The implication that there is air in contact with the sphere of the stars (which include the sun and moon) is explicitly embraced in 2.9: "if indeed the bodies of the stars are moving either in a quantity of air or of fire spread through the universe, *as everyone says*" (291a18–20). But it is also suggested by the following text: "We say that [1] what is upper (*to anô*) as far as the moon (*mechri selênês*) is [2] a body distinct from air or fire, but varying in purity and freedom from admixture, and admitting of difference (*diaphoras echein*), especially [3] toward its limit on the side of the air, and the cosmos surrounding the earth" (*Mete.* 1.3.340b6–10). For since [2] refers to ether (primary body) and the variation of affections in it, especially as it gets closer to (roughly) the earth and its atmosphere, [1] must refer to the upper region of the cosmos *down* as far as the moon. The fieriness of the lunar region is evidenced by the following texts: (1) "The outermost part of what is called 'the air' has the capacity of fire" (8.345b33–34). (2) "The air . . . is composed of . . . vapor, which is wet and cold, . . . and smoke, which is hot and dry" (2.4.360a21–25). (3) "The fourth genus [of animals] must not be sought in these places [land, water, air], although there certainly wants (*bouletai*) to be one corresponding to fire in the order. For it is counted as the fourth of the [simple] bodies. But fire always appears to have a shape [= form] that is not special to it, on the contrary, it is always in another of the bodies. For what is on fire appears to be either air, smoke, or earth. Instead, this fourth genus must be sought on the moon. For it appears to participate in [the body] at the fourth remove [= fire]" (*GA* 3.11.761b15–22). No parallel explanation of the light from the stars is given, but one is easily provided by appeal to the account of light in *DA* 2.7: "It is not insofar as something is water or insofar as it is air that it is visible, but because there is a certain nature in it that is the same in both of them and in the [eternal] body above [= ether]. And light is the activity of this, of the transparent insofar as it is transparent. But whatever this is present in, so potentially is darkness. For light is a sort of color of the transparent, when it is made actually transparent by fire or something of that sort, such as the body above. For one and the same [affection] also belongs to it" (418b7–13). Thus as the air mixed in with the ether explains, via friction, the heat from the stars, so the ether mixed in with the air explains their light.

wood, stones, and iron. It is more reasonable, then, for it to do the same to what is closer to fire, and air is closer to fire—as, for example, in the case of spatially moving missiles; for these are themselves ignited to such an extent that lead balls melt, and, since these are ignited, it is necessary for |289ᵃ25| the air around them to be affected in the same way. These missiles themselves, then, are heated up because of their spatial movement in air, which becomes fire because of a blow struck by the movement.[92]

Each of the upper things spatially moves in a sphere, so that, though they themselves cannot ignite, the air beneath the sphere of the rotating body is necessarily |ᵃ30| heated up, especially there where the sun happens to be fixed. That is why heat comes about when the sun gets closer, rises, and is over us.

About the fact that the stars are neither fiery nor spatially move in fire, then, let us say this much. |ᵃ35|

De Caelo 2.12.291ᵇ24–293ᵃ14

There are two puzzles, which it makes perfect sense for anyone to puzzle over, about which we must try to state what appears to be so, |ᵇ25| thinking such audaciousness to be reverence rather than rashness, if someone, because of his thirst for philosophy,[93] is content to become a little more puzzle-free concerning the things about which we have the greatest puzzlement.

Among the many things of this sort, not the least wondrous is what the cause is due to which |ᵇ30| it is not those bodies that are more distant from the primary spatial movement that always have more movements,

92. "We see that movement is capable of disaggregating (*diakrinein*) and igniting air, so that even things in spatial movement often appear to melt. The sun's spatial movement, then, is sufficient by itself to produce warmth and provide heat. For to do so it must be fast and not too far away. Now, the spatial movement of the [fixed] stars, though fast, is far off, while that of the moon, though close by, is slow. But that of the sun has enough of both characteristics. That more heat should be generated when the sun itself is there is reasonable, if we take the similarity from what comes about where we are. For here too it is the air that is closest to what is spatially moving by force that becomes most hot. And this happens quite reasonably. For the movement of a solid object disaggregates it most. This, then, is one cause due to which heat reaches this place here. Another is that the fire encompassing the air is often dispersed by the [sun's] movement and by force carried downward" (*Mete.* 1.3.341ᵃ17–31).

93. "The mathematical science that is most akin to philosophy [is] astronomy" (*Met.* 12.8.1073ᵇ4–5).

but rather that the intermediate ones have the most. For it would seem reasonable, since the primary body has one spatial movement, for what is closest to it moves with the fewest movements—for example, two, the next three, or that there be some other order of this sort. But as things stand, the contrary is the case; for the sun and the moon move with fewer |b35| movements than some of the wandering stars.[94] And yet these are farther |292a1| away from the center and closer to the primary body. And in some cases this has even been made clear by sight; for we have seen the moon, when half-full, move under the star of Ares [Mars], which was occulted by |a5| the dark half of the moon, and come out on its light and bright side.[95] The ancient Egyptians and Babylonians, who have kept a close watch for the most years, speak similarly about the other stars as well, and from them we have acquired many convictions about each of the stars.

One might justly raise this puzzle and also that of what exactly the cause is due to which |a10| the multitude of stars in the primary spatial movement is so great that their whole order seems to be uncountable, whereas each of the others has one separate star, and two or more do not appear fixed on the same spatial movement.

Where these issues are concerned, then, it is well to seek to increase our comprehension, even though we have few things |a15| to start from and are at such a great distance from what happens concerning them. Nonetheless, for those who get their theoretical grasp on the basis of things of the following sort, what is presently puzzling would not seem to be at all unreasonable. We think about these stars as bodies only, that is, as units having a certain order, altogether inanimate. But we should conceive of them as participating |a20| in action and life; for in this way what happens will not seem at all contrary to reason.[96] For it seems that the good belongs without

94. I.e., planets. In *Met.* 12.8, three versions of the theory of homocentric spheres are considered: Eudoxus', Callippus', and Aristotle's own theory. In Eudoxus' theory, the sun and the moon have three movements each, the other planets four each. So they have fewer movements than *all* of the planets. In Callippus' theory, the sun and the moon have five movements each, as do Venus, Mercury, and Mars, while Jupiter and Saturn have four. So in his theory they have fewer movements than none of the planets.

95. Dating the sighting to May 4, 357 BC between 7:49 and 8:00 pm, Athens mean time. This, however, is subject to a "clock error" of about 1000 seconds.

96. Compare: "We consider that we have adequately demonstrated in accord with reason (*logos*) things unapparent to perception if we have led things back to what is possible" (*Mete.* 1.7.344a5–7).

action to what is in the best state,[97] to what is closest by means of one small action, and to what is further away by means of several actions. It is just as in the case of the body: one is in a good state without exercising, another

97. What is being described, as *Met.* 12.7.1072^{b}22–30 shows, is the primary god (the immovable mover of the primary heaven). What is puzzling about the description is that it characterizes the primary god as possessing the good "without action" while at the same time identifying him with contemplative activity, which is itself a sort of action. We find the very same puzzle in *NE* 10.8.1178^{b}17–23. To resolve the puzzle, our first port of call must be another puzzling text: "the [primary] god always enjoys a single simple pleasure. For there is not only an activity of moving but also an activity of immobility (*akinêsias*), and pleasure is found more in rest than in movement" (*NE* 7.13.1154^{b}26–28). Now, "in the case of what movement belongs to, immobility is rest" (*Ph.* 3.2.202^{a}5), but to the primary god, as we see, movement does not belong, so its immobility is not simply rest or privation of movement. Thus step one in the resolution of our puzzle is that god's immobility is not simply one of rest. That opens up the requisite possibility that it involves something else. Second step: the paradigm cases of *actions*, as we understand them, are temporally extended bodily movements appropriately related to (perhaps by being caused by) beliefs, desires, and intentions. Hence "action" is clearly a somewhat misleading translation of *praxis*. Nonetheless, there is one type of action that *praxeis* seem to resemble quite closely, namely, so-called *basic actions*—actions we do directly without having to do anything else. This is especially true, if, as Aristotle himself seems to believe, these are thought to be *internal* mental acts of some sort: "we say that in the most controlling sense the ones who above all do actions, even in the case of external actions, are the ones who by means of their thoughts are their architectonic craftsmen" (*Pol.* 7.3.1325^{b}21–23). Like *praxeis*, in any case, these sorts of mental acts are not bodily movements and do not seem to take time to perform. Moreover, just as we do not perform basic actions by doing something else first, the same seems true of *praxeis*, so that a human being, for example, "is a starting-point and begetter of *praxeis* just as he is of children" (*NE* 3.5.1113^{b}18–19; also 6.2.1139^{b}5). So what we should say, then, is that the good belongs without *external* action to what is in the best state. But that, of course, is quite consistent with its not doing so without internal actions, such as the contemplative ones in which the primary god's life exclusively consists. Third step: some actions are done both for their own sake and for the sake of other things, which may themselves be actions (*NE* 10.7.1177^{b}6–15). Other actions or activities, by contrast, are done solely for their own sake, and these (or this) are the ones in which happiness consists: "It is not necessary, as some suppose, for an action-involving (*praktikon*) life to be lived in relation to other people, nor are those thoughts alone action-involving that arise for the sake of the consequences of doing an action, rather, much more so are the acts of contemplation and thought that are their own ends and are engaged in for their own sake. For doing well in action is the end, and so action of a sort is the end too" (*Pol.* 7.3.1325^{b}17–21). In *Cael.* itself, Aristotle will soon rely on this very point (2.12.292^{b}4–7). Putting the three steps together, the entire solution to our puzzle is now before us: that the good belongs without any action that is either *external* action or *not exclusively an end* to what is in the best state. Compare this passage from ††*De Mundo*: "[The god] needs no contrivance or the service of others, in the way that rulers among us need many helping hands because of their weakness. On the contrary, what is most divine would be this: to produce multifarious kinds (*ideas*) of things with ease and with a simple movement, just as consummate craftsmen do, by using as their instrument a single release mechanism, to accomplish many different activities. In the same way puppeteers, by pulling a single string, make the neck, hand, shoulder, eye, and sometimes all the parts, move with rhythmic movement" (6.398^{b}10–19).

by walking around a little, |a25| a third needs running, wrestling, and hard training, while to another again this good would not yet belong no matter how much exertion he undergoes, but rather a distinct one.[98]

It is difficult, though, to attain success either in all things or often—for example, to make ten thousand Chian throws at knucklebones is inconceivable, but one or two is comparatively easy.[99] And, again, when it is necessary |a30| that one do this for the sake of that, and that for the sake of something else, it is easy to succeed at one stage or two,[100] but when it is through a greater number, it is more difficult.

That is why one should think the action of the stars to be |292b1| like that of animals and plants. For here the actions of human beings are in fact most numerous; for it is possible to attain many goods, so that it is possible to do many things in action, and for the sake of other ones. (What is in the best state, by contrast, has no need of action; for it is itself the |b5| for-the-sake-of-which[101]; action, though, is always in two [varieties], namely, when it is the for-the-sake-of-which and when it is what is for the sake of that.[102]) The actions of the other animals, on the other hand, are fewer, and of the plants perhaps one small one; for either there is some one thing which they may attain, as there is for a human being too, or the many things are a route toward the best one. |b10| One thing, then, has and participates in the best, one reaches close[103] to it by means of few [steps], another by means of many, and another does not even try, but it is sufficient for it to come close to the ultimate [end]. For example, if health is the end, one thing, then, is always healthy, another is slimming down [to be healthy], another running and slimming down, another does some other action for the sake of running, so that its movements are more numerous; a distinct one, |b15| though, is incapable of reaching being healthy, but only of running or slimming down (and one or the other of these is the end for them). For on the one hand it is best of all for each to attain the end; but on the other, if this is not [possible], it would always be better to the degree that it got closer to the best one.

---

98. I.e., the next best thing. See *Cael.* 2.12.292b17–19.

99. An *astragalos* is an ancient form of die made from the knucklebone of a sheep (Google "astragalus" for images). To have the bones land in a Chian configuration would evidently be like landing ten thousand double sixes in throwing dice.

100. Reading ἑνὶ καὶ δυσὶ, but understanding (and translating) καὶ as equivalent in meaning to ἤ.

101. See *EE* 7.12.1245b16–19, *Met.* 12.9.1074b33–35.

102. See *Cael.* 2.12.292a22–23n.

103. Reading ἐγγὺς.

And this is why the earth does not move at all, and things close to it have few |b20| movements; for they do not reach the ultimate [end], but as far as is possible attain the most divine starting-point.[104] The primary heaven, however, attains this[105] directly by means of a single movement. But the bodies intermediate between the first and the last ones, though they do attain it, do so by means of more movements.

As to the puzzle that in the |b25| primary spatial movement, though it is one, a great number of stars is involved, whereas each of the others has separately received its own movement, one might reasonably think this holds primarily because of one thing; for one should understand that in the case of each one's life and starting-point[106] the primary one has a great superiority over the others, and this superiority would turn out to be |b30| proportional; for the primary movement, though one, moves many divine bodies, whereas the others, though many, each moves only one; for any one of the planets spatially moves with several |293a1| spatial movements. In this way, then, nature both equalizes things and produces a certain order, having given many bodies to the one spatial movement, and many spatial movements to the one body.

And, further, it is because of this that the other spatial movements have one body, namely, that the spatial movements before the |a5| final one, which has one star, move several bodies; for the final sphere is carried fixed on many spheres, and each sphere is a body. The work of this final sphere, then, would be common [to all of them]; for while each sphere has a spatial movement that is by nature special to it, this spatial movement is, as it were, added on, and the capacity of every limited body is related to |a10| a limited one.[107]

About the stars spatially moving with circular movement, it has been stated what they are like with respect to their substance and with respect to their shape, as well as where their spatial movement and order are concerned.

---

104. See *Met.* 12.7.1072b1–14.

105. Not the ultimate end (which only the primary god attains), but rather getting as close to it as possible.

106. "The soul is as it were a starting-point of living things" (*DA* 1.1.402a6–7).

107. See *Cael.* 1.7.274b33–275b4.

4. Later Intimations

Coming to Be and Passing Away 2.10.336^{b}27–337^{a}1

[W]e say that in all cases nature always desires what is better, and that being is better than not being[1] (in how many ways things are said to *be* has been stated elsewhere[2]), but this cannot belong to all things, because of their being too far removed from the starting-point,[3] although in the remaining way, the god has completed the whole, and made coming to be perpetual; for in this way being would most of all be connected together, because the closest things to being in the fullest sense are perpetual coming to be and coming to be.[4] The cause of this, as has often been said, is circular spatial movement; for it alone is continuous.[5]

De Anima 1.1.402^{b}5–8

And we must be careful not to neglect to consider whether there is one account of the soul, as of animal, or whether there is a distinct account of each (for example, of horse, dog, human, god)—animal, the universal, being either nothing or posterior.[6]

---

1. An example: "It is clear that most human beings are willing to endure much misery in order to cling to living, on the supposition that there is a sort of joy in it and a natural sweetness" (*Pol.* 3.6.1278^{b}28–30).

2. At *Met.* 4.2.1003^{a}33–^{b}10, 5.7, 6.2, 7.1, 9.1, 10.

3. I.e., "the sort of starting-point on which the heaven and nature depend" (*Met.* 12.7.1072^{b}13–14), which is the unmoved mover of the primary heaven, and so of all the other celestial spheres, including that of the sun, on which sublunary coming to be and passing away depend (*GC* 2.10.336^{a}32–^{b}3), and which is the good that all other beings desire or aspire to.

4. *Ousia*, usually "substance," is here "being in the fullest sense." The being that is in the fullest sense an *ousia* is "the simple one and an activity" (*Met.* 12.7.1072^{a}31–32), namely, the primary god, who is always and at every instant achieving the end or best good, which is at once the teleological cause of himself and of everything else.

5. See *Ph.* 8.8.261^{b}26–265^{a}12.

6. The universal would be nothing if there were no universal to which the souls of things in different species all belonged. In this case "soul" would be homonymous or ambiguous, like "bank" or "key": there is no universal that all banks—river banks, savings banks—instantiate. It would be posterior if knowledge of the universal soul was not possible until after all the various sorts of soul had been defined.

De Anima 1.1.403^{a}3–^{b}16

There is a puzzle too about the affections of the soul, as to whether they are all also shared by what has the soul or whether there is also some affection that is special to the soul itself; for it is necessary to get [a resolution of] this, but it is not easy. But it appears that |^{a}5| in most cases the soul is neither affected by nor does it act without the body—for example, being angry, being confident, having an appetite for things, perceiving in general—whereas understanding seems to be most of all special to the soul. Yet if it too is a sort of imagination, or does not exist without imagination, it would not be possible even for it to exist without a body.

If, then, some function or |^{a}10| affection of the soul is special to it, it will be possible for it to be separated. But if there is nothing special to it, it will not be separable, but will be like the straight, to which, insofar as it is straight, many coincidents belong—for example, it will touch a bronze sphere at a point, although, if separated, the straight will not touch it in this way; for it is inseparable, if indeed it always involves some body. |^{a}15|

So too the affections of the soul—spiritedness, mild-manneredness, fear, pity, confidence, and, further, joy, loving, and hating—would all seem to involve the body; for at the same time as these, the body is affected in a certain way. This is evidenced by the fact that sometimes, though strong and vivid affections take place in us, we are not provoked or |^{a}20| frightened, whereas at other times we are moved by small and faint ones, as when the body is aroused (*orga[i]*) and its condition is like when someone is angry (*orgizêtai*). It is yet more evident that this is so; for sometimes, though nothing frightening is occurring, people come to have the affections of a frightened person.

If this is so, however, it is clear that the affections of the soul are enmattered accounts.[7] So their definitions |^{a}25| will be of this sort, for example: "Being angry is a sort of movement of such-and-such a sort of body, or of a part or a capacity, as a result of this for the sake of that." And that is why it already belongs to the natural scientist to get a theoretical grasp on the soul, either all soul or this sort of soul.

But a natural scientist and a dialectician would define each of these differently—for example, what anger is. For a dialectician it is a desire for retaliation |^{a}30| or something like that, whereas for a natural scientist it is a boiling of the blood and hot stuff around the heart. Of these, the natural scientist gives the matter, whereas the dialectician gives the |403^{b}1| form and the account. For this is the account of the thing, although it must be

7. I.e., accounts that include a reference to matter. See *Met.* 6.1.1025^{b}3–1026^{a}32.

in matter of such-and-such a sort if it is to exist. And so of a house the account is this, that it is a shelter to prevent destruction by winds, rain, and heat. But one person will say that it is stones, |^{b}5| bricks, and timbers, and another that it is the form in them for the sake of these other things.

Which of these people, then, is the natural scientist? Is it the one concerned with the matter but ignorant of the account, or the one concerned with the account alone? Or is it rather the one concerned with what is composed of both? Who, then, is each of the others? Or is there not someone who is concerned with the affections of the matter that are not separable and insofar as they are not separable? Or |^{b}10| is the natural scientist rather the one who is concerned with everything that is a function or affection of this sort of body and this sort of matter? And isn't anything, insofar as it is not of this sort, the concern of someone else, in some cases a craftsman, if there happens to be one, such as a builder or a doctor? And aren't those things that are not separable, but are considered insofar as they are not affections of this sort of body and in abstraction from it, the concern of the mathematician? And insofar as they are separate, |^{b}15| that of the primary philosopher?

De Anima 1.4.408^{b}18–29

The understanding, though, seems to be born in us as a sort of substance, and not to pass away. For if it could pass away, it would most of all be due to the feebleness of old age, but as things stand perhaps it is presumably what happens in the case of |^{b}20| the perceptual organs; for if an old man could get such-and-such a sort of eye, he would see as well as a young one does. So old age is not due to the soul's being affected in a certain way, but rather what the soul is in, as in the case of drunkenness and disease. And, in particular, understanding and contemplating are extinguished because something else within passes away, but it is unaffectable. For thinking |^{b}25| and loving or hating are not affections of that but of this thing here that has that, insofar as it has that. That is why when this passes away it neither remembers nor loves[8]; for they were not [affections] of that, but of what is

8. "That" refers to so-called passive understanding, "it" to so-called productive or active understanding (*DA* 3.5.430^{a}23–24).

common,[9] which has passed away. But the understanding is perhaps something more divine and is unaffectable.[10]

De Anima 2.1.412ᵇ27–413ᵃ9

As, then, cutting and seeing are, so too is being awake an actuality, and as sight and the capacity of the instrument are, so is the soul, |413ᵃ1| whereas the body is what is potentially [alive]. But just as the eye-jelly[11] plus sight is an eye, so in this case the soul plus the body is an animal. Hence that the soul is not separable from the body—or that certain parts of it are not, if it naturally has parts—is not unclear; for of some parts |ᵃ5| the actuality is of the parts themselves. Nevertheless nothing prevents some of them,[12] at any rate, from being separable, because of being the actualities of no body. Further, it is unclear whether the soul is the actualization of the body in the way a sailor is of a ship.[13]

9. I.e., the rational animal to whom both the soul and the understanding belong is common.

10. See *DA* 2.1.413ᵃ6–7, 3.5.430ᵃ18–23.

11. *Korê*: Sometimes translated as "pupil."

12. Namely, the understanding (*DA* 1.4.408ᵇ18).

13. The previous sentences (413ᵃ5–7) have distinguished between parts of the soul that are inseparable from the body, since they are actualizations of its parts (sight and the eye-jelly are examples), and parts—of which the understanding is an example—that are or may be separable from the body because they are not actualizations of any of its parts. The question arises, therefore, of how we should see the whole soul, which includes the understanding, as relating to the body it is in: Is it the actualization of the body in the way a sailor is of a ship? A ship, for its part, typically has many sailors, organized to perform in harmony the various functions involved in sailing it: "Sailors are dissimilar in their capacities (for one is an oarsman, another a captain, another a lookout, and others have other sorts of titles); it is clear both that the most exact account of the virtue of each sort of sailor will be special to him and that there will also be some common account that fits them all alike. For the preservation of the ship while sailing is a function of all of them, since this is what each of the sailors desires" (*Pol.* 3.4.1267ᵇ20–27). For simplicity, however, we may think, as Aristotle does, of a ship small enough to be sailed by just one sailor, since this is a closer analog to the case of body and soul. When the sailor enters the ship from outside—as the understanding does the body (*GA* 2.3.736ᵇ27–29)—he transforms what is potentially a functioning ship, as yet incapable of autonomous sailing, into a functional ship, possessed of the capacity (= first actuality) to sail, which is the analog of the alive but sleeping animal. It is in this way that he is its actualization.

De Anima 2.4.415^{a}26–^{b}2

It is the most natural function in those living things that are complete and not disabled or spontaneously generated, to produce another like itself—an animal producing an animal, a plant a plant—in order that they may partake in the eternal and divine insofar as they can. For all desire that, and it is for the sake of it that they do whatever they do by nature.

De Anima 3.5.430^{a}10–25

But since, just as in the whole of nature, there is something that is matter for each genus (and this is what is potentially all those things [that are in the genus]), while there is something else that is causal and productive,[14] because of producing them all (which, for example, is the role of a craft in relation to its matter[15]), in the soul too there must be these differences.[16] And one sort of understanding exists by becoming all things, another sort by producing all things, as a sort of state, like light, does; for in a

14. "In the things that come to be by nature or by craft, what is potentially such-and-such comes to be due to what is actually such-and-such" (*GA* 2.1.734^{a}29–31).

15. "Since what comes to be, comes to be as a result of something (by which I mean the starting-point that the coming to be is from) and from something . . . and comes to be something (and this is either a sphere or a circle or whichever of the others it happens to be), just as the producer does not make the underlying subject (the bronze), so he does not make the sphere either, except coincidentally, because the brazen sphere is a sphere and he does make the former. For to make the this something is to make from what is wholly the underlying subject a this something. I mean that to make the bronze round is not to make the round or the bronze but a distinct thing, namely, this form in something else. For if the producer makes something, he must make it from something else (for we assumed this). For example, he makes a brazen sphere, but in such a way that from this, which is bronze, he makes this, which is a sphere. If, then, he also made this [matter] itself, it is clear that he will make it in the same way, and the productions will go on without limit. It is evident, therefore, that neither does the form itself—or whatever we ought to call the shape that is in the perceptible thing—come to be, nor is there any coming to be of it, or of the essence (for it is this that comes to be in something else, whether as a result of craft or as a result of nature or of some capacity). But the producer does make a brazen sphere be. For he produces it from bronze and sphere. For in this he produces the form, and the result is a brazen sphere" (*Met.* 7.8.1034^{a}9–^{b}10).

16. When, through perception or learning or whatever, intelligible forms become imprinted on X's passive understanding, X can activate them by himself (*DA* 3.4.429^{b}5–9). There must therefore be something "causal and productive" in his soul that enables him to do so. This is so-called productive understanding.

way light too makes potential colors into active colors.[17] And this [productive] understanding is separable, unaffectable, and unmixed, being in substance an activity; for the producer is always more estimable than the thing affected,[18] and the starting-point than the matter. But active scientific knowledge is the same as its object, whereas |^{a}20| potential scientific knowledge is prior in the individual, but in general, is not even prior in time; on the contrary, it is not sometimes understanding and at other times not.[19] But, when separated, it is alone precisely that which it is,[20] and it alone is immortal and eternal (but we do not remember because this is

17. A transparent medium stands to color as the passive understanding does to intelligible objects: as the one must be colorless to be able to take on the form of any color without the matter, so the other must be unmixed to be able to take on every intelligible form without the matter. Light is the activity of such a medium: "the activity . . . of the transparent insofar as it is transparent" (*DA* 2.7.418^{b}9–10). Hence things that are potentially colored become actively so when a phosphorescent or self-illuminated light source activates it. Similarly, we may infer, the productive understanding, as in substance or essence an actively self-intelligible object (430^{a}18), makes what is potentially intelligible (namely, an intelligible object already received by passive understanding) into something actively intelligible.

18. "That the activity is also better and more estimable than the excellent capacity is clear from the following considerations. For in the case of those things that are said to be with reference to being capable, the same one is capable of contraries—for example, the same thing that is said to be capable of being healthy is also capable of being sick, and at the same time. . . . For the contraries to be present at the same time, however, is impossible (for example, to be healthy and to be sick), so that it is necessary for the good to be one or the other of them. But being capable is of both alike, or of neither. So the activity is better" (*Met.* 9.9.1051^{a}4–15). The relevant producer here is the productive understanding and the matter is the passive understanding and the various forms stamped on it that productive understanding, by being in essence an activity, activates.

19. The implicit inference is from being in substance (essence) an activity to being unmixed, impassive, and separable. What the productive understanding is separable from and unmixed with is matter (passive understanding): "the primary essence [= the divine understanding with which the primary god is identical] does not have matter, since it is an actuality [= activity]" (*Met.* 12.8.1074^{a}35). But matter in the final analysis is potentiality and form (= substance, essence) is actuality (9.6.1048^{a}35–^{b}6). Thus what is in substance or essence an activity cannot involve any matter, since, as pure actuality, it cannot involve any potentiality.

20. To say that A is *hoper* B (as the productive understanding when separated is here said to be *hoper* an activity) is to say that B is precisely what A is. The claim, then, is that when the productive understanding is separated from passive understanding and the rest of the essentially embodied soul, it is precisely an activity pure and simple, with no associated material or passive element.

unaffectable,[21] whereas the passive understanding is capable of passing away[22]), and without this nothing understands.[23] |^{a}25|

Prophecy in Sleep 1.462^{b}12–463^{b}11

Where the prophecy that takes place in sleep is concerned, and is said to come from dreams, it is not an easy matter either to despise it or to believe it. For the fact that all, or many, people suppose that dreams have some significance inclines us to believe it |^{b}15| as something said on the basis of experience; and that there should be prophecy in dreams in some cases is not incredible; for there is some reason for it. That is why one might think

---

21. Memory, like understanding, has a lot in common with perception: "A problem might be raised as to how, when the affection is present but the thing producing it is absent, what is not present is ever remembered. For it is clear that one must understand the affection, which is produced by means of perception in the soul, and in that part of the body in which it is, as being like a sort of picture, the having of which we say is memory. For the movement that occurs stamps a sort of imprint, as it were, of the perceptible object, as people do who seal things with a signet ring. That is also why memory does not occur in those who are subject to a lot of change, because of some affection or because of their age, just as if the change and the seal were falling on running water. In others, because of wearing down, as in the old parts of buildings, and because of the hardness of what receives the affection, the imprint is not produced" (*Mem.* 1.450^{a}25–^{b}5). Thus *memory wax*, as we may call it, is stamped with a perceptible form, but not the matter, and as a result, provided the memory wax is up to the task of retaining what is imprinted on it, the soul acquires the capacity to remember the thing causally responsible for the stamping. If we are to remember at time t_2 anything that occurred at time t_1, then we must have had memory wax at t_1 and at t_2. Hence if the understanding were actively understanding some intelligible object at a time when it was separated from memory wax, and was unaffectable by the movements that stamp things on it, as it would be if it were separated from passive understanding and the body, we would not remember this: "Even the memory of intelligible objects does not occur without an appearance. So memory will belong coincidentally to the understanding, but intrinsically to the primary perceptual part" (450^{a}12–14). Thus the eternal existence of our active understanding in separation from memory wax and other concomitants of embodiment is consistent with our inability to remember anything of that existence. This disposes of one objection to our accepting that it existed then.

22. Since it, like memory wax, requires a body (*DA* 1.4.408^{b}25–29).

23. This could mean (1) without passive understanding, productive understanding understands nothing; or (2) without productive understanding, passive understanding understands nothing. Initially, (1) seems to conflict with the fact that active understanding, as in essence an activity, can be actively understanding—and so understanding some intelligible object—when separated from memory wax, mortal passive understanding, and the body, making (2) seem the more attractive option, since this has already been stated at the opening of the chapter (*DA* 3.5.430^{a}10–17).

likewise about other dreams as well. But the fact that we see no reasonable cause why such prophecy might occur makes it difficult to believe it. For it is absurd to hold both that the sender of such dreams is the god and, in addition to |b20| its other unreasonableness, that he sends them not to the best and most practically wise, but to people at random. But if the causality of the god is set aside, none of the other causes appears reasonable; for that some people should have foresight in dreams about events at the Pillars of Heracles, or on the banks of the Borysthenes,[24] |b25| seems to be something whose starting-point is beyond us to discover.

It is necessary for dreams to be either causes or signs of the events, or else coincidences;[25] either all of these, some of them, or only one. By "cause" I mean as the moon is of an eclipse of the sun, or as fatigue is of fever; by "sign" as the entrance of a star[26] into the shadow is a sign of the eclipse, |b30| or roughness of the tongue a sign of fever; by "coincidence" the fact that someone is walking when the sun is eclipsed; for the walking is neither a sign nor a cause of the eclipse, nor the eclipse of the |463a1| walking. That is why no coincidence occurs always or for the most part.

Is it, then, that some dreams are causes and others signs, for example, of things happening in the body? At any rate, even sophisticated doctors[27] say that one should pay close attention |a5| to dreams; and to hold this view is likewise reasonable also for those who are not practitioners of the craft, but are investigating [the subject] and engaging in philosophy. For the movements that occur in the daytime, unless very great and very strong, escape notice alongside the waking movements, which are greater. But during sleep the contrary occurs; for then even |a10| small movements seem great. This is clear from what often happens during sleep—for example, people think that there is thunder and lightning, when there are only faint ringings in their ears; or that they are enjoying honey or other sweet juices, when only a tiny drop of phlegm is running down [their throats]; or that they are walking through fire, and feeling intense heat, |a15| when certain parts of the body are slightly warmed. When they wake up, though, these things appear to them the way they really are. But since the starting-points of all things are small, it is clear that those of the diseases and other affections about to occur

24. The Pillars of Heracles are the rocks on either side of the Strait of Gibraltar; the Borysthenes is the Dnieper, which flows into the Black Sea.

25. *Sumptômata*: As at *Ph.* 2.8.199a1 and *Rh.* 1.9.1367b25, where it is equivalent to "by luck."

26. Probably the appearance of a star when the sky is darkened by a solar eclipse.

27. "Of doctors, those who are sophisticated and curious say something about physics and claim to derive their starting-points from it" (*Juv.* 21.480b26–28). These are the doctors earlier described as being more philosophical: "Of doctors who pursue their craft in a more philosophical way, the vast majority begin with physics" (*Sens.* 1.436a19–b1).

in our bodies are as well. It is evident, then, that it is necessary for these to be more manifest in sleeping |^{a}20| moments than in the waking state.

Moreover, it is not unreasonable that some, at least, of the appearances in sleep are causes of the actions corresponding to each of them. For, as when we are about to act, or are engaged in actions, or have performed them, we often take part in them or perform them in a vivid dream (and the cause of this is that |^{a}25| the movements starting in the daytime have paved the way for the movement in the dream), in the same way, it is also conversely necessary in many cases for the movements in sleep to be starting-points of daytime actions, because the way has been conversely paved in the nighttime appearances for the intentions related to these actions. In this way, then, it is possible for some dreams |^{a}30| to be signs and causes.

Many dreams, however, seem to be coincidences, especially all the inaccessible ones, that is, those |463^{b}1| in which the starting-point is not in the dreamers themselves but concern sea battles or things taking place far away. For where these are concerned it is likely that matters stand in the same way as when something someone has mentioned happens to come to pass; for what prevents this also from happening in sleep? |^{b}5| On the contrary, it is more likely that many such things happen. Just as, then, mentioning someone is neither a sign nor a cause of his showing up, so also in this case the dream is neither a sign nor a cause of its coming to pass, but a coincidence. That is why many dreams do not come to pass; for coincidences do not occur either always or |^{b}10| for the most part.

Prophecy in Sleep 2.463^{b}12–464^{b}18

In general, though, since some of the other animals also dream,[28] dreams could not be sent by a god, nor do they come about for the sake of this[29] (they are daimonic,[30] nonetheless; for nature is daimonic but not divine).

---

28. See *HA* 4.10.536^{b}27–32.

29. I.e., prophecy.

30. Usually a *daimon*—like Socrates' famous *daimonion*—is a god, or the child of a god (*Rh.* 3.18.1419^{a}8–12; Plato, *Ap.* 27d), but here the term seems intended to mean something like "beyond human power": (1) "Is it possible or impossible to foresee the future? And if it is possible, in what way? Also, does the possibility extend only to the results of human action, or also to those of which what is daimonic (*to daimonion*) is the cause, that is, what comes about by nature or due to chance?" (*Somn.* 1.453^{b}20–24). (2) "Nature's contribution is clearly not up to us, but because of some divine causes is present in those who are truly lucky" (*NE* 10.9.1179^{b}21–23).

A sign is this: utterly worthless human beings are capable of foreseeing things |b15| and of having vivid dreams,[31] implying that these are not sent by a god; but merely that all those with a garrulous and passionate[32] sort of nature see multifarious dream visions; for because they experience many multifarious movements, they just happen to have visions resembling [real events], doing so by luck, like those who play at odd and even. For as is said indeed, |b20| "If you make many throws, your luck will change," and so it happens too in the case we are discussing.

That many dreams do not come to pass is not at all strange; for this is also the case with many signs in the body and in the heavens—for example, those of rains and those of winds. For if another movement with more control occurs, |b25| then the movement that was about to occur, which resulted in the sign, will not occur. For many things that should occur, though nobly planned, are done away with by other starting-points that have more control. For, in general, what was going to happen does not always happen, nor is what will happen the same as what is going to happen.[33] But, nonetheless, it must be said that there are certain starting-points from which nothing is fulfilled, and these are natural signs |b30| of events that do not come to pass.

But where dreams are concerned that involve no such starting-points as we have described, but are beyond the frontier[34] |464a1| in times, or places, or magnitudes—or which, though not so in any of these respects, nevertheless those who see the dream do not have the starting-points within themselves, unless the foresight comes about by coincidence—the following would be better than what Democritus says, |a5| who treats images and emanations as causes.[35] It is like when something causes movement in water or air, so that one part moves another and, though the first has stopped, such movement advances to a certain point, although the first mover is not present. In the same way there is nothing to prevent a certain movement and perception, |a10| stemming from the objects Democritus makes the source of images

31. Here meaning veridical ones.

32. A *melagcholikos* ("passionate") person is not melancholy in our sense of the term but is someone with intense desires (*NE* 7.4.1154b11–13), easily affected by imagination and dreams: "Passionate people (*melagcholikous*) most of all are moved by appearances (*phantasmata*)" (*Mem.* 2.453a19).

33. "For of a thing that it is true to say that it will be, it must at some time be true to say that it is. On the other hand, of that of which it is now true to say that it is going to be, there is nothing to prevent its not coming to be; for someone who is going to take a walk may not take a walk" (*GC* 2.11.337b4–7).

34. *Huperorias*: Notice *xenikôn* at *Div. Somn.* 2.464a26.

35. See Sextus Empiricus, *Against the Mathematicians* 9.19.

and emanations, from reaching souls that are dreaming. And, in whatever way they arrive, since they are more perceptible at night, because in the daytime they are more liable to be carried away and dissipated (for the air is less disturbed at night, because there is then less wind), they produce a perception in the body |a15| as a result of sleep, because people perceive even slight internal movements more when asleep than when awake. And it is these movements that produce images, on the basis of which sleepers foresee what is going to happen in these sorts of cases.

And that is why this affection occurs in random people, and not in those who are most practically wise. |a20| For if it were a god who sent the movements, they would occur both in the daytime and to the wise; but, this way, it makes perfect sense that random people should have foresight; for the thought of such people is not skilled at wise thinking, but is like a desert empty of everything, and, when once set moving, is moved as the mover carries it. And the cause due to which some excitable people have foresight is that the movements that properly belong to them do not |a25| cause trouble [to the alien movements] but are driven away by them. So they most perceive the alien movements.[36]

With regard to the fact that some persons who are liable to derangement have this foresight, its cause is that their normal movements do not impede the alien movements, but are beaten off by them. Thus they have an especially keen perception of the alien movements.

. . .[37]

The most craftsman-like judge of dreams is the one who has the capacity to see resemblances; for anyone can judge vivid dreams. By "resemblances" I mean that dream images are similar to images reflected in water, as was said before. In the latter case, if the movement in the water is great, |b10| the reflection has no resemblance to its original, nor do the images resemble the real objects. Someone would be skillful, indeed, at judging such reflections, if he could quickly discern, and see at a glance, the scattered and distorted fragments of such images, so as to perceive that one of them is a man, or a horse, or anything whatever. Likewise, in the present case, the

---

36. Aristotle's account of prophetic dreams seems, then, to be wholly naturalistic (or non-supernatural). A small event E_1, which will, if not interrupted by something with more control, lead to a significant event E_2, affects a sleeper S, as it might affect an actual perceiver of E_1, by setting up small movements in his thought. This thought is especially susceptible to such small movements, because it is empty of wise thoughts. Then just as an actual observer of E_1 might rationally calculate that E_2 would (everything else being equal) follow, so S might "foresee" it as following, without reasoning, due to his thought being carried on by E_1 to E_2, which might or might not actually occur.

37. I omit 464a27–b5, which adds some details to the theory already described.

dream produces a similar effect; |b15| for the internal movement effaces the clearness of the dream.

What sleep and dreams are, then, and due to what sort of cause they occur, and further the prophecy in dreams in its entirety, have now been discussed.

Parts of Animals 1.5.644b23–645a36

Of the substances composed by nature, some are un-generated and incapable of passing away for all eternity, while others participate in coming to be and passing away. But it has happened that where the former are concerned, though they are estimable and divine, our branches of theoretical knowledge are less developed |b25| (for both about the things on the basis of which one would investigate them and the things about them we long to know, the things evident to perception are altogether few). But where the plants and animals that are capable of passing away are concerned, we are better equipped with a view to knowledge because of living together with them. For many things can be grasped about each genus if one wishes |b30| to take sufficient pains. Each of the two has its charms. For even if our contact with the eternal things is small, nonetheless because they are the most estimable ones, knowing them is more pleasant than knowing all the things around us, just as a random small glimpse of the ones we love is a greater pleasure than seeing many other great things in exact detail. |b35| But because of knowing the others more and in greater number they take |645a1| preeminence in scientific knowledge. Further, because they are nearer to us and more of our own nature, they provide some compensation in comparison to the philosophy concerned with divine things. But since where these are concerned we are through with stating what seems to be so to us,[38] it remains |a5| to speak about animal nature, if possible omitting nothing whether less estimable or more estimable.

For even in the theoretical knowledge of animals disagreeable to perception, the nature that handicrafts them likewise provides enormous pleasures to those capable of knowing the causes by nature. |a10| For it would in fact be unreasonable, even absurd, if we enjoyed getting theoretical knowledge of the likenesses of animals because of at the same time getting it of the craft (for example, painting or sculpture) that handicrafted them, while not loving even more the theoretical knowledge of the ones composed by nature, at any rate, when we are capable of seeing their causes distinctly.

38. Presumably, in *De Caelo*.

That is why we must not be childishly disgusted at the investigation of the less estimable animals.[39] For in all natural things there is something wondrous present—as indeed Heraclitus is said to have told those strangers who wished to meet him but stopped as they were approaching on seeing him warming himself at the oven.[40] For he told them to enter confidently, "for there are gods even here."[41] In this way too one must approach inquiry concerning each of the animals without disgust, on the supposition that in each one there is something natural and nobly beautiful. For what is not random, but rather for the sake of something is present most of all in the works of nature, and the end for the sake of which each has been composed or has come to be has taken the place of the nobly beautiful.

But if someone has considered the theoretical knowledge of the other animals to be without esteem, he must think the same thing about himself as well. For it is impossible to look at what the human genus is composed of—for example, blood, flesh, bones, blood vessels, and other parts of this sort—without considerable disgust. But in the same way as someone discussing the parts or the equipment of anything whatever must be considered as doing so not to produce a record concerning the matter, nor for the sake of it, but rather for the sake of the whole shape [or form] (for example, concerning the house in fact, and not bricks, mortar, and timbers), so where nature is concerned too one must consider the discussion to be about the composition and the whole substance, but not about those things that do not occur in separation from their substance.[42]

---

39. "The differentiae that determine whether the genus of the thing being composed is more estimable or non-estimable lie in the enclosure of the soul-involving starting-point" (*GA* 3.11.762^{a}24–26).

40. *Theromenon pros tô[i] ipnô[i]*: This may be a euphemism for going to the bathroom. This would explain the story's relevance to disgust, which is difficult to do otherwise. The idea would be that as the strangers came within sight of Heraclitus they saw him going into the bathroom (which may have been an outhouse). He told them to enter (not the bathroom, of course, but the house) confidently, since even in the place he was going to there are gods present (to those capable of seeing causes clearly).

41. DK 22A9 = TEGP 162.

42. I.e., the functional parts of the animal whose parts they are: "Now, since the soul of animals (for this is substance of the animate) is the substance that is in accord with the account and is the form and the essence of such-and-such sort of body (certainly each part, if it is to be defined correctly, will not be defined without its function, which it could not have without perception), it follows that the parts of this are prior, either all or some, to the compound animal, and similarly, then, to each particular animal, whereas the body and its parts will be posterior, and what is divided into these as into matter is not the substance but the compound. These bodily parts, then, are in a way prior to the compound, but in a way not, since they cannot even exist when they are separated. For it is not a finger in any and every state that is the finger of an animal, rather, a dead finger is only homonymously a finger" (*Met.* 7.10.1035^{b}14–25).

Parts of Animals 4.10.686^{a}25–687^{a}2

Instead of having forelegs and forefeet, the human has arms and so-called hands. For the human is the only animal that stands upright, and this is because its nature, that is, its substance, is divine. Now, the function of that which is most divine is understanding and thinking; and this would not be easy if there were a great deal of the body at the top pressing it down, for |^{a}30| weight hampers the movement of understanding and the common perceptual capacity.[43] . . . That is why, when the weight—that is, the body-like quality—becomes too great, the body itself must lurch forward toward the ground; and then, for preservation's sake, nature provides forefeet instead of arms and hands, as has happened in quadrupeds |^{a}35| . . . because their soul could not sustain |686^{b}1| the weight bearing it down. . . . In fact, compared with the human, all other animals are dwarf-like [= top-heavy]. For something is dwarf-like when its upper part is large, while its lower part is small. And the upper part is what is called the "chest," |^{b}5| extending from the head to the outlet for the residues [that is, the anus]. Now, in human beings this part is proportional to the lower part. But when they are young the contrary is the case, the upper part being large, the lower small, which is why they crawl and are incapable of walking. . . . For all children are dwarfs. . . . That is also why all animals are less practically wise than human beings. Even among human beings, indeed, children in comparison to grown men, and among the latter in their prime the naturally dwarf-like, |^{b}25| even if they have a surplus of some other capacity, are deficient in the possession of understanding. And the cause of this . . . is that in very many[44] the starting-point of the soul[45] is movement-hampered and body-like in quality. And if the heat that raises

43. The capacity common to the special perceptual capacities (sight, hearing, smell, and so on), to discern common perceptibles (such as movement, rest, shape, magnitude, number, and oneness), or things perceptible to more than one special perceptual capacity. See *DA* 3.13.425^{a}14–30.

44. Reading πολλοῖς for the mss. πολλῷ ("in many respects").

45. I.e., what the male seed or semen contributes to the female menses in embryogenesis: "The male is a certain starting-point and cause, and it is male insofar as it is capable of something, female insofar as it is incapable, and the defining mark of the capacity, and of the incapacity, is being capable of concocting, or being incapable of concocting, the last stage of the nourishment (which in the blooded animals is called 'blood' and in the others its analog). . . . And by 'last stage' I mean what is carried to each [part], which is also why what comes to be is like its progenitor. . . . But the seed of the male differs from that of the female because it contains a starting-point within itself of such a sort as to cause movement in the animal too and to concoct the last stage of the nourishment, whereas that of the female contains matter alone. When it has mastered [the latter] it draws [it] to itself, but when it has been mastered it changes to its contrary or comes to ruin. And contrary to the male is the female, female due to the non-concoctedness and coldness of its sanguineous nourishment" (*GA* 4.1.766^{a}30–^{b}18).

becomes less and the earthy material becomes greater, the bodies of animals also become smaller |b30| and many footed, and finally they lose their feet altogether and lie full length on the earth. Proceeding in this way a little further, even the starting-point they have is below, and the part corresponding to the head is incapable of movement and perception, and the creature becomes a plant, having the upper parts below, and the lower parts above. For the roots of plants have the capacity of a mouth |b35| and a head, while the seed has the contrary. |687a1| For it comes to be up above, on the uppermost shoots.

Generation of Animals 2.3.736a24–b29

The next puzzle to be stated is this. If, in the case of the animals in which semen is emitted into the female, what enters is no part |a25| of the embryo that comes to be, where is the corporeal part of it diverted to, if indeed it does its work by means of the capacity it has within itself? It is necessary to determine whether what is being composed in the female receives something, or not, from what has entered her, but also, concerning the soul in virtue of which an animal is so called (and it is an animal in virtue of the perceptual part of the soul), |a30| whether it is present within the seed and the fetus or not, and where it comes from [if it is]. For one could not regard the fetus as soulless, as in every way lacking in life. For both the seeds and the embryos of animals are no less alive than plants, and are fertile up to a certain point.[46] That they have nutritive |736a35| soul, then, is evident (and why they must acquire this first is evident from the determinations about the soul made elsewhere[47]), but as they proceed they also have perceptual soul in virtue of which they are animals {***}.[48] |736b1| For they do not at the same time become animal and human, or animal and horse, and likewise in the case of the other animals; for the last thing to come to be is the end, and the end of the coming to be of each thing is what is special to it.[49] That is why where understanding is concerned, when, how, and from where it is acquired |b5| by those that participate in this starting-point involve a very great puzzle, and we must try hard to get a grasp on [these things] in accord with our capacity and to the extent possible.

As for the seeds and fetuses that are not yet separable, it is clear that they must be regarded as possessing nutritive soul potentially, but not actively,

46. Like the wind-eggs of birds. See *GA* 1.21.730a4–9.

47. In *DA* 2.4.

48. There is a lacuna in the mss. at this point.

49. See *GA* 4.3.767b29–36.

until, like |b10| separated fetuses, they are drawing in nourishment and performing the function of this sort of soul; for at first all things of this sort seem to live the life of a plant. And it is clear that perceptual soul and understanding soul must be spoken about accordingly; for it is necessary for all soul to be possessed potentially before being possessed actively. |b15|

For [1] either they must all be produced [in the menses or matter] without existing beforehand, or they must all preexist, or some must, but not others; and [2] they must be produced in the matter either without having entered in the male's seed, or having come from there; and [3] in the male they must either all be produced [in the seed] from outside it, or none from outside, or some but not others. |b20| Now, it is evident from the following that it is impossible for all to be present beforehand; [4] for it is clear that it is impossible for all starting-points whose activity is bodily to be present without body (for example, walking without feet). [5] So they cannot enter from outside; for they can neither enter by themselves, being inseparable, |b25| nor enter in a body; for the seed is a residue produced by a change in the nutriment. [6] It remains, then, that the understanding alone enters additionally from outside and alone is divine; for bodily activity is in no way associated with its activity.[50]

---

50. Here [1] concerns the menses and what it contributes to the fetus; [2] concerns the seed and what it contributes; and [3] concerns the male progenitor and what he contributes to the seed. And the line of descent, as we know, is from formative movements in the *pneuma* contained in the male progenitor's blood to his seed, from seed to menses, and so to fetus. [4] restricts our attention to starting-points of psychological functions whose active varieties are bodily, in that they require bodily organs, as walking requires feet and seeing requires eyes. [5] tells us the two conditions under which these could enter something "from the outside." This signals, as [3] makes clear, that the something they enter is the male seed. [5] then shows that the starting-points cannot meet either of the conditions: they cannot enter by themselves, apart from body, because they are not separate from it; they cannot enter the body of the seed as the starting-points of an already formed body, because seed, as a residue produced by nutriment, does not contain things like feet and other bodily parts. On the other hand, [6] because bodily activity is in no way associated with the activity of understanding, understanding does enter the male seed from outside. But just how understanding manages to enter the seed from outside, however, is left unexplained. All that we are told is that in embryogenesis it is transmitted along with the seed yet separate from it (*GA* 2.3.737a7–11). As a result of being transmitted in this way, however, the understanding "seems to be born in us as a sort of substance, and not to pass away" (*DA* 1.4.408b18–25) and to be "presumably something more divine" (408b29). Moreover, it is "in substance an activity," and so is not "sometimes understanding and at other times not," but rather of all the elements in the human soul "it alone is immortal and eternal" (*DA* 3.5.430a18–23). These characteristics make it reasonable to suppose that understanding is transmitted along with the male seed as movements in ether that "code" for it. The description of ether in *Cael.* 1.3.270a12–35 makes the supposition all but certain. For if understanding is coded for by anything other than the circular movements in ether, then it seems that it could not itself be immortal, eternal, or ever-active. And what moves this ether in the proper direction is presumably the sun. See *Met.* 12.5.1071a13–17.

Movement of Animals 4.699b32–700a5

Well, then, must there be something immovable and at rest outside the moved thing, which is no part of it, or not? In particular, is it necessary for this to be so also in the case of the universe? For it would seem strange if the starting-point of the movement were inside. That is why to those who think of it in this way Homer would appear to have spoken well:

> But you could not drag from sky to earth
> Zeus, the highest counsellor, not even if you toiled very hard.
> Take hold, all you gods and all you goddesses![51]

For what is wholly immovable cannot be moved by anything. Therein lies the resolution of the puzzle mentioned previously[52]—of whether it is possible or impossible for the structure of the heaven to be broken asunder: [it is impossible] if it depends on an immovable starting-point.[53]

Metaphysics 1.2.982a4–983a11

Since this is the science we are inquiring into, this is what we should investigate, namely, what sorts of causes and what sorts of starting-points |a5| are the concern of the science that is theoretical wisdom. Well, if we were to get hold of the suppositions we have about the theoretically-wise person, perhaps the answer will thereby become more evident.

First, then, we take it that [1] what a wise person has scientific knowledge about is *all things*, insofar as they admit of it, without his having particular scientific knowledge of them. Next, we take it that [2] the person who has the capacity to know difficult things, that is, |a10| things that are not easy for humans to know—*he* is wise; for perception is common to all, which is why it is easy and involves no wisdom. Further, we take it that someone is wiser in any science if [3] he is a more exact knower of it and [4] a better teacher of the causes. Also, we take it that among the sciences [5] the one choiceworthy for the sake of itself, and for the knowing of it, is |a15| more theoretical wisdom than one choiceworthy for the sake of its results. Also, we take [6] a more ruling science to be wisdom more than a

51. *Iliad* 8.21, 22, 20.

52. At *MA* 4.699b12–13.

53. See *Met.* 12.7.1072b13–14.

subordinate one; for a wise person should prescribe, not be prescribed to, and should be obeyed by the less wise, not obey someone else. Such, then, are the sort and number of suppositions we hold about theoretical wisdom |a20| and theoretically-wise people.

Of these, [Response 1] scientific knowledge of all things necessarily belongs to the person who most of all has universal scientific knowledge; for he in a way knows all the things that fall under it. [R2] The most universal things of all, however, are almost the most difficult for humans to know; for they are furthest from perception.[54] [R3] And the most exact |a25| of the sciences are the ones concerned most of all with the primary things; for the sciences which proceed from fewer things (for example, arithmetic) are more exact than those that proceed from an addition (for example, geometry). [R4] But then too the one that provides theoretical scientific knowledge of the causes is more teachable; for teaching is what those people do, that is, those who state the causes of each thing. [R5] And knowing or knowing scientifically |a30| for its own sake most of all belongs to the science of what is most scientifically knowable of all; for the person who chooses to know scientifically because of itself will most of all choose to have what is most of all scientific knowledge, and this is the science of what is most |982b1| scientifically knowable of all. And what is most scientifically knowable of all are the primary things and causes; for it is through these and proceeding from these that we know the other things, not these because of the ones that fall under them. [R6] But the most ruling of the sciences—that is, the one that is ruling rather than subordinate—is the one that knows that for the sake of which |b5| each thing is to be done, and this is the good of each of them, and in general the best good in all of nature.

So based on all that has been said, the name we are inquiring into applies to the same science [as has all these features]; for this must be the one that gets a theoretical grasp on the primary starting-points and causes, and the good or the for-the-sake-of-which is one of these causes. |b10|

That it is not a productive science is clear too from those who first turned to philosophy; for it is because of wondering at things[55] that humans, both now and at first, began to do philosophy. At the start, they

54. "I call 'prior and more knowable to us' what is closer to perception, 'unconditionally prior and more knowable' what is further away. What is most universal is furthest away, and particulars are closest" (*APo.* 1.2.72a1–5).

55. "To learn and to wonder is for the most part pleasant, since in wondering there is an appetite for learning, so that what is wondered at is appetitively desired, and in learning there is a settling down that is in accord with nature" (*Rh.* 1.11.1371a31–34).

wondered at those of the puzzles that were close to hand,[56] then, advancing little by little, they puzzled over greater issues—for example, about the |b15| affections of the moon and about issues concerning the sun and stars, and how the universe comes to be. Someone who puzzles or wonders, however, thinks himself ignorant (it is because of this, indeed, that the philosopher is in a way a myth-lover[57]; for myth is composed of wonders). So if indeed it was because of [a desire] to avoid ignorance that they engaged in philosophy, it is evident that it was because of [a desire] |b20| to know that they pursued scientific knowledge, and not for the sake of some sort of utility.

What in fact happened is witness to this; for it was when pretty much all the necessities of life, as well as those related to ease and passing the time, had been supplied that such wisdom[58] began to be sought. So clearly we do not inquire into it because of its having another use, but just as a human |b25| being is free, we say, when he is for his own sake and not for someone else, in the same way we pursue this as the only free science; for it alone is for its own sake.

It is because of this indeed that the possession of this science might be justly regarded as not for humans; for in many ways the nature of humans is enslaved, so that, according to Simonides, "a god alone can have this |b30| privilege,"[59] and it is not fitting that a human should not be content to inquire into the science that is in accord with himself.[60] If, then, there is something in what the poets say, and envy is natural to the divine, it would probably occur in this case most of all, |983a1| and all those who went too far [in this science] would be unlucky. The divine, however, cannot be envious—but, as the proverb says, "Bards often do speak falsely." Moreover, no science should be regarded as more estimable than this. For the most divine science is also the most estimable. And a science would be most divine in only two ways: if the [primary] god most of all would have it, or if it were a science of divine things. And this science |a5| alone is divine in both these ways; for the [primary] god seems to be among the causes of all things and to be a sort of starting-point, and this is the sort of science that the [primary] god alone, or that he most of all, would have.[61]

---

56. Reading τὰ πρόχειρα τῶν ἀπόρων.

57. Reading φιλόμυθος ὁ φιλόσοφος πῶς.

58. *Phronêsis*, which is often specifically *practical* wisdom, is here, as frequently elsewhere, a synonym for wisdom of any sort, including the theoretical wisdom (*sophia*) sought by the early philosophers.

59. Fr. 3 Hiller.

60. See *NE* 10.7.1177b31–34.

61. See *Met.* 12.9.1074b15–1075a5.

All the sciences are more necessary than this one, then, |^{a}10| but none is better.[62]

Metaphysics 3.2.997^{b}5–12

But while [Platonic] Forms involve difficulties in many places, none is stranger than to say that there are certain natures beyond those in the heaven as a whole, and that these are the same as perceptibles, except that they are eternal whereas the latter pass away; for they say that there is man-itself and horse-itself and health-itself, and nothing else[63]—like those who introduce gods, but say that they are human in form[64]; for those people were making the gods nothing but eternal human beings, and these are making the Forms nothing but eternal perceptibles.

Metaphysics 5.5.1015^{b}9–15

Of some things, then, another thing is the cause of their being necessary, of others nothing is such a cause, rather, because of them other things are necessary. And so the necessary in the primary and full way is the simple; for it is not possible that this should be in more than one state, or even to be both in one state *and* another; for it would thereby be in more than one state. Hence if there are certain things that are eternal and immovable, there is nothing forced or contrary to nature in them.

---

62. Sciences are necessary in the relevant sense when they are concerned with providing the necessities of life, as, for example, the mathematical sciences are not (*Met.* 1.1.981^{b}21–22). Nonetheless, nothing prevents such sciences from being "coincidentally useful to us where many of the necessities of life are concerned" (*EE* 1.6.1216^{b}15–16). Theoretical wisdom, by contrast, does not even coincidentally "have a theoretical grasp on any of the things from which a human will come to be happy" (*NE* 6.12.1143^{b}19–20).

63. I.e., man-itself is man taken by himself, with nothing added that is extraneous to what makes him a man, and similarly for the others.

64. See *Met.* 12.8.1074^{a}38–12.9.1075^{a}10.

Metaphysics 6.1.1025^{b}3–1026^{a}32[65]

The starting-points and causes of beings are what we are inquiring into, and clearly qua beings. For there is some cause of health and of good physical condition, and there are starting-points and elements and causes of the objects of mathematics, and in general |^{b}5| every science that proceeds by thinking or that has some share in thinking[66] is concerned with causes and starting-points, whether more exactly or more simply considered. All these sciences, however, mark off a certain being, a certain genus, and busy themselves with it, but not with being unconditionally or qua being, nor do they produce any account of the what-it-is. Instead, starting from the what-it-is—|^{b}10| some making it clear by means of the perceptual capacities, some getting hold of it as a hypothesis—they in this way proceed to demonstrate the things that belong intrinsically to the genus with which they are concerned, either in a more necessary or in a weaker way. Which is why it is evident from such an induction[67] that there is no demonstration of substance nor of the what-it-is, but some other way of |^{b}15| making it clear. Similarly too they say nothing as to whether the genus they busy themselves with does or does not exist, because it belongs to the same sort of thinking to make clear both its what-it-is and whether it exists.

But since natural science too is a science concerned with a particular genus of being (for it is concerned with the sort of substance in which the starting-point of movement and |^{b}20| of rest is internal to itself), it is clear that it is neither a practical science[68] nor a productive one (for in the case of producible things the starting-point is in the producer, whether this is understanding or craft or some capacity, whereas in the case of things doable in action it is in the doer, namely, deliberate choice; for what is doable in action and what is deliberately choosable are the same), so that if all thought is either practical or productive or theoretical,[69] |^{b}25| natural science would have to be some sort of theoretical science—but a theoretical science that is concerned with such being as is capable of being moved and with the substance that in accord with its account holds for the most part only, because it is not separable.

---

65. Compare *Met.* 11.7.

66. The thinking at issue is presumably deduction from starting-points or causes, so that the contrast is to sciences that deal with starting-points themselves (1025^{b}15–16).

67. The "induction" referred to is the review of the various special sciences that Aristotle has just summarized.

68. One dealing with action (*praxis*), such as ethics or politics.

69. As Aristotle thinks it is. See *Met.* 11.7.1064^{a}16–19.

But we must not neglect to consider the *way* the essence or its account is, because, without this, inquiry produces no result. Of things defined, however, |^{b}30| that is, of the whats that things are, some are the way the snub is, others the way the concave is. And these differ because the snub is grasped in combination with the matter (for the snub is a concave *nose*), whereas the concavity is without perceptible matter. If, then, all natural things are said the way the snub is (for example, nose, eye, face, flesh, bone, |1026^{a}1| and, in general, animal, and leaf, root, bark, and, in general, plant—for the account of none of these is without [reference to] movement, but always includes matter[70]), the way we must inquire into and define the what-it-is in the case of natural things is clear, as is why it belongs to the natural scientist to get a theoretical grasp even on some of the soul,[71] |^{a}5| that is, on as much of it as is not without matter.

That natural science is a theoretical science, then, is evident from these considerations. Mathematics too is a theoretical one, but whether its objects are immovable and separable is not now clear; however, it is clear that *some* parts of mathematics get a theoretical grasp on their objects insofar as they are immovable and insofar as they are separable.[72] But if there is something that is eternal and immovable and |^{a}10| separable, it is evident that knowledge of it belongs to a theoretical science—not,

70. "The activation of what is potential, insofar as it is such, is what I say movement is" (*Met.* 11.9.1065^{b}16), and matter is what is potential (9.8.1050^{a}15). Hence anything capable of moving in a certain way must have matter for that sort of movement (*Met.* 8.1.1042^{b}5–6).

71. See *DA* 1.1.403^{a}3–^{b}16, 3.4.429^{a}22–25.

72. "About these things [the sun, the moon, and certain affections of theirs] both the natural scientist and the mathematician do all the work they do, but the mathematician does not get a theoretical grasp on each of them as the limit of a natural body, nor on their coincidents as coincident with such bodies. That is why he separates them. For they are separable from movement in the understanding, and so it makes no difference, nor does any falsity result, if they are separated. Those who speak about the Forms [namely, Platonists] do the same, but they fail to notice it. For they separate the objects of natural science, although these are less separable than the objects of mathematics. This becomes clear when we try to state in each of the two cases the definitions of the things and of their coincidents. For odd and even, straight and curved, and similarly number, line, and figure, can be defined without movement, whereas flesh, bone, and human cannot, but rather all these are said like snub nose and not like curved. This is also clear from the more natural-science-like parts of mathematics, such as optics, harmonics, and astronomy. These are in a way the reverse of geometry. For whereas geometry investigates natural lines, but not insofar as they are natural, optics investigates mathematical lines, but not insofar as they are mathematical" (*Ph.* 2.2.193^{b}31–194^{a}12).

however, to *natural* science (for natural science is concerned with certain moveable things[73]) nor to mathematics, but to something prior to both. For natural science is concerned with things that are inseparable but not immovable,[74] while certain parts of mathematics are concerned with things that are immovable and not separable but as in matter. |a15| The primary science, by contrast, is concerned with things that are both separable and immovable. Now, all causes are necessarily eternal, and these most of all; for they are the causes of the divine beings that are perceptible.[75] There must, then, be three theoretical philosophies: mathematical, natural, and theological; for it is not unclear that if the divine belongs anywhere, it belongs in a nature of this sort.[76] |a20| And of these, the most estimable must be concerned with the most estimable genus. Thus, of the various sciences, the theoretical are the more choiceworthy, and this of the theoretical ones.[77]

For we might raise a puzzle as to whether the primary philosophy is universal or concerned with a particular genus and one particular nature (for it is not the same way even in |a25| the mathematical sciences, but rather geometry and astronomy are concerned with a particular nature,

73. Reading περὶ κινητῶν γάρ τινων ἡ φυσική.

74. Reading περὶ ἀχωριστὰ μὲν ἀλλ᾽ οὐκ ἀκίνητα.

75. I.e., the stars and heavenly bodies. The causes of these are their immovable movers (*Met.* 12.8).

76. (1) There are three different sorts of accounts of the "whats" that things are, or of the substances or essences that they have, depending on whether they are natural objects, objects of mathematics, or divine objects. (2) These essences, or the accounts or definitions of them, are starting-points of the different theoretical sciences (natural, mathematical, and theological). (3) The philosophies associated with these sciences are concerned with their starting-points. (4) Therefore, there must be three theoretical philosophies (which, at *Met.* 11.7.1064b1–3, are described as theoretical sciences).

77. See *NE* 10.7–8.

whereas universal mathematics is common to all[78]). If, then, there is no other substance beyond those composed by nature, natural science will be the primary science. But if there is some immovable substance, this [that is, theological philosophy] will be prior and will be primary philosophy, and it will be universal in this way, |a30| namely, because it is primary.[79] And it

78. Many theorems in mathematics are special to some branch of it, such as arithmetic or geometry, but there are also "certain mathematical theorems of a universal character" (*Met.* 13.2.1077a9–10). Here is an example: "That proportionals alternate might seem to apply to numbers insofar as they are numbers, lines insofar as they are lines, solids insofar as they are solids, and times insofar as they are times, as used at one time to be demonstrated of these separately, although it is possible, at any rate, to prove it of all cases by a single demonstration. But because all these things—numbers, lengths, times, solids—do not constitute a single named [genus] and differ in form from one another, they used to be taken separately. But now it is proved universally; for it did not belong insofar as they are lines, or insofar as they are numbers, but insofar as they are *this* [unnamed thing], which they suppose belongs universally" (*APo.* 1.5.74a17–25). Nonetheless, the universality of the demonstration is open to challenge on the grounds that lines and numbers differ in genus. For "it is necessary for the extreme and middle terms in a demonstration to come from the same genus" (1.7.75b10–11), so that trans-generic demonstrations are ruled out: "it is impossible that what is proved should cross from one genus to another" (1.23.84b17–18). Hence "the why [that is, why the theorem about proportionals holds in the case of lines and of numbers] is different" (2.17.99a8–9), and so separate demonstrations seem to be needed in the case of each. Nonetheless, "qua such-and-such an increase in quantity" (2.17.99a9–10) the demonstration is the same, so that the theorem "holds in common of all *quantities*" (*Met.* 11.4.1061b19–21). For "while the genera of the beings are different, some affections belong to quantities and others of qualities alone, with the help of which we can prove things" (*APo.* 1.32.88b1–3). But though the universal theorem holds of all quantities, it does so *by analogy*: "Of the things used in the demonstrative sciences some are proper to each science while others are common, but common by analogy, since something is useful, in fact, [only] to the extent that it functions in the genus that falls under the science: proper ones—for example, that a line is such-and-such and straight such-and-such; common ones—for example, that if equals are subtracted from equals the remainders are equal" (*APo.* 1.10.76a37–41). Thus the kind to which lines, numbers, and so on belong, which is the ontological correlate of a theorem of universal mathematics, is not a first-order genus, but an analogical unity—a quantity.

79. This is Aristotle's resolution to the puzzle. Natural, mathematical, and theological sciences or philosophies deal with beings of different "natures," which together exhaust the beings and their starting-points and causes, and so must include those of the beings qua beings. The one that is primary among these must deal with the starting-points and causes that are prior to those of the others, so that those starting-points and causes too fall within its explanatory scope. Since together with its own starting-points and causes, these are all the ones there are, its explanatory scope is indeed universal—it includes the starting-points and causes of all the beings, and so of them qua beings. The primary starting-points and causes, however, are the immovable movers that are the starting-points and causes of the "divine beings that are evident." But if "the divine belongs anywhere, it belongs in a nature of this sort." But this is the "nature" with which theological science or philosophy is concerned. Therefore, theological science or philosophy must be the universal science of being qua being. It is universal, though, not in dealing with a universal genus, for "being is not a genus" (*APo.* 2.7.92b14), but in the way that universal mathematics is. See *Met.* 12.4–5.

will belong to it to get a theoretical grasp on being qua being, both what it is and the things that belong to it qua being.

Metaphysics 11.7.1063b36–1064b14[80]

Every science inquires into certain starting-points and causes for each of the things of which it is the science—for example, medicine and athletic training and each of the rest of the sciences whether productive or mathematical. |1064a1| For each of these marks off a certain genus and busies itself with it, as something that exists and is a being, although not qua being, since the science that does *this* is another science that is beyond the former ones. And each of the sciences just mentioned somehow gets hold of the what-it-is in |a5| each genus and tries to prove the rest in a weaker or more exact way. Some get hold of the what-it-is through perception, others by hypothesizing it. Hence it is clear from an induction of this sort that there is no demonstration of substance or the what-it-is.

However, since there is a science concerned with nature, it is clear that |a10| it must be distinct both from practical and from productive science. For in the case of productive science the starting-point of movement is in the producer and not in the product, and is either a craft or some other sort of capacity. Similarly, in practical science too the movement is not in the action done but in the doer of the action. But the natural scientist is concerned with things that have within |a15| themselves a starting-point of movement. It is clear from these considerations, therefore, that natural science is neither practical nor productive but theoretical (for it must fall in some one of these kinds). And since each of the sciences must somehow know the what-it-is and use it as a starting-point, |a20| we must not fail to notice the *way* the natural scientist must define things and the *way* he must get hold of the account of the substance—whether like snub or like concave. For of these the account of the snub is said together with the matter of the thing, whereas that of the concave is said separate from the matter; for it is in a nose that the snubness occurs, which is why the account of it is theoretically grasped together with this. |a25| For the snub is concave nose. It is evident, then, that the account of flesh too and of the eye and of the other parts must always be given together with the matter.

Since, though, there is a science of being qua being and separable, we must investigate whether this should be posited as the same as natural

80. Compare *Met.* 6.1.

science or, rather, as distinct from it. |^{a}30| Natural science is concerned with things that have a starting-point of movement within themselves. Mathematics on the other hand is theoretical and is a science of things that remain the same but are not separable. Concerning things that are separable, therefore, and immovable, there is a science distinct from both of these—if indeed there is some substance of that sort (I mean separable and immovable), |^{a}35| which is just what we shall try to prove.[81] And if indeed there is a nature of this sort among beings, there is where the divine too would surely be, and this would be the primary and most controlling starting-point. Accordingly, it is clear that there are three |1064^{b}1| kinds of theoretical sciences—natural, mathematical, and theological. The best kind of science is that of the theoretical sciences, and of these themselves the last named one; for it is concerned with the most estimable of beings, and each science is said to be better or worse |^{b}5| in accord with the scientifically knowable object that properly belongs to it.

We might raise a puzzle, however, as to whether or not the science of being qua being should be posited as universal at all. For each of the mathematical sciences is concerned with some one definite genus, whereas universal mathematics is common, concerned with all alike.[82] If, then, the natural substances are primary among beings, natural science will also be |^{b}10| primary among the sciences, but if there is another nature and substance, separable and immovable, the science of it must be distinct from and prior to natural science, and universal by being prior.

Metaphysics 12.1.1069^{a}18–^{b}2

The theoretical knowledge [we are seeking] is concerned with substance; for it is the starting-points and the causes of substances that are being inquired about. For if in fact the All is a whole of some sort,[83] substance is its primary part, and even if it exists by being a succession,[84] in this way too substance is primary, |^{a}20| then quality or quantity. At the same time, these

81. In *Met.* 12.6–7.

82. See *Met.* 6.1.1026^{a}27n.

83. At *Met.* 10.1.1052^{a}22 a whole (*holon*) is what has a certain shape and form by nature, and at 5.6.1016^{b}12–13 not being "some sort of whole (*ti holon*)" is identified with "not possessing one form." At 8.6.1045^{a}10 it is something beyond the parts that is the cause of their being one, namely, a form (1045^{a}23). Notice "the substance of the universe" at 12.10.1076^{a}1.

84. A view like that of Speusippus, described at *Met.* 12.10.1075^{b}34–1076^{a}4.

latter things are not, so to speak, unconditionally beings, but qualities and movements—or else even the not-white and the not-straight will be beings (at any rate, we say that even these things *are*—for example, that something *is* not-white). Further, none of the others is separable.

. . .[85]

There are, though, three sorts of substances. One is perceptible (which everyone agrees about), of which [1] one sort is eternal, |^{a}30| [2] another capable of passing away—for example, plants and animals; of this it is necessary to grasp the elements, whether one or many. And [3] another sort that is immovable, and this [3a] certain thinkers say is separable, some dividing it into two, the Forms and the objects of mathematics, [3b] others positing these two as one in nature, |^{a}35| and [3c] others only one of these, namely, the objects of mathematics.[86] The first two sorts belong to natural science (for they involve movement), but the third to another science, if no |1069^{b}1| starting-point is common to these.[87]

Metaphysics 12.2.1069^{b}24–26

All things that change have matter, however, but of distinct sorts. And of eternal things those that do not admit of coming to be but do admit of spatial movement have matter—not matter for coming to be, however, but for movement from where to where.

Metaphysics 12.4.1070^{b}11–35

Perhaps the elements of perceptible bodies are: as form, the hot and, in another way, the cold, which is the privation; and, as matter, what is potentially these

85. Omitting 1069^{a}25–1069^{a}30.

86. [3a] Plato (*Met.* 7.2.1028^{b}19–20); [3b] Xenocrates (1028^{b}24–27); [3c] Speusippus (1028^{b}21–24, 13.1.1076^{a}20–21).

87. The meaning is presumably that if there is no starting-point common to [3] immovable substances and [1] perceptible ones capable of passing away or [2] eternal, then natural science (*phusikê*) will deal with [1] and [2], and another science will deal with [3]. But if there is a starting-point common to both, as Aristotle has suggested there is (*Met.* 6.1.1026^{a}27–31), then a single science (namely, primary philosophy) will deal with [3] and with [1] and [2], while natural science will deal with [1] and [2] exclusively.

directly and intrinsically. And both these and the things composed of them are substances, of which these are the starting-points, that is, anything that comes to be from the hot and the cold that is one [something-or-other], such as flesh or bone; for what comes to be from these must be distinct from them. |b15| These things, then, have the same elements and starting-points (although distinct things have distinct ones). But that all things have the same ones is not something we can say just like that, although by analogy they do. That is, we might say that there are three starting-points—the form, the privation, and the matter. But each of these is distinct for each category—for example, in color they are white, black, and surface, |b20| or light, darkness, and air, out of which day and night come to be.

But since not only the things present in something are causes, but also certain external things, for example, the mover, it is clear that starting-point and element are distinct. Both, though, are causes, and the starting-point is divided into these, while what is so as a mover or a cause of rest is a starting-point and a substance. So—by analogy—there are three elements, |b25| and four causes and starting-points. But distinct things have distinct ones, as was said,[88] and the direct cause as mover is distinct for distinct things. Health, sickness, body—the mover is the craft of medicine. Form, disorder of such-and-such sort, bricks—the mover is the craft of building. And since the mover in the case of natural things |b30| is for a human a human, and in those that come from thought it is the form or its contrary, there will be in a way three causes, while in a way there are four. For the craft of medicine is in a way health, and the craft of building is the form of a house, and human begets human; and, furthermore, beyond these there is what as the first of all [movers] moves all things.[89] |b35|

88. At *Met.* 12.4.1070b17.

89. Once form, privation, matter, and the mover have been introduced as analogical unities, we can see what <health, sickness, body, the craft of medicine> has in common with <form, disorder of such-and-such sort, bricks, the craft of building>, and with <a human begetting a human>. In each case we have a form (house, health, human form), a privation (sickness, disorder of such-and-such sort, privation of human form), matter (body, bricks, flesh and bones), all of which are internal to the thing that comes to be, and an external mover (the craft of medicine, the craft of building, the father). If we lead back the craft to the form, the effect is to bring more clearly into view the analogy between craft production, where the mover is external, and natural reproduction, where it is internal and encoded in the form. Generalizing on these structures we get: <form, privation, matter, external mover>. Now ask the general question, Why is form (actuality, activity) of any sort present in the universe? By analogy with the particular cases there must be a first mover responsible for it. In one way, this must be external to and so beyond the universe, just as in the case of crafts. But in another way, if we lead back the external mover to an internal formal one, as in the case of natural beings, it will be internal to the universe. Compare *Met.* 12.5.1071a13–17, 10.1075a11–25.

Metaphysics 12.5.1070^{b}36–1071^{b}2

But since some things are separable and others are not separable, the former are substances. And because of this the same things are causes of all things, because without substances, |1071^{a}1| there are no affections or movements. Next, these causes will presumably be soul and body, or understanding and desire and body.[90]

Further, there is another way in which the causes are—by analogy—the same, namely, activity and potentiality.[91] But these too are not only distinct for distinct things but also apply to them |^{a}5| in distinct ways. For in some cases the same thing is sometimes active and sometimes potential—for example, wine or flesh or human.[92] But these also fall under the aforementioned causes[93]; for the form actively is, if it is separable[94]; as is what is composed of both [matter and form]; as is the privation—for example, darkness or sickness[95]; but the matter potentially is; for it is what

90. In *Met.* 12.3.1070^{a}5–6 Aristotle refers to both (1) natural things and (2) artifacts as substances. (1) The natural things are (1a) the animals and plants, (1b) their parts, (1c) the natural bodies (earth, water, fire, air), and (1d) the heaven and its parts, the stars, sun, and moon (7.2.1028^{b}8–13). 7.16.1040^{b}5–10 excludes both (1b) and (1c) from being substances, so that only (1a) and (1d) remain (17.1041^{b}28–30). In the case of (1a) we can see right away why body and soul should be their causes, since all living things have souls and bodies of some sort, by reference to which their various movements (growth, spatial movement, alteration) are explained, while human beings have, in addition, an understanding, responsible together with desire for their deliberately chosen actions. What makes these same factors responsible for the movements of the various celestial beings is that these beings too are in various ways like living things (*Cael.* 2.12.292^{a}18–21). (2) Artifacts may not be substances, as *Met.* 8.3.1043^{b}21–23 suggests, or not substances in the fullest sense. But whatever about that, they too have understanding, desire, and body as their causes, since they come to be as a result of human bodily movements caused by the understanding and desire of the craftsman (7.7.1032^{a}33–^{b}6, 9.5.1048^{a}10–21).

91. The causes are form, privation, and matter (*Met.* 12.4.1070^{b}25–34). Another way in which these are analogically the same is from the perspective of activity and potentiality—for example, form is activity, matter potentiality (5.1071^{a}8–11).

92. Something is actively wine when the form of wine is the relevant causal factor, and potentially wine when its matter is the relevant causal factor. Similarly for flesh or human.

93. Form, privation, and matter.

94. I.e., the forms of matter-form compounds (such as that of a house), which can exist in separation from the matter in the soul of the craftsman. The forms of natural compounds are active, although they are not inseparable from matter at all (*Met.* 9.8.1050^{b}2–3).

95. We are not explicitly told how to see these from the perspective of potentiality and actuality, but since each is a privation, and "the privation too is form in a way" (*Ph.* 2.1.193^{b}19–20), we are presumably to group them with the form.

is |ª10| capable of becoming both.[96] But actively and potentially differ in another way in the case of things whose matter is not the same, things of which the form is not the same but distinct—just as, for example, the cause of a human is both his elements, fire and earth as matter and the special form [as form], and furthermore some other external thing, such as the father,[97] and beyond these the sun[98] and its |ª15| movement in an inclined circle,[99] which are not matter, form, or privation, and are not the same in form [as father or son], but are, rather, movers.

Further, it must be observed that some causes can be stated in universal terms, whereas others cannot. The this [something][100] that is first active, then, and a distinct thing that is potential, are the starting-points of all

---

96. See *Met.* 12.4.1070ᵇ12–13.

97. X's father E is X's moving or efficient cause. X's matter is m_1, a specific quantity of fire and earth, which is obviously distinct from E's matter m_2. Prior to X's coming to be, m_1 was potentially but not actually a human being, whereas E was actually a human being. These two causes, m_1 and E, differ both with respect to their matter ($m_1 \neq m_2$) and with respect to their form (m_1 does not yet have human form, E does).

98. X's father E and the sun S are efficient causes of X. But they are not efficient causes in the same way. For though S and E both differ in their matter and in their form from X, S is not in actuality what X's matter (m_1) is potentially. Thus there are two ways in which a potential being (material cause) and an actual being (efficient cause) can be joint causes of a matter-form compound.

99. "Since we have posited and proved that things are subject to continuous coming to be and passing away, and since we say that spatial movement is the cause of coming to be, it is evident that if the spatial movement is one, it will not be possible for both processes to occur, because they are contraries (for what is the same, and remains in the same state, by its nature always produces the same thing, so that either coming to be will always occur or passing away will), so the spatial movements must be more than one and must be contraries, either because of the direction of their movement or because of its irregularity; for contraries have contraries as their causes. That is why it is not the primary spatial movement that is the cause of coming to be and passing away, but the one in the inclined circle; for in this there is both continuity and being moved with two movements; for it is necessary, if coming to be and passing away are always to be continuous, for there to be, on the one hand, something that is always moved, so that these changes do not fail, and, on the other hand, for there to be two movements, in order that not only one of the two processes will occur. The spatial movement of the whole, then, is the cause of the continuity, whereas the inclination is the cause of the approach and retreat; for this results in its becoming further away at one time and closer at another, and, since the distance is unequal, the movement will be irregular. So, if it causes coming to be by approaching and being close, this same thing causes passing away by retreating and becoming further away; and if it causes coming to be by repeatedly approaching, it also causes passing away by repeatedly retreating; for contraries have contraries as their causes, and passing away and coming to be in accord with nature occur in equal periods of time. That is why the times—that is, the lives—of each [sort of] thing have a number that determines it" (*GC* 2.10.336ª23–ᵇ12).

100. I.e., the particular substance.

things. Well, these are not universals; for the particular is the starting-point of the |^{a}20| particulars; for while human is the starting-point of human universally, no particular human is—instead, Peleus is of Achilles, and your father of you, and this B of this BA, and B in general of BA unconditionally.

Next, [the causes and elements] of substances (but distinct ones of distinct ones) are, as has been said, the causes and elements of things that are not in the same kind—|^{a}25| of colors, sounds, substances, quantity—save by analogy. And those of things in the same species are distinct, not in species, but because the causes of the particular ones—your matter and form and moving cause and mine—are distinct, but in universal account they are the same.

When we inquire, then, about the starting-points or elements of substances, relations, and qualities, |^{a}30| as to whether they are the same or distinct, it is clear that when they are said of things in many ways they are the same, but when these are distinguished the starting-points and elements are not the same but distinct—except that in a way the causes of all are the same. And in one way they are the same or analogous because matter, form, privation, and mover are omnipresent; in another way the causes of substances may be considered as the causes of all things, because if substances are done away with, all things are done away with; furthermore, |^{a}35| the first in terms of actuality is a cause of all things.[101] In another way, though, there are distinct direct causes, namely, the contraries that are said of things neither as genera nor in many ways, and furthermore the matters.

What the starting-points of perceptible things are, |1071^{b}1| how many they are, and in what way they are the same and in what way distinct has now been stated.

Metaphysics 12.6.1071^{b}3–1072^{a}18

Since there were three sorts of substances, two of them natural and one immovable,[102] concerning the latter it must be said that it is necessary for there to be an eternal immovable substance; for substances are primary among beings, |^{b}5| and if they are all capable of passing away, everything is capable of passing away. But it is impossible that movement either came into being or passed away (it, we saw,[103] exists always), or that time did; for there cannot be

101. See *Met.* 12.4.1070^{b}34–35.

102. See *Met.* 12.1.1069^{a}30–^{b}2. The focus now is on eternal immovable substances.

103. See *Ph.* 8.1.251^{a}8–252^{a}5.

a before and an after if there is no time. Movement too is continuous, then, in the way that time also is; for time is either the same thing as movement or an affection of it. But there is no continuous movement |^{b}10| except movement in place, and of this only that which is circular is continuous.[104]

But then if there is something that is capable of moving things or acting on them, but that is not actively doing so, there will not [necessarily] be movement; for it is possible for what has a capacity not to activate it. There is no benefit, therefore, in positing eternal substances, as those who accept the Forms do, unless there is to be present in them some starting-point that is capable of |^{b}15| causing change. Moreover, even this is not enough, and neither is another substance beyond the Forms[105]; for if it will not be active, there will not be movement. Further, even if it will be active, it is not enough, if the substance of it is a capacity; for then there will not be *eternal* movement; for what is potential may possibly not be. There must, therefore, be such a starting-point, the substance of which is activity. Further, accordingly, |^{b}20| these substances must be without matter; for they must be eternal, if indeed anything else is eternal. Therefore, they must be activities.[106]

. . .[107]

If, then, there is a constant cycle, something [A] must always remain, acting in the same way. And if |1072^{a}10| there is to be coming to be and passing away, there must be something else [B] that is always acting now in one way, now in another.[108] This [B] must, therefore, act in one way intrinsically and in another in virtue of something else—either of a third thing [C], therefore, or of the first [A]. It must, then, be in virtue of this one [A]. For otherwise this [A] again causes the movement of that one [C] and of the other one [B]. Accordingly, it is better to say "the first" [A].[109] |^{a}15| For it was the cause of things always occurring in the same way, and something else the cause of their occurring in another way, and of their always occurring in another way clearly both are the cause. This, therefore, is the way the movements actually take place. Why, then, inquire after other starting-points?[110]

---

104. See *Ph.* 8.7–8.

105. I.e., "the one," from which, together with the indefinite dyad, the Forms are composed (*Met.* 1.6.987^{b}20–22).

106. Reading ἐνέργειαι.

107. I omit 1071^{b}23–1072^{a}9, which discusses Leucippus, Plato, Anaxagoras, and Empedocles.

108. See *Met.* 12.6.1071^{b}15n.

109. A is required anyway to explain the constant cycle. B acting in way$_1$ causes coming to be and in way$_2$ passing away. But B's acting in these ways is itself a constant cycle. If C is introduced to cause it, we have an unnecessary extra cause.

110. Such as, for example, Platonic Forms.

5. Aristotle's God

Metaphysics 12.7.1072^{a}21–1073^{a}13

[T]here is something that is always moved with an unceasing movement,[1] which is in a circle (and this is clear not from argument alone but also from the facts[2]). So the primary heaven would be eternal.[3] There is, therefore, also something that moves it.[4] But since what is moved and moves something is an intermediate, there is then something that moves without being moved, being eternal, substance, and activity. |^{a}25|

This, though, is the way the object of desire and the intelligible object move things: they move them without being moved.[5] Of these objects, the primary ones are the same.[6] For the [primary] object of appetite is the apparently noble, and the primary object of wish is the really noble.[7] But we desire something because it seems [noble] rather than its seeming so

1. See *Met.* 12.6.1071^{b}12–22. The eternality (1071^{b}19) of the movement entails its being unceasing and is entailed by its being in substance or essence an activity (1071^{b}19–20).

2. Of astronomical observation.

3. I.e., the outermost transparent sphere of the fixed stars, which moves in a simple circular movement (*Cael.* 2.12.292^{b}22–23).

4. I.e., the primary mover of *Met.* 12.6.1071^{b}19–20.

5. It follows that the primary heaven must have an understanding with which to grasp that object and a desire that is moved by it: "desire and the desiring part cause movement when being moved" (*MA* 6.700^{b}35–701^{a}1). It follows that "the heaven is animate, that is, has a starting-point of movement" (*Cael.* 2.2.285^{a}29–30).

6. *Met.* 12.7.1072^{a}30–34 argues that within the column of intrinsically intelligible opposites, which are the objects of understanding, is the sub-column of substances, which is further divided into substances of different degrees of primacy, with unqualified primacy assigned to a substance that is both simple and an activity. 1072^{a}34 locates the real good in the same place, on the grounds that what is best (the good or best good) has the sort of primacy among objects of choice that the most primary substance has among intelligible objects. For the primary object of wish is the real good, which is identical to the primary mover, or mover of the primary heaven, which is itself a substance and an activity, and so an intelligible object.

7. (1) "Should we say that unconditionally and in truth the object of wish is the good, but to each person it is the apparent good? To an excellent person, it is what is truly the proper [= primary] object; to a base one, it is whatever random thing it happens to be. . . . In the case of ordinary people, however, deception seems to come about because of pleasure, which appears to be a good thing when it is not. So they choose what is pleasant as good and avoid what is painful as bad" (*NE* 3.4.1113^{a}23–^{b}2). (2) "Appetite is concerned with what is pleasant and what is painful" (2.1111^{b}16–17). As we see from these texts, Aristotle often speaks of the good rather than the noble in making this point. His reason for switching to *kalon* here is given at *Met.* 13.3.1078^{a}31–32: "the good is always found in action, whereas the noble is found also in immovable things."

because we desire it.[8] For the starting-point is the active understanding. And understanding is moved by intelligible objects, and what is intrinsically intelligible |a30| is the one column [of opposites],[9] and in this substance is primary, and in *this* the simple one and an activity[10]—but the one and the simple are not the same; for one signifies a measure, whereas simple signifies how the thing is. But the good too, and what is choiceworthy because of itself, are in the same column, |a35| and what is primary is always best or analogous to the best.

That the for-the-sake-of-which does exist among the |1072b1| immovable things is made clear by a distinction; for the for-the-sake-of-which is both for something and of something,[11] and of these the one is moved and the other is not. And it produces movement insofar as it is loved,[12] whereas it is by being moved that the other things move.

Now, if something is moved, it admits of being otherwise than it is, so that if its activity is the primary spatial movement, insofar as it is being moved, |b5| in this respect it admits of being otherwise—with respect to place, even if not with respect to substance. But since there is something that moves while it itself is immovable, though it is in activity,[13] it can in no way admit of being otherwise. For spatial movement is primary among

---

8. (1) "Both of these, therefore, can produce movement with respect to place, understanding and desire—understanding, though, that rationally calculates for the sake of something and is practical, and which differs from theoretical understanding with respect to its end" (*DA* 3.10.433a13–15). (2) "That which produces movement will be one in kind (*eidos*), the desiring part qua desiring—and the first mover of all is the object of desire. For this produces movement without being moved, by being actively understood (*noêthênai*) or actively imagined" (433b10–12). (3) "Understanding evidently does not move anything without desire—for wish is a desire, and when movement is in accord with calculation, it is in accord with wish. . . . Hence what moves us in every case is the desired object, which is either the good or the apparent good; and not every good but the good doable in action" (433a22–29).

9. The two columns of opposites are columns of starting-points (*Met.* 1.5.986a23), which, as such, are objects of understanding. One of them, however, because it consists of privations (*Met.* 11.9.1066a14–16), is not intrinsically intelligible (8.2.1046b10–12).

10. *Met.* 12.6.1071b20–22 recognizes the existence of a number of substances that are activities, among which it is now claimed that the simple one is primary. The basis for the claim is not specified, but one way to cash it out is in terms of the sort of movement that the desiderative understanding of it causes in the primary heaven. See *Cael.* 2.12.292b17–25.

11. "The for-the-sake-of-which is twofold—the purpose for which and the beneficiary for whom" (*DA* 2.4.415b2–3).

12. An important point of continuity between Aristotle's account and that of philosophers such as Parmenides and Empedocles who also assign a fundamental cosmological role to love (*Met.* 1.4.984b24, 985a6).

13. See *NE* 7.14.1154b26–27.

the sorts of change, and of these, that in a circle is primary; and this it produces. Therefore, it [the primary mover] of necessity is; and insofar as it is of necessity, |b10| it is in noble fashion, and in this way a starting-point [of movement]. For something is said to be necessary in a number of ways—as what is forced contrary to natural impulse, as that without which what is good does not exist, and as what does not admit of being otherwise, but is unconditionally necessary.[14]

This, therefore, is the sort of starting-point on which the heaven and nature depend. And its pastime is like the best that we can have[15]—and have for a short time (for it is always in that state [of activity], |b15| whereas we cannot be)—since its activity is also pleasure.[16] And because of this, waking, perceiving, and active understanding are a very great pleasure, and expectation and memory because of these.

Active understanding, though, is intrinsically of what is intrinsically best, and the sort that is to the highest degree best is of what is to the highest degree best.[17] And the understanding actively understands itself by partaking of the intelligible object; for it becomes an intelligible object |b20| by touching and understanding one, so that understanding and intelligible object are the

14. See *Met.* 5.5.1015b11–15, which associates unconditional necessity with simplicity.

15. See *NE* 10.7.1177a25–27, 1178a19–24, and leisure.

16. "Presumably, though, it is even necessary that if there are indeed unimpeded activities of each state, no matter whether happiness is the activity of all of them or of one of them in particular, then this activity, insofar as it is unimpeded, is the most choiceworthy. But this *is* pleasure. So the best good might be some sort of pleasure, even if most pleasures turned out to be bad—even unconditionally bad" (*NE* 7.13.1153b9–14).

17. Since understanding is like "the visual perception of intelligible things" (*Protr.* B24), and it is on vision in particular that the account of understanding is modeled—"as that which is capable of perceiving is to perceptibles, so must the understanding be to intelligible ones" (*DA* 3.4.429a17–18)—the following text explains: "Since every perceptual capacity is active in relation to its perceptible object, and completely so when it is in good condition in relation to the noblest of its perceptibles (for a complete activity seems to be most of all something of this sort, but whether it is the perceptual capacity itself that is said to be active, or what it is in, makes no difference), in the case of each perceptual capacity, the best activity will be, then, the activity of the subject that is in the best condition in relation to the most excellent of its objects. And this activity will be the most complete and most pleasant. For with every perceptual capacity there is a pleasure connected, and the same holds for both thought and contemplation. But the most pleasant is the most complete, and the most complete is the activity of a subject that is in good condition in relation to the most excellent of the relevant objects" (*NE* 10.5.1174b14–23).

same.[18] For what is receptive of the intelligible object and of the substance is the understanding, and it is active when it possesses it,[19] so that the former rather than the latter[20] seems to be the divine thing that understanding possesses, and contemplation seems to be most pleasant and best.[21] If, then, that good state [of activity], which we are sometimes in, the [primary] god is always in, that is a wondrous thing, and if to a higher degree, that is yet |^{b}25| more wondrous. And this is his state. And life too certainly belongs to him; for the activity of understanding is life, and his activity is that[22]; and his intrinsic activity is life that is best and eternal. We say, then, that the god is a living being who is eternal and best, so that living and a continuous and everlasting eternity belong to the god; for this is the god.[23]

. . .[24]

It is evident from what has been said, then, that there is a substance that is eternal and immovable and separate from perceptible things. And it has also been proved that |1073^{a}5| this substance cannot have any magnitude, but must be without parts and indivisible[25] (for it moves something for an unlimited time, and nothing finite has unlimited capacity; and, since every magnitude is either unlimited or finite, it cannot have a finite magnitude, because of what we said, and it cannot have an unlimited magnitude because there is no unlimited |^{a}10| magnitude at all). But then it has also been proved that it is impassive and inalterable[26]; for all the other movements are posterior to that with respect to place.

It is clear, then, why things are this way.

---

18. "The understanding is in a way the intelligible objects potentially, although it is none actually before it understands [them]—and it is potentially [these] in the same way as there is writing on a wax tablet on which there is nothing actually written. That is just how it is in the case of the understanding. And it is an intelligible object in just the way its intelligible objects are, since, in the case of those things that have no matter, that which understands and that which is understood are the same, since theoretical scientific knowledge and what is known in that way are the same. In those that have matter, each of the intelligible objects is present potentially" (*DA* 3.4.429^{b}30–430^{a}7). On the metaphor of touching and its importance, see *Met.* 9.10.1051^{b}24.

19. See *DA* 3.5.430^{a}10–25.

20. Reading ἐκεῖνο μᾶλλον τούτου.

21. See *NE* 10.8.1178^{b}7–23.

22. Reading ἐκεῖνο.

23. See *Cael.* 1.9.279^{a}11–28.

24. I omit 1072^{b}30–1073^{a}3, which criticizes the Pythagoreans and Speusippus.

25. What has been explicitly shown is that the primary god moves the primary heaven for an unlimited time (*Met.* 12.6.1072^{a}12–20). The next sentences explain why it must, therefore, be without parts and indivisible.

26. What has been explicitly shown is that the primary god is immovable with respect to place. The next clause explains why this entails impassivity and inalterability.

Metaphysics 12.8.1073^{a}14–1074^{b}14

We must not neglect to consider, though, whether we should posit one substance of this sort or several, and, if several, how many. On the other hand, we should remind ourselves too about the |^{a}15| views of the others, namely, that they have said nothing that can even be perspicuously stated about how many they are. . . .[27] We, however, must discuss the topic on the basis of the assumptions and determinations already made.

The starting-point and primary being is immovable both intrinsically and coincidentally, but it causes the primary eternal and single movement. |^{a}25| But since what is moved must be moved by something, and the primary mover must be intrinsically immovable, and eternal movement must be caused by something eternal, and a single movement by a single thing,[28] and since we see that beyond the simple spatial movement of the universe, which we say the primary and immovable substance causes, there are other spatial movements—|^{a}30| those of the planets—that are eternal (for the body with a circular movement is eternal and un-resting, as has been proved in our works on natural science[29]), each of *these* spatial movements must be caused by a substance that is both intrinsically immovable and eternal.[30] For the nature of the stars is eternal, because it is a certain sort of substance, and the mover is eternal and prior to the moved, |^{a}35| and what is prior to a substance must be a substance.[31] It is evident, accordingly, that there must be this number of substances that are in their nature eternal and intrinsically immovable, and without magnitude (due to the cause mentioned earlier[32]).

It is evident, then, that the movers are substances, |1073^{b}1| and that one of these is first and another second in accord with the same order as the spatial movements of the stars. But when we come to the number of these spatial movements, we must investigate it on the basis of the mathematical science that is most akin to philosophy, namely, astronomy; for

27. I omit 1073^{a}15–22, which criticizes Platonists.

28. Argued for at *Met.* 12.8.1074^{a}17–22.

29. I.e., *Ph.* 8.8–9, *Cael.* 1.2.

30. Each thing that has a spatial movement distinct from the simple circular movement of the primary heaven needs an immovable mover of its own to move it, which is why each of them must have understanding and desire. They are animals, after all, and their movements are explicable in the same way as those of other relevantly similar animals, such as ourselves. See *EE* 8.2.1248^{a}25–29. What moves each immovable mover's understanding, however, is its intelligible object, namely, the primary mover (*Met.* 12.7.1072^{a}26–27).

31. See *Met.* 12.1.1069^{a}20.

32. At *Met.* 12.7.1073^{a}5–11.

it is about |^{b}5| substance that is perceptible but eternal that this produces its theoretical science, whereas the others are not concerned with any substance at all—for example, the one concerned with numbers and geometry.

. . .[33]

There is a tradition handed down from the ancients of the earliest times and bequeathed to posterity in the shape of a myth |1074^{b}1| to the effect that the heavenly bodies are gods and that the divine encompasses the whole of nature. The rest of the tradition has been added later in a mythical way with a view to the persuasion of ordinary people and with a view to its use for legal purposes and for what is advantageous.[34] |^{b}5| For they say that these gods are human in form[35] or like some of the other animals, and also other features that follow from or are similar to those just mentioned. But if we separate the first point from these additions and grasp it alone, namely, that they thought that the primary substances were gods, we would have to regard it as divinely said, and that while it is likely |^{b}10| that each craft and each philosophy has often been developed as far as possible only to pass away again, these beliefs about the gods have survived like remnants until the present.[36] In any case, the belief of our forefathers and of our earliest predecessors is to this extent alone illuminating to us.

---

33. I omit 1073^{b}8–1074^{a}38, which deals with these astronomical investigations.

34. When Aristotle assigns an important role to traditional religion in his ideal city (see *Pol.* 7.8.1328^{b}2–23), he seems to have these sorts of goals primarily in mind. See 5.11.1314^{b}38–1315^{a}4.

35. See *Met.* 3.2.997^{b}5–12.

36. "We should take it, indeed, that pretty much everything else too has been discovered many times—or, rather, an unlimited number of times—in the long course of history. For our needs are likely to teach the necessities, and once they are present, the things that add refinement and abundance to life quite naturally develop" (*Pol.* 7.10.1329^{b}25–30; also *Cael.* 1.4.270^{b}19–20, *Mete.* 1.3.339^{b}27–29). For (1) the world and human beings have always existed (*Mete.* 1.14.352^{b}16–17, *DA* 2.4.415^{a}25–^{b}7, *GA* 2.1.731^{b}24–732^{a}3); and (2) human beings are naturally adapted to form largely reliable beliefs about the world and what conduces to their welfare in it (*Met.* 2.1.993^{a}30–^{b}11, *Rh.* 1.1.1355^{a}15–17).

Metaphysics 12.9.1074^{b}15–1075^{a}10

Issues concerning the [divine] understanding involve certain puzzles; for while it seems |^{b}15| to be the most divine of the appearances,[37] the question of how it can have that character involves certain difficulties. For if on the one hand it understands nothing, where is its dignity? It would be just like someone asleep. And if on the other hand it does understand something, but this other thing controls it (for what it is, its substance, is not active understanding, but a capacity), it would not be the best substance; for it is because of |^{b}20| actively understanding that esteem belongs to it.[38]

Further, whether it is understanding [as a capacity] or active understanding that is the substance of it, what does it understand? For it is either itself or something else. And if something else, then either always the same thing or sometimes this and sometimes that. Does it, then, make a difference or none at all whether it actively understands the noble or some random object? Or are there not certain things that it would be absurd for it to think of? It is clear, therefore, that |^{b}25| it actively understands what is most divine and most estimable and does not change [its object]; for change would be for the worse, and would already be a sort of movement.

First, then, if its substance is not active understanding, but rather a capacity [to understand], it is reasonable to suppose that the continuity of its active understanding is laborious for it.[39] Next, it is clear that something else would be more estimable than the understanding, namely, what is understood. |^{b}30| For both [the capacity] to understand and active understanding will belong even to someone who actively understands the worst thing, so that if this is to be avoided (for there are in fact some things that it is better not to see than to see), the active understanding would not be

---

37. Aristotle refers to the heaven itself as "the most divine of perceptible things (*ta theiotata tôn phanerôn*)" (*Ph.* 2.4.196^{a}33–34), and speaks of other things "that are far more divine in nature even than human beings, the most perceptible ones (*phanerôtata*), certainly, being those from which the cosmos is composed" (*NE* 6.7.1141^{a}34–^{b}2). It seems likely, therefore, that his characterization of the divine understanding is metonymic: the bodies attached to the first heaven are perceptible, so by transference from part to whole, the heaven and its mover are perceptible phenomena.

38. See *Met.* 12.7.1072^{a}30–^{b}1.

39. See *Ph.* 8.10.267^{b}3–4n.

the best thing. It is itself, therefore, that it understands,[40] if indeed it is the most excellent thing, and the active understanding is active understanding of active understanding.[41]

It appears, though, that scientific knowledge, perception, |b35| belief, and thinking are always of something else, and of themselves only as a by-product. Further, if to understand and to be understood are distinct, in virtue of which of them does the good belong to it? For the being for an act of understanding is not the same as the being for a thing understood. Or is it that in some cases the scientific knowledge *is* the thing? In the case of the productive sciences |1075a1| isn't it the substance and the essence without the matter? In the case of the theoretical sciences isn't it the account, the thing, and its active understanding? In the cases, then, where the thing understood and the active understanding of it are not distinct, namely, in

40. A parallel passage from the †*Magna Moralia* seems to contradict this conclusion: "[1] For since, [the argument] says, the god has all the goods and is self-sufficient, what will he do? For he will not lie asleep. He will, then, contemplate something, it says. For this is most noble and most appropriate. What, then, will he contemplate? For if he will contemplate something else, he will contemplate something better than himself. But this is absurd, namely, that there is something better than the god. Therefore, he will contemplate himself. But this is absurd. For if a human being were [to spend his time] looking closely at himself, we would rebuke him as indifferent [to other things]. It is absurd then, it says, if the god will contemplate himself" (2.15.1212b38–1213a7). But when we see [1] in the context of the immediately preceding sentence (1212b35–38) a different picture emerges: [2] "For if the god is self-sufficient and needs no one, it does not follow because of this that we need no one. For there is in fact an argument of this sort stated about the god" (= [1]). The point of [1–2], it is now clear, is that we cannot draw immediate inferences about ourselves from truths about the god, or vice versa. The god is self-sufficient, and so does not need friends, but it does not follow that a human being has no need of them. To think otherwise would be like arguing [2] that because a human being who spends all his time in self-scrutiny is senselessly narcissistic, so the god would have the same absurd defect were he to contemplate only himself. The argument fails precisely because such a person is not the primary god, not the best thing, and so not a worthy object of eternal contemplation. The god, by contrast, as the best thing, is a worthy object of it. For him to contemplate himself, therefore, is not absurd at all.

41. The divine understanding (= the primary god) is thus apparently a form of reflexive conscious awareness—active reflexive awareness that is otherwise objectless: "exercising wisdom and contemplating are the soul's function, and this is the most choiceworthy of all things for human beings—comparable, I think, to seeing for the eyes, which one would choose to have even if nothing else were going to come into being because of it beyond sight itself" (*Protr.* B70). From the inside, then, from the point of view of the subject experiencing it, it is apparently a state of consciousness of a sort familiar from the writings of the mystics, in which both subject and object merge in an awareness that yet remains fully and truly attentive. Insofar as we have any experience-based evidence of what a beatific state is like, this one is surely a candidate, giving us some reason to credit Aristotle's glowing description of it (*Met.* 12.7.1072b14–28).

those where the thing understood has no matter, they will be the same, and the active understanding will be one with the thing understood.[42]

A further puzzle remains as to whether the thing understood is composite; |^{a}5| for if it were, then the [divine] understanding would undergo change in understanding the parts of the whole.[43] Or is not everything that has no matter indivisible? (Just as the human understanding [of such things] is, or the understanding even of composite things in a certain time—for it does not possess the good in [understanding] this or that [part], rather, in [understanding] a certain whole it possesses the best, being something else.) And is not this the condition of this understanding which, for all eternity, is an understanding of itself? |^{a}10|

Metaphysics 12.10.1075^{a}10–27, 1076^{a}3–4

We must also investigate in which way the nature of the whole[44] possesses the good and the best—whether as something separated and

42. See *Met.* 12.7.1072^{b}19–21.

43. That the object of divine understanding is non-composite follows also from the fact that it itself is "without parts and indivisible" (*Met.* 12.7.1073^{a}6–7), since it is its own object (1074^{b}33–34).

44. The whole = the universe. Is its nature (1) something beyond the individual natures of the beings that constitute the universe or (2) not something beyond them—as it would be, for example, if it were epiphenomenal on them? The analogy Aristotle draws between the universe and the household (*Met.* 12.10.1075^{a}19) suggests not only that (1) is correct but also helps explain the appeal of (2). For the order of a household is dependent on the constitution of the city of which it is a part (*Pol.* 1.13.1260^{b}13–20). To explain why the members of a household have, for example, a socialized or second nature that suits them for life in an aristocracy rather than an oligarchy, then, we have to appeal to the constitution of the city in which their household is located. For the constitution and its laws are what cause the members of the household to have the second natures they do. But the constitution is the governing body (*politeuma*) (3.6.1278^{b}11)—since what sort a constitution is, is determined by the number and nature of its rulers. A kingship, for example, is a monarchical constitution aiming at the common advantage (7.1279^{a}32–34). In a way, then, it is the fact that the constitution has such a ruler that explains why its members, including those of its constituent households, have the second natures they do. By parity of reasoning, it is the fact that the universe is a kingship (*Met.* 12.10.1076^{a}4) that explains why the beings that constitute it have the (first) natures that they do (1075^{a}22–23).

intrinsic, or as its organization.[45] Or is it rather in both ways, like an army? For the good of an army is in its organization, and is also the general—and more so the latter; for he is not due to the organization, but it is due to him. |1075a15| All things are jointly organized in a way, although not in the same way—even swimming creatures, flying creatures, and plants. And the organization is not such that one thing has no relation to another, but rather there is a relation.[46] For all things are jointly organized in relation to one thing—but it is as in a household,[47]

45. *Met.* 12.9 argues that the divine understanding (the primary god) is the best or most excellent thing (1074b30–35), and explains how it possesses the good and the best, which is in fact itself (1075a6–10). The question now raised is how "the nature of the whole" possesses that best good. Three options are canvassed: (1) the divine understanding is an intrinsic being separated from the nature of the whole; (2) it is the order of that nature; (3) it is both. Although none of these is explicitly identified as the correct answer, a preference is shown for (3). The divine understanding is outside space and time, the universe is inside it (*Cael.* 1.9.279a11–28). So the divine understanding is (1) separated from the nature of the whole. At the same time, as an object of desire its existence is detectable within the universe in the shape of the order that desire induces in it (*Met.* 12.10.1075a15–25).

46. Compare the following text, which runs things in the opposite direction: "it is not necessary for even those cities to be inactive that are situated by themselves and have deliberately chosen to live that way; for actions can take place even among their parts; for the parts of the city have many communal relations with each other. Similarly, this also holds of any individual human being; for otherwise the [primary] god and the entire cosmos could scarcely be in a noble condition, for they have no external actions beyond the [internal] ones that are proper to them" (*Pol.* 7.3.1325b23–30).

47. "Every household is part of a city" (*Pol.* 1.13.1260b13), which "is prior in nature to the household, because the whole (*to holon*) is necessarily prior to its parts" (2.1253a18–20). Since "the virtue of a part must be determined by looking to the virtue of the whole," those of the household and its parts must be determined by looking to the city of which it is a part, and its constitution (*politeia*) (1.13.1260b14–15). Moreover, the household itself provides a model for one sort of political constitution: "There is a fifth kind of kingship, when one person controls all matters, just as each nation and each city controls common matters. It is ordered on the model of household management. For just as household management is a sort of kingship of a household, so this kingship is household management of a city or a nation or several nations" (3.14.1285b29–32). Like other constitutions, this one is "a certain order (*taxis*) of the inhabitants of a city" (3.1.1274b38), and is thus the relevant analog of the sort of cosmic order referred to throughout *Met.* 12.10.1075a11–25—notice *politeuesthai* ("governed") and *koiranos* ("ruler," "king") at 1076a3–4.

where the free people least of all do things at random,[48] but all or most of the things they do |^{a}20| are organized, while the slaves and beasts can do a little for the common thing, but mostly do things at random; for this is the sort of starting-point that the nature is of each of them. I mean, for example, that all must at least come to be disaggregated [into their elements][49]; and similarly there are other things which they all share for [the good of] the whole.[50]

However, we must not neglect to consider the impossibilities and absurdities that follow |^{a}25| for those who say otherwise, and what sorts of things

48. A free person is, in the first instance, someone who is not a slave. In this sense the farmer citizens of a democracy are free people. But a farmer has to work in order to get the necessities of life; he is not a man of leisure. Hence, there is another sense in which he is not free. A person free in this second sense has distinctive character traits, education, and outlook. Unlike a slavish or unrefined person, he is not obsessed with practical or useful things (*Pol.* 7.14.1333^{b}9–10, 8.3.1338^{b}2–4), but is "the sort of person whose possessions are more noble and profitless than profitable and beneficial; for that is more characteristic of a self-sufficient person" (*NE* 4.3.1125^{a}11–12). Because he is a well-educated person he has a broad perspective on the world, rather than a narrow-minded or overly specialized one. Hence he is able to judge or assess the credibility and appropriateness of discussions belonging to different professions and disciplines in which he is not himself an expert: "A doctor, however, may be either an ordinary practitioner of the craft, an architectonic one, or thirdly, someone well educated in the craft. For there are people of this third sort in (one might almost say) all crafts. And we assign the task of judging to well-educated people no less than to those who know the craft" (*Pol.* 3.11.1282^{a}3–7). Moreover, he has the virtues of character and thought, and so what appears to be the good to him is what is in fact the best good (*NE* 3.4.1113^{a}23–^{b}2), namely, the sort of theoretical contemplation that the primary god also engages in (10.8.1179^{a}22–32). Hence he alone has what it takes to be a full citizen in the city with the best sort of constitution: "the one consisting of those who are unconditionally best in accord with virtue . . . is the only constitution that it is just to call an 'aristocracy'; for only in it is the same person unconditionally a good man and a good citizen" (*Pol.* 4.7.1293^{b}3–6). Since this city insures that he has the resources needed for leisure (7.9.1329^{a}17–26), he does not need to work for a living, and so does not "live in dependence on" (*Rh.* 1.9.1367^{a}32–33) or "for the sake of" (*Met.* 1.2.982^{b}26) another, which is another mark of being free. The art and music he enjoys, and the use he makes of his leisure, further distinguish him from those who are crude or uncivilized (*Pol.* 8.7.1342^{a}19–32, 7.15.1334^{a}11–40, *Po.* 26.1461^{b}26–1462^{a}4). But even such a citizen is often under the authority of others, whom he must obey. There are thus substantial limitations on his freedom or self-determination.

49. The elements into which things are disaggregated contribute to the whole by being "ever active" and imitating "the things that cannot pass away" (*Met.* 9.8.1050^{b}28–30).

50. See *DA* 2.4.415^{a}26–^{b}2.

are said by those who speak in a more sophisticated way, and what sorts involve the fewest puzzles.

. . .[51]

Beings, however, do not wish[52] to be badly governed: "To have many rulers is not good; let there be one ruler."[53]

51. Omitting 1075ª28–1076ª3, in which Aristotle argues that his own theory is superior to those of Empedocles, Anaxagoras, Plato, and other Platonists.

52. *Bouletai* with subjects not obviously possessed of wish is often best translated as "tends"—as in the phrase *bouletai hê phusis* (*GA* 4.10.778ª4–9, and elsewhere). Here, however, the beings are being treated as if they were the citizens of a city ruled by a monarch, and so as things that do have wish. Compare *Met.* 12.7.1072ª28.

53. Homer, *Iliad* 2.204.

6. The Gods and Us

Nicomachean Ethics 1.9.1099^{b}11–18

Well, if anything is a gift from the gods to human beings, it is reasonable to suppose that happiness is also god given—especially since it is the best of human goods. But though perhaps this issue properly belongs more to a different investigation, it is evident that, even if happiness is not a godsend but comes about through virtue and some sort of learning or training, it is one of the most divine things; for virtue's prize and end is evidently something divine and blessed.

Nicomachean Ethics 1.11.1101^{b}18–21, 23–25

This is also clear from awards of praise involving the gods; for these are evidently ridiculous if it is by reference to us that they are awarded. But this happens because awards of praise involve such a reference. . . .[1] We call the gods both blessed and happy and call the most divine of men this as well.

Nicomachean Ethics 3.10.1118^{a}32–^{b}1

A certain gourmand[2] prayed for his gullet to become longer than a crane's, showing that it was the touching that gave him pleasure.

1. By praising the gods, we imply that the standard to which their actions are referred is human virtue, even though this is absurd. See *NE* 10.8.1178^{b}8–22.

2. Identified at *EE* 3.2.1231^{a}12–17 as Philoxenus, the son of Eryxis.

Nicomachean Ethics 4.2.1122^{b}18–20, 1123^{a}9–10

Also, the virtue of a work—its magnificence—lies in its magnitude. And this is found in the sorts of expenditure that are called "estimable"—for example, those concerning the gods (votive offerings, ritual objects, and sacrifices) . . . (for the same things are not fitting for gods and human beings or for a temple and a tomb).

Nicomachean Ethics 4.3.1123^{b}17–21

But worth is said of things in relation to external goods; and we would take the greatest of these to be the one we award to the gods, the one that the most worthy people most aim at, and the one awarded as the prize for the noblest accomplishments. But honor is like that; for it surely is the greatest of external goods.

Nicomachean Ethics 5.1.1129^{b}1–6

Since the unjust person is greedy, he will be concerned with goods—not with all of them but with those that are matters of good and bad luck, which are always good, unconditionally speaking, but for this or that person, not always so. (These are the ones human beings pray for and pursue. But they should not. Instead, they should pray that unconditionally good things will also be good for them, while choosing the ones that are good for them.)

Nicomachean Ethics 5.7.1134^{b}24–30

It seems to some people, though, that all cases of justice are like this, because what is by nature is unchangeable and has the same capacity everywhere, just as fire burns here and in Persia; whereas what is just they see as changing. This is not the case, however, but in a way it is. Among the gods, no doubt, it is presumably not at all this way, but among us, while there is such a thing as what is by nature, everything is changeable all the same.

Nicomachean Ethics 5.9.1137^{a}26–30

What is just is found among people who have a share in unconditionally good things,[3] who can have an excess of these or a deficiency; for, for some beings (as presumably for gods) there is no such thing as an excess of them, whereas for others (the incurably bad ones) no amount of them is beneficial but they are all harmful, and, for yet others, they are beneficial up to a point. That is why the just is something human.

Nicomachean Ethics 6.2.1139^{b}9–11

That is why Agathon is correct: "Of one thing alone is even a god deprived, To make undone what is done and finished."[4]

Nicomachean Ethics 6.13.1145^{a}6–11

But yet [practical wisdom] does not control either theoretical wisdom or the better part any more than medicine controls health; for it does not use it but sees to its coming into being. So it prescribes for its sake, not to it. Besides, it would be like saying that politics rules the gods, because it prescribes with regard to everything in the city.

Nicomachean Ethics 7.1.1145^{a}22–27

So if, as they say, human beings become gods because of an excess of virtue, it is clear that the state opposed to the sort that is beast-like will be of this sort. And just as there is in fact neither vice nor virtue of a wild beast,

---

3. These are (1) intrinsically good things, such as the virtues, that are good for everyone; (2) things, such as money, honor, or external goods generally, that taken in isolation are good but that may not be good for this or that person. (2) is the relevant sort here. See *NE* 5.1.1129^{a}34–^{b}6.

4. Fr. 5 Nauck.

neither is there of a god. But his state is more estimable than virtue, while that of a wild beast is of a different kind than vice.

Nicomachean Ethics 7.14.1154^{b}20–31

In no case, though, is the same thing always pleasant, because our nature is not simple but also has another element in it, in that we are mortals.[5] So if one of the two is doing something, it is contrary to the nature of our other nature, and when the two are equally balanced, what we are doing seems neither painful nor pleasant; since if the nature of some being was simple, the same action would always be most pleasant. That is why the god always enjoys a single simple pleasure[6]; for there is not only an activity of moving but also an activity of immobility, and pleasure is found more in rest than in movement.[7] "Change in all things is sweet," as the poet says,[8] because of a sort of wickedness; for just as a wicked human being is an easily changeable one, a nature that needs change is also wicked; for it is neither simple nor decent.

Nicomachean Ethics 8.7.1158^{b}33–1159^{a}12

When a great disparity in virtue, vice, resources, or something else comes about . . . then the parties are no longer friends and do not even claim that they deserve to be. This is most evident in the case of the gods; for they are the most superior to us in all good things. . . . In cases like this there is no exact definition of the point up to which people can remain friends; for much can be taken away and the friendship will still last, but if the separation is large—for example, between us and a god—it no longer does.[9] And

5. Our soul contains a divine element—understanding—which is our true nature or what we are most of all (*NE* 10.7.1177^{b}26–1178^{a}8, 9.8.1168^{b}31–33). In contrast to the other element referred to here, which we have in us insofar as we are mortal, it is immortal. See *DA* 1.4.408^{b}18–19, 3.5.430^{a}17–23.

6. Aristotle's primary god is a simple and entirely immovable being (*Met.* 12.7.1072^{a}21–^{b}1), whose one activity—contemplating himself—"is a pleasure" (1072^{b}16).

7. See *Cael.* 2.12.292^{b}1–25.

8. Euripides, *Orestes* 234.

9. *NE* 8.5.1157^{b}5–13 discusses the effects of spatial separation on friendship. Here the separation between the two parties is a measure of their differences in virtue, resources, and so on.

from this the puzzle arises as to whether friends really wish the greatest of goods for their friends (for example, that they be gods); for then they will no longer be friends to them, and not good things either then; for friends are good things.[10] If, then, we were correct to say that one friend wishes good things for the other for the other's own sake, it should be the case that the other remains whatever sort of thing he is. It is for him insofar as he is a human being, then, that he will wish the greatest goods. But perhaps not all of them[11]; for it is most of all for himself that each person wishes good things.[12]

Nicomachean Ethics 8.9.1160^{a}18–28

Some communities, though, seem to come about because of pleasure—namely, religious guilds and dining clubs; for these come about for the sake of sacrifices and companionship. All of these, however, seem to be subordinate to the political community; for it seeks not the advantage that is present at hand but the one that is for all of life {. . .}[13] [even when its

10. If we wished the greatest goods for our friends, we would wish them to become gods. But then (1) they would be too separate from us and other human beings to have friends, which would deprive them of the greatest of external goods, since that is just what friends are (*NE* 9.9.1169^{b}9–10). Alternatively, (2) in depriving ourselves of their friendship, we would deprive *ourselves* of the greatest external goods. Although both interpretations are possible, (2) is perhaps more plausible, since the puzzle is one about whether friends really wish for their friends the greatest goods that they wish to themselves—friendship itself being one of these.

11. (1) It is to his friend *as a human being* that a friend wishes the greatest goods, which excludes the possibility of wishing him to become a god. (2) "But perhaps not all of them," might seem at first to mean that there are some greatest goods that the good man does not wish for his friend. But that conflicts with the later claim that a good person "is related to his friend as he is to himself; for his friend is another himself" (9.4.1166^{a}30–32), since that entails that a good person will wish some greatest goods for himself that he will not wish for his friend, and so his friend will not be a second himself after all. What (2) must mean, therefore, is that there are some greatest goods that the good man does not wish for his friend *as a human being*, but as the thing he most of all is, namely, his immortal and divine understanding (*NE* 9.8.1168^{b}28–34, 10.5.1176^{a}24–29, 7.1178^{a}2–8)—this being the way he wishes good things most of all for himself (9.4.1166^{a}19–23). So the person who raises the puzzle is partly right and partly wrong. He is right in thinking that there are some greatest goods that a good man does not wish for his friend *as a human being*, but wrong in thinking that there are therefore some greatest goods that he does not wish for his friend *at all*.

12. See 9.8.

13. There is a lacuna in the text here.

members are] performing sacrifices, arranging gatherings related to these, giving honors to the gods, and providing pleasure-involving relaxations for themselves. For ancient sacrifices and gatherings seemed to take place after the harvesting of the crops, as a sort of offering of first fruits; for it was at these times that people were most at leisure.

Nicomachean Ethics 8.12.1162ᵃ4–5

The friendship of children toward parents, as of human beings toward gods, is as toward something good and superior.

Nicomachean Ethics 8.14.1163ᵇ15–17

For friendship seeks what is possible, not what is in accord with worth; for that is not even possible in all cases, such as in cases of honor to the gods or to parents; for here no one could ever make a return of equal worth, but the one who serves them as far as he can seems to be decent.

Nicomachean Ethics 9.1.1164ᵇ3–6

For the worth of philosophy is not measured in money, nor would honor serve as its counterweight, but it is perhaps enough—as in the case of gods and parents—to do what we can.

Nicomachean Ethics 9.2.1165ᵃ24

And honor too, it would seem, one should give to parents just as to the gods.

Nicomachean Ethics 9.4.1166^{a}20–23

But no one chooses, by becoming someone other than himself, to have everything (for even as things stand the god has the good).[14] Rather, he chooses to have it while being whatever it is that he is. But each person would seem to be his understanding part, or it most of all.

Nicomachean Ethics 9.8.1168^{b}31–33

But just as a city too, or any other complex system, seems to be most of all its most controlling part,[15] so also does a human being.

Nicomachean Ethics 10.7.1177^{a}12–1178^{a}8

But if happiness is activity in accord with virtue, it is reasonable that it should be in accord with the one that is most excellent; and this would be the virtue of the best element. Whether, then, this element is understanding or something else that seems in accord with nature to rule, lead, and understand noble things and divine ones, whether by being something divine itself |^{a}15| or by being the most divine element in us—the activity

14. (1) "The god" could refer to the primary god and "the good" to happiness. The thought would then be that no one would choose to have happiness or the good if he had to become a god to get it. (2) "The god" could refer to the understanding (as at *NE* 1.6.1096^{a}24–25, 12.1101^{b}30) and "the good" to the good under discussion, that is, the excellent person's ongoing life. The thought would then be that the excellent person, to whom life is a good, wishes good things for himself and so wishes for his ongoing life to be preserved, since this is a condition of his having these other good things. In other words, he wishes to become something at each next moment that will have those good things. If the something in question were *something else*, its having those things would not be a case of *his* having them. For, as things stand, there is something in him that already has ongoing life (the good in question), namely, his own understanding, since it is immortal and eternal. Moreover, his understanding is not something other than himself, since it is what he is or is most of all. On balance, (2) seems to make better sense of the entire argument than (1).

15. "The governing body controls the city everywhere, and the constitution is governing body" (*Pol.* 3.6.1278^{b}10–11).

of it, when in accord with the virtue that properly belongs to it, would be complete happiness.[16] That it is contemplative activity we have said.[17]

And this would seem to be in agreement both with what was said before and with the truth. For this activity is also most excellent (for not only is understanding the most excellent element in us, but also, of |^{a}20| knowable objects, the ones that understanding is concerned with are the most excellent ones). And, further, it is the most continuous activity; for we can contemplate more continuously than we can do any action whatever.[18]

Moreover, we think that pleasure must be mixed in with happiness, and the most pleasant of the activities in accord with virtue is agreed to be the one in accord with theoretical wisdom. Philosophy, at any rate, seems to involve pleasures that are wondrous |^{a}25| in their purity and stability, and it is reasonable that those who have attained knowledge pass their time more pleasantly than those who are seeking it.

Moreover, the self-sufficiency that is meant would belong most of all to contemplative activity; for while a theoretically-wise person, a just one, and people with the other virtues all need the things necessary for living, when these are adequately supplied, the just one still needs |^{a}30| people to do just actions for and with, and similarly for the temperate person, the courageous person, and each of the others.[19] But the theoretically-wise person, even when by himself, is able to contemplate, and the more theoretically wise he is, the more he is able to do so. But he does it better, presumably, if he has co-workers. Nonetheless, he is most self-sufficient.

Moreover, this activity, and only this, would seem to be liked because of itself [alone]; |1177^{b}1| for nothing arises from it beyond having contemplated, whereas from the practical ones we try—to a greater or lesser extent—to get for ourselves something beyond the action.

Moreover, happiness seems to reside in leisure; for we do unleisured things in order to be at leisure, and wage war in order to live in peace. |^{b}5| Now, the activity of the practical virtues occurs in politics or in warfare, and the actions concerned with these seem to be unleisured and those in warfare completely so (for no one chooses to wage war for the sake of

---

16. Aristotle has said that happiness is activity in accord with complete virtue (*NE* 1.10.1101^{a}14–15) or with the best and most complete one (1.7.1098^{a}16–18) and that it itself is something complete, but he has not previously distinguished complete happiness from happiness of another sort, as he seems to do here and explicitly does at 10.7–8.1178^{a}7–10. On the features attributed to understanding, see 3.3.1113^{a}5–7, 9.8.1169^{a}17–18.

17. This has not in fact been said in so many words, but see *NE* 1.5.1095^{b}14–1096^{a}5, 6.7.1141^{a}18–^{b}3, 12.1143^{b}33–1144^{a}6, 13.1145^{a}6–11.

18. See *NE* 1.10.1100^{b}11–17.

19. A reference back to *NE* 1.7.1097^{b}7.

waging war, or to foment war either; for someone would seem completely bloodthirsty |^{b}10| if he made enemies of his friends in order to bring about battles and killings). But the activity of the politician too is unleisured, and beyond political activity itself he tries to get positions of power and honors or, at any rate, happiness for himself and his fellow citizens—this being different from the exercise of politics and clearly something we seek on the supposition of its being different. |^{b}15|

If, then, among actions in accord with the virtues, those in politics and war stand out in nobility and magnitude, but these are unleisured and aim at some end rather than being choiceworthy because of themselves, whereas the activity of understanding seems to be superior in excellence because it is contemplative, to aim at no end beyond itself, and to have its |^{b}20| own proper pleasure, which increases the activity by its own increase, and if in addition the self-sufficiency, leisured quality, and un-weariness (so far as this is possible for a human being), as well as all the other affections assigned to the blessed, are evidently affections of it, then this activity would be the complete happiness of a human being, if it receives a complete span of life[20] (for nothing is incomplete |^{b}25| that is characteristic of happiness).

But such a life would be more excellent than one in accord with the human element; for it is not insofar as he is a human being that someone will live a life like that but insofar as he has some divine element in him, and to the degree that this element is superior to the compound,[21] to that degree will its activity also be superior to that in accord with the other sort of virtue. If, then, understanding is something divine in comparison with the human element, so also a life in accord with it |^{b}30| is divine in comparison with human life. One must not, however, in accord with the makers of proverbs,[22] "think human things, since you are human" or "think mortal things, since you are mortal," but rather one must as far as possible

---

20. See *NE* 1.7.1098^{a}18.

21. This could be either (1) the compound of soul and body or (2) the compound of the understanding and the other less divine elements in the soul. The reference to virtues of character and feelings (*NE* 10.8.1178^{a}9–14) suggests (2); the association of some of these specifically with the body (10.8.1178^{a}14–15) suggests (1).

22. See *Met.* 1.2.982^{b}22–983^{a}11.

immortalize,[23] and do everything to live in accord with the element in oneself that is most excellent; for even if it is small in bulk, in its capacity and esteem it far |1178^{a}1| exceeds everything.

It would seem too that each person actually is this, if indeed it is the controlling and better element.[24] So it would be strange if he were to choose not his own life but that of something else. Moreover, what we said before will fit now as well; for what properly belongs to each thing by nature is most excellent |^{a}5| and most pleasant for each of them; for each human being, then, the life in accord with understanding is so too, if indeed this most of all is a human being.[25] Therefore, this life will also be happiest.[26]

Nicomachean Ethics 10.8.1178^{a}9–1179^{a}32

Happiest, but in a secondary way, is the life in accord with the other virtue; for the activities in accord with it are human. For just actions, courageous actions, and |^{a}10| other actions that we do in accord with the virtues, we do in relation to each other in contracts, catering to needs, and in every sort of action and in feelings as well, by keeping closely to what is appropriate to each person. And all of these are evidently human. Indeed, some of them even seem to arise from the body, and virtue of character seems in many ways to be intimately related to feelings. |^{a}15|

Practical wisdom too is coupled together with virtue of character, and it with practical wisdom, if indeed the starting-points of practical wisdom

---

23. The verb *athanatizein* is rare and its precise meaning difficult to determine. However, its one other occurrence in a text of Aristotle's (although it may be spurious) helps somewhat with its interpretation (F645). Aristotle's advice, accordingly, is to immortalize ourselves by contemplating, that is, by living in accord with the immortal element in us, which is what we most of all are. Compare Plato, *Timaeus* 90b1–c4: "If a man has become wholly engaged in his appetites or spirited love of victory and takes great pains to further them, all his beliefs must become merely mortal. And so far as it is at all possible, he will become thoroughly mortal, and not fall short of it even to the least degree, seeing that he has strengthened these all along. On the other hand, if someone has seriously devoted himself to the love of learning and to truly wise thoughts, if he has exercised these aspects of himself above all, then there is absolutely no way his thinking can fail to be immortal and divine. And to the degree that human nature can partake of immortality, he can in no way fail to achieve this."

24. See *NE* 9.8.1168^{b}31–33.

25. "What increases something by its own increase properly belongs to that thing, and to things that differ in form, things that also differ in form properly belong" (*NE* 10.5.1175^{a}35–36).

26. See *Protr.* B63–70.

are in accord with the virtues of character and the correctness of these virtues is in accord with practical wisdom.[27] And connected as these virtues also are with feelings, they would be concerned with the compound.[28] But the virtues of the compound |a20| are human. So too, then, are both the life and the happiness that is in accord with them. But the virtue of understanding is separated.[29] (About it, in fact, let just this much be said; for to develop an exact account of it is a greater task than the one we have set before us.[30])

It would seem too that it has little need of external supplies[31] or less need than virtue of character does. For let us grant that they both need the necessary ones |a25| and to an equal extent, even if the politician does labor more in relation to the body and such-like; for any differences here would be small.[32] As regards the activities, though, there will be a large difference. For the generous person will need money for doing generous actions, and so will the just one, of course, for repaying debts (for wishes are not manifest things, |a30| and people who are not just pretend to wish to do just actions). And the courageous person will need capacity, if indeed he is to bring to completion anything that is in accord with his virtue. And the temperate one will need authority; for how else would it be manifest that he or any of the others is what he is?

Moreover, it is disputed[33] whether it is deliberate choice or action that is the more controlling element in virtue, on the supposition that it depends on both. |a35| Well, its completeness clearly does depend on both; but for |1178b1| the actions many things are needed and more of them the greater and more noble the actions are.

---

27. See *NE* 6.12.1144a28–b1, 13.1144b20–32, 7.8.1151a18–19.

28. See *NE* 10.7.1177b28–29.

29. Active understanding is separate from the body and from the other elements in the soul that are the body's form (*DA* 1.4.408b18–25, 3.5.430a17–23, *GA* 2.3.736b27–29, 737a7–11). Theoretical wisdom is separate from the body and the other psychic elements, in turn, because it is the virtue of something separate from them.

30. I.e., to make a contribution to politics (*NE* 1.2.1094b10–11, 13.1102a12–13) which, as the same state of the soul as practical wisdom (6.8.1141b23–24), does not control or use theoretical wisdom but "sees to its coming into being" (6.13.1145a6–11).

31. Elsewhere referred to as external goods.

32. The politician aims to develop the virtues of character in the citizens (*NE* 1.13.1102a7–10). These involve bodily appetites and feelings and so also the bodily pleasures and pains (2.3) that allow the citizens to be properly habituated through rewards (pleasures) and punishments (pains) (*NE* 10.9.1179b4–1180b28).

33. See *NE* 8.13.1163a22–23, also 3.2.1111b4–6, 9.1.1164b1–2.

The person who is contemplating, by contrast, needs none of these things, at any rate, for the activity. On the contrary, one might almost say that they are even impediments, at any rate, to his contemplating. But insofar as he is a human being and living with many other people, |^{b}5| he chooses to do the actions that are in accord with virtue and so will need such things for living a human life.

But that complete happiness is a sort of contemplative activity would also be evident from the following considerations. For we suppose the gods to be the most blessed and happy of all. But what sorts of actions must we assign to them? Just ones? |^{b}10| Won't they appear ridiculous if they engage in transactions, return deposits, and so on? Courageous ones, then, enduring what is frightening and facing danger because it is a noble thing to do? Or generous ones? To whom will they give? It will be a strange thing if they actually have money or anything like that. And their temperate actions, what would they be? |^{b}15| Or isn't the praise unrefined, because they do not have base appetites? If we were to go through them all, it would be evident that everything to do with actions is petty and unworthy of gods. Nonetheless, everyone supposes them to be living, at any rate, and therefore in activity; for surely they are not sleeping like Endymion.[34] If, then, living has doing actions taken away from it and still |^{b}20| more so producing, what is left except contemplating?[35] So the activity of a god, superior as it is in blessedness, would be contemplative. And the activity of humans, then, that is most akin to this would most bear the stamp of happiness.

A further sign of this is that other animals, being completely deprived of this sort of activity, do not share in happiness. For |^{b}25| the life of the gods is blessed throughout, that of human beings is so to the extent that it has something similar to this sort of activity, but of the other animals, none is happy, since they in no way share in contemplation. Happiness extends, then, just as far as contemplation does, and those to whom it more belongs to contemplate, it also more belongs to be happy, not coincidentally, |^{b}30| but in accord with contemplation; for this latter is intrinsically estimable. And so happiness would be some sort of contemplation. But to the extent

---

34. Loved for his great beauty by Selene, goddess of the moon, Endymion was made immortal by her, but was cast into a deep sleep in a cave on Mount Latmus in Caria so that she might descend and visit him during the dark phase of the lunar month.

35. Happiness is activity in accord with some sort of virtue. This activity could be (1) practical, and so in accord with practical wisdom and the virtues of character, (2) productive, and so in accord with the virtues associated with craft (*NE* 6.7.1141^{a}9–12) and—ultimately—with practical wisdom (6.2.1139^{b}1), or (3) contemplative, and so in accord with theoretical wisdom. (1) is excluded by the previous considerations, and (2) is implicitly excluded by them too, leaving (3) as the only possibility (6.1–2.1138^{b}35–1139^{b}4).

that someone is a human being, he will also need external prosperity; for his nature is not self-sufficient for contemplation, but his body must be healthy and provided with food and other sorts of service. |^{b}35| Nonetheless, one must not think that a person who is going to be happy needs many things and grand ones, |1179^{a}1| even if it is not possible for him to be blessed without external goods; for self-sufficiency does not lie in an extreme amount of these and neither does action. But it is possible to do many noble actions even without ruling land and sea; for even from moderate resources a person can do actions |^{a}5| in accord with virtue. (This is plain enough to see; for private individuals seem to do decent actions no less, or even more, than people in positions of power.) It is enough, then, to have that amount; for the life of a person who is active in accord with virtue will be happy.

Solon[36] too was presumably depicting happy people correctly when he described them as moderately |^{a}10| supplied with external goods but as having done what he regarded as the noblest actions and lived their lives temperately; for it is possible with moderate possessions to do the things one should. Anaxagoras also seems to have supposed the happy person to be neither rich nor in a position of power when he said that it would be no wonder if the happy one appeared to be a strange sort of person to ordinary people; for these |^{a}15| judge by external goods; for these are the only ones they can perceive.[37] The beliefs of wise people, then, would seem to be in harmony with our arguments.

But while these sorts of considerations also carry a certain conviction, the truth in practical matters must be judged from the works and the life; for these are what have the controlling vote.[38] When we examine what has been previously said, then, it must be judged by bringing it to bear on the works and |^{a}20| the life, and if it is in harmony with them, one must accept it, but if it clashes, one must suppose it mere words.

---

36. Croesus, the fabulously wealthy and powerful king of Lydia, confident that he was the "most blessed (*olbiôtaton*)" of human beings (Herodotus, 1.30.2), invited Solon to confirm his self-estimation. Solon famously demurred, citing Tellus the Athenian as most happy, and justifying himself by describing Tellus' life as follows: "In the first place, Tellus' city was in a prosperous condition when he had sons who were noble and good, and he saw children in turn born to all of them, and all surviving. Secondly, when he himself had come prosperously to a moment of his life—that is, prosperously by our standards—he had an ending for it that was most glorious: in a battle between the Athenians and their neighbors in Eleusis he made a sally, routed the enemy, and died most nobly, and the Athenians gave him a public funeral where he fell and so honored him greatly" (1.30.3–5).

37. See *NE* 10.9.1179^{b}7–31, especially 15–16, 26–28.

38. See *NE* 1.5.1095^{b}14–16, 1.8.1098^{b}9–12.

The person whose activity is in accord with understanding, however, and who takes care of it, would seem to be both in the best condition and the one most loved by the gods. For if the gods exercise a sort of supervision over human affairs, as indeed they seem to,[39] it would also be reasonable |^{a}25| both that they should enjoy what is best and most akin to themselves (and this would be the understanding) and that they should reward those who most like and honor it for taking care of what they themselves love and for acting correctly and nobly. But that all these qualities belong most of all to the wise person is not unclear. Therefore, he is most loved by the gods. |^{a}30| And the same person is also likely to be the happiest. So in this way too the wise person would be most happy of all.

Eudemian Ethics 1.1.1214^{a}21–25

Or is [living well] in accord with none of these ways, but one of the two following ones: like human beings who are taken possession of by nymphs or gods, by being inspired by a sort of daimonic thing, like those who are in ecstasy; or else due to luck (for many people say that happiness and good luck are the same).

Eudemian Ethics 1.7.1217^{a}21–24

Now, happiness is surely agreed to be the greatest and best of human goods. We say "human" because perhaps there could also be happiness for some other superior being—for example, for a god.

39. The gods live exclusively contemplative lives (*NE* 10.8.1178^{b}8–23) and so whatever supervision they exercise over human affairs must be of a somewhat special sort. Aristotle does not tell us what it is, but his identification of these gods with the heavenly spheres (*Met.* 12.8.1074^{a}38–^{b}14) suggests an answer. For the orderly revolutions of these spheres govern the seasons as well as the cycles of fertility and infertility of land and animals (*GA* 4.10.778^{a}4–9). Hence they confer benefits on all beings, but especially on those wise people who, through astronomical contemplation of the heavens, learn about these cycles, and adjust their lives accordingly.

Eudemian Ethics 2.6.1222^{b}20–23

Among starting-points, however, those of the sort from which movements first stem are said to be controlling, and most rightly so those from which what does not admit of being otherwise stems, by which, presumably, the [primary] god rules.

Eudemian Ethics 7.3.1238^{b}27–28

For it would be ridiculous if someone were to reproach the god, because he does not reciprocate love in the same way as he is loved.

Eudemian Ethics 7.4.1239^{a}17–19

But whenever the degree is excessive, not even the inferior parties themselves demand that they should be reciprocally loved, or be reciprocally loved to the same degree—for example, no one[40] expects the god to do so!

Eudemian Ethics 7.10.1243^{b}11–12

Even the god is content with receiving sacrifices that are in accord with our capacity.

Eudemian Ethics 7.12.1244^{b}2–11, 1245^{b}13–19

For someone might raise a puzzle as to whether, if someone were self-sufficient in all respects, he will have {. . .}[41] a friend, if a friend is sought in

40. Reading οὐθείς.

41. There is a lacuna in the manuscripts of at least twelve letters, perhaps to be filled by something meaning "any need of."

accord with a need. Or is this not so? Or will the good person be most self-sufficient? If the person with virtue is happy, why would he need a friend? For it is characteristic of a self-sufficient person to need neither useful people, nor amusing ones, nor living together; for to be with himself is sufficient for him. This is especially evident in the case of a god; for it is clear that needing nothing added, he will not need a friend either, nor will there be [one] for him, nor anything of a master.[42] So also a human being who is the happiest will least of all need a friend, except to the extent that it is impossible for him to be self-sufficient.

. . .

For although the comparison [with a god] is true, the resolution is in accord with the putting together.[43] For because the god is such as not to need a friend, we think that the one who is like him is too.[44] Yet according to this argument the excellent person will not even understand[45]; for it is not in this way that the god is in a good state [of activity], instead, he is better than to understand something else beyond himself.[46] And the cause of this is that for us the good is in accord with something else, whereas for that being he himself is the good for himself.[47]

Eudemian Ethics 8.2.1247a23–31, 1248a22–b7

Or is [being lucky] due to being loved, as they say, by a god, and the correctness due to something external? For example, a badly built ship often sails better, although not because of itself, but because it has a good navigator. Does the lucky person, in this way, have a daimonic thing as his good navigator?[48] It would be strange, though, for a god or a daimon to love someone of that sort rather than the best and most practically-wise

42. Reading οὐδ' ἔσται αὐτῷ οὐθὲν δεσπότου.

43. Rejecting the addition of οὐκ.

44. Reading καὶ τὸν ὅμοιον ἀξιοῦμεν.

45. If the excellent person does not need friends because the god does not, then he should not need something beyond himself to understand, since the god does not.

46. See *Protr.* B64.

47. "The eternally noble and true things, that is, the primarily good one that is not good at one time and not at another, is too divine and too estimable to be [so] in relation to something else (*pros heteron*)" (*MA* 6.700b32–35).

48. See *Div. Somn.* 2.463b14n.

person.[49] If, then, it is necessary for someone to be correct either by nature, or by understanding, or by [divine] protection, and it is not two of these, |^{a}30| then it would be by nature that the lucky are lucky.

. . .

Or is there some starting-point with no other external to it, which, because it is itself of this sort, is capable of doing that sort of thing? This is what we are seeking, namely, what the starting-point of movement in the soul is. It is clear, |1248^{a}25| then, that just as in the universe, so there too, [the] god moves everything.[50] For the divine thing in us in a way moves everything.[51] Of reason, however, the starting-point is not reason, but something superior. But what besides god is superior even to scientific knowledge and understanding?[52] For virtue is an instrument of understanding.[53] And it is because of this, as I said earlier,[54] that people are called "lucky" who, if they are impelled to, |^{a}30| do the correct thing, though they are without reason.[55] And for them it is not advantageous to deliberate. For they have the sort of starting-point that is stronger than understanding and deliberation (whereas those who have reason do not have this) and are divinely inspired,[56] but cannot [deliberate]. For though non-rational they are successful. Also, the prophesizing of these practically-wise and theoretically-wise people is quick, and |^{a}35| the only thing it must not receive is the prophesizing based on reason, though in some people it is due to experience, in others due to intimacy with the use of examination.[57] These

49. Compare *NE* 10.8.1179^{a}24–32.

50. Reading καὶ πᾶν ἐκεῖ κινεῖ.

51. Namely, the understanding. But this understanding, unlike god's, has an external starting-point: "of understanding, then, the starting-point is the end" (*EE* 2.11.1227^{b}32–33).

52. Since the primary god just is a sort of understanding (*Met.* 12.9.1074^{b}34–35), the understanding referred to here must be human understanding.

53. I.e., virtue of character, as part and parcel of practical wisdom, prescribes for the sake of theoretical wisdom, which is the virtue of understanding. See *NE* 6.13.1145^{a}6–11, and compare †*Pr.* 30.5: "science is an instrument of understanding (for it is useful to understanding, just as flutes are to flute players)" (955^{b}36–38). The primary god, on the other hand, has no such virtues to serve as his instruments. See *NE* 10.8.1178^{b}8–21.

54. At *EE* 8.2.1247^{b}21–28.

55. In the sense of lacking a rational argument for something, just as understanding is "without reason" (*EE* 5.8.1142^{a}25–26). Hence the involvement of understanding is not in jeopardy. Compare *Rh.* 2.17.1391^{a}33–^{b}3.

56. Reading (. . . ἔχουσι) καὶ ἐνθουσιασμοί.

57. Reading ἀπολαβεῖν. The examination may be, in particular, that of dreams and their significance. Notice the reference to dreams at *EE* 8.2.1248^{a}40 and see *Div. Somn.* 2.464^{b}5–16.

prophesizings are due to the god,[58] and it sees well what will be and what is, especially in those whose reason is released in this way.[59] That is why passionate people[60] also have vivid dreams. For the starting-point seems to be |^{a}40| stronger because reason is released, just as blind people remember better, |1248^{b}1| when released from looking at visible things, because what does the remembering is stronger. It is evident, then, that there are two kinds (*eidos*) of good luck, the one divine (which is why the lucky person seems to be correct because of a god, and this is the one who in accord with impulse tends to be correct), whereas the other is the one who goes contrary to impulse. Both, though, are non-rational. And the former is a continuous sort of good luck, |^{b}5| whereas the latter is not continuous.

Eudemian Ethics 8.3.1249^{a}21–^{b}25

But since there is a certain defining mark[61] also for the doctor, by reference to which he judges what is healthy for a body and what is not, and up to what point each thing must be produced (and if it is produced well the body is healthy, but no longer so if it is too little or too much), in a similar way too where actions and choices that are good by nature but not praiseworthy are concerned, |^{a}25| the excellent person must have a certain defining mark for the possession and choice—|1249^{b}1| and concerning the avoidance of abundance or scarcity—of wealth and of other results of good

58. Reading τῷ θεῷ. The reference is to the understanding, which grasps things without (discursive) reason. For the (primary) god does not see well "what will be and what is," since he is exclusively a self-contemplator. Compare *Div. Somn.* 2.463^{b}12–22.

59. Reading οὕτως.

60. See *Div. Somn.* 2.463^{b}16n.

61. Here, as often elsewhere (*Pol.* 1.9.1258^{a}18, 2.8.1267^{a}29, 7.4.1326^{a}35, ^{b}12, 23, 32, 7.1327^{b}19), a *horos* is what gives definition to what would otherwise lack it. The root meaning of *horos*, indeed, is that of a stone marking the boundary of a territory or piece of land in a visible way. Hence the doctor's *horos* is that by reference to which he judges what is healthy for a body and what isn't. For example, the *horos* of health in a muscle might be a certain uniform or smooth state, which the doctor can detect by touch (*Met.* 7.7.1032^{b}6–10). The *horos* is not the *skopos*, or target itself then, but the target's defining mark: "the politician must have certain *horoi*, derived from nature and from the truth itself, by reference to which he will judge what is just, what is noble, and what is advantageous" (*Protr.* B47). Notice *skopos* at *EE* 8.3.1249^{b}24.

luck.[62] Earlier it was certainly said[63] that this [defining mark] was "as reason [prescribes]," but this is as if someone were to say in matters of nutrition that it is "as medicine and its reason [prescribe]." It |b5| is true, but not perspicuous.

Well, just as in other areas, one must live by reference to the ruling element, and by reference to the state, in accord with its activity, of the ruling element, as a slave by reference to that of his master, and each thing by reference to its own ruling starting-point.[64] But since a human being too is by nature composed of a ruler and a ruled, |b10| each one would also have to live by reference to its own proper ruling starting-point. But this is twofold; for medicine and health are ruling starting-points in distinct ways (the former is for the sake of the latter). This is the way it is as regards what contemplates.[65] For the god is not a prescriptive ruling starting-point, but that for the sake of which practical wisdom prescribes. But the for-the-sake-of-which is twofold (the distinction has been made elsewhere), |b15| since [the god], at any rate, is in need of nothing. Whatever choice and possession, then, of natural goods—whether goods of the body, wealth, friends, or other goods—will most of all produce the contemplation of the god,[66] this is the best one, and this the noblest defining mark; and whatever choice, whether because of deficiency or because of excess, prevents serving the god and contemplation, |b20| is a base one. And this holds for the soul, and this for the soul is the best defining mark—[namely,] to perceive as little as possible the other part of the soul, [3] insofar as it is such.[67]

What the defining mark is for noble-goodness, then, and what the target is for the unconditional goods, let it be stated thus. |b25|

62. Reading σώματι.

63. See, for example, *EE* 2.3.1220b28, 5.1222a34, 6.1233b6. More often the formula also mentions the correctness of the reason. See, in particular, *NE* 6.1.1138b20.

64. *Archê* is usually translated as "starting-point"; I have added "ruling" to make explicit the connection to *to archon* ("ruling element") at *EE* 8.3.1249b8 and 1249b10.

65. I.e., the understanding: "the understanding . . . the contemplative capacity" (*DA* 2.2.413b24–25).

66. Reading τὸν θεὸν.

67. Reading τὸ ἥκιστα αἰσθάνεσθαι τοῦ ἄλλου μέρους τῆς ψυχῆς.

Politics 1.2.1252b24–27, 1253a27–29

And it is because of this that all people say that the gods too are ruled by a king, namely, that they themselves were ruled by kings in ancient times, and some still are. And human beings model not only the forms of the gods on their own, but their way of life as well. . . . And anyone who cannot live in a community with others, or who does not need to because of his self-sufficiency, is no part of a city, so that he is either a wild beast or a god.[68]

Politics 1.5.1255a34–36

If people were to become in body alone as distinguished as the statues of the gods, everyone would say that those who fell short deserved to be their slaves.

Politics 3.9.1280b29–1281a2

It is evident, therefore, that a city is not a community of location, nor one either for the sake of preventing mutual injustice |b30| or for the sake of exchange. On the contrary, while these must be present if indeed there is to be a city, when all of them are present it is still not yet a city. Rather, the city is the community for both households and families in living well, namely, complete and self-sufficient living. But in fact this will not be possible unless they inhabit one and the same |b35| location and practice intermarriage. That is why marriage connections arose in cities, as well as brotherhoods, religious sacrifices, and the pastimes characteristic of living together. And things of this sort are the function of friendship, since the deliberate choice to live together is friendship. The end of the city is living well, then, but these other things are for the sake of the end. And the city is the community of families and villages |b40| in complete and self-sufficient living, which we |1281a1| say is living happily and nobly.

68. See *NE* 7.1.1145a22–27.

Politics 3.13.1284ᵃ3–11

If, however, there is one person, or more than one (though not enough to fill up a city), who is so outstanding in extreme virtue that neither the virtue nor the political capacity of all the others is comparable to his (if there is only one) or theirs (if there are a number of them), then such people can no longer be taken to be part of the city; for they would be treated unjustly if they were thought worthy of equal shares despite being so unequal in virtue and political capacity; for anyone of that sort would probably be like a god among human beings.

Politics 3.16.1287ᵃ28–32

The one who bids the law to rule, then, would seem to be bidding the god and the understanding alone to rule, whereas the one who bids a human being to do so adds on a wild beast as well; for appetite is a thing of that sort, and spirit[69] distorts [the judgment of] rulers even when they are the best men.[70] That is why law is understanding without desire.

Politics 4.1.1288ᵇ22–24

[Politics must get a theoretical grasp on] what the best constitution is and what it would have to be like to be most of all in accord with our prayers, provided that no external impediments stand in its way.

---

69. Aristotle sometimes uses *thumos* ("spirit") and *orgê* ("anger") interchangeably (*Rh.* 1.10.1369ᵇ11) and very often uses the former in contexts where its aggressive side is highlighted (for example, *NE* 3.8.1116ᵇ15–1117ᵃ9). In other places, however, he says that anger is only "in (*en*)" the spirited element (*Top.* 2.7.113ᵃ36–ᵇ1, 4.5.126ᵃ10) alongside other feelings, such as fear and hatred (4.5.126ᵃ8–9). In one passage, indeed, he identifies spirit as the source not just of "negative" feelings but also of love and friendship: "spirit is what produces friendliness (*philêtikon*), since it is the capacity of the soul by which we love (*philoumen*)" (*Pol.* 7.7.1327ᵇ40–1328ᵃ1).

70. The distortion is the sort that feelings generally produce because of their involvement with pleasure and pain: "What is pleasant or painful does not ruin or distort every sort of supposition (for example, that triangles do or do not contain two right angles), but it does do this to the one about what is doable in action" (*NE* 6.5.1140ᵇ13–16).

Politics 4.11.1295ᵇ28–34

Also, of all the citizens, those in the middle are the ones that preserve themselves most in cities. For they neither desire other people's property, as the poor do, nor do other people desire theirs, as the poor desire that of the rich. And because they are neither plotted against nor plot, they pass their time free from danger. That is why Phocylides did well to pray: "Many things are best for those in the middle. In the middle is where I want to be in a city."[71]

Politics 5.11.1314ᵇ38–1315ᵃ4

Further, a tyrant should always be seen to be outstandingly serious where matters concerning the gods are concerned. For people are less afraid of suffering something contrary to the law at the hands of such people. And if they think their ruler is a god-fearing man, and one who takes thought of the gods, they plot against him less, on the supposition that he has even the gods on his side. In appearing to be someone of this sort, however, the tyrant must avoid silliness.

Politics 6.8.1322ᵇ18–29

Another kind (*eidos*) of supervision, however, is that concerned with the gods—for example, priests, supervisors of matters relating to the temples (such as the preservation of existing buildings, the restoration |ᵇ20| of decaying ones), and all other things that are ordered in relation to the gods. In some places it happens that a single office supervises all of this—for example, in small cities. But in other places there are many officials who are separate from the priesthood—for example, supervisors of sacrifices, temple-guardians, and treasurers of sacred funds. |ᵇ25| Next after this is the office set aside for all the public sacrifices that the law does not assign to the priests, but which have the honor [of being celebrated] from the

71. Fr. 10 Diehl.

communal hearth.[72] These officials are called "archons" by some, "kings" or "presidents" by others.

Politics 7.1.1323b21–26

Let us take it as agreed, then, that to each person falls just as much happiness as he has virtue, practical wisdom, and action done in accord with them. We may use the [primary] god as evidence of this, who is happy and blessedly so, not because of any external goods but because of himself and by being in his nature of a certain quality.[73]

Politics 7.3.1325b23–30

Moreover, it is not necessary for even those cities to be inactive that are situated by themselves and have deliberately chosen to live that way; for actions can take place even among their parts[74]; for the parts of the city have many communal relations with each other. Similarly, this also holds of any individual human being; for otherwise the [primary] god and the entire cosmos could scarcely be in a noble condition; for they have no external actions beyond the [internal] ones that are proper to them.[75]

Politics 7.4.1325b35–1326a5

The starting-point for the remainder of our investigation is first to discuss the sorts of hypotheses |b35| there should be concerning the city that is going to be set up so as to be in accord with our prayers. For the best constitution cannot come into existence without commensurable resources.

72. A city's communal hearth derived from the hearth in a king's palace, which was of both practical and religious significance.

73. See *Met.* 12.7.1072b24–30, 8.1178b7–23.

74. Although normally a city lives a political life in relationship to other cities. See *Pol.* 7.6.1327b4–6.

75. See *Met.* 12.10.1075a11–23.

That is why we should hypothesize many things in advance, just as when we are praying, although none of them should be impossible. I mean, for example, the size of the citizenry and of the territory. |^{b}40| For just as other craftsmen—for example, a weaver or a shipbuilder—must also be supplied with matter suitable for the work, |1326^{a}1| and the better the matter has been prepared, the nobler the product of their craft must be, so too a politician and legislator must be supplied with proper matter in a suitable condition.

Politics 7.8.1328^{b}2–23

But we must also investigate the question of how many of these things there are that a city cannot exist without; for in fact what we are calling the parts of a city would of necessity be included among them. So we must determine the number of functions there are, since this will make the answer clear. First, |^{b}5| there should be a food supply. Second, crafts—for living needs many instruments.[76] Third, weapons—for the members of the community must also have weapons of their own, both in order to rule (since there are people who disobey) and in order to deal with outsiders who attempt to do injustice. Further, a ready supply of wealth, |^{b}10| both for their needs among themselves and for military needs. Fifth, but of primary importance, the supervision of religious matters, which is called a "priesthood." Sixth, and most necessary of all, judgment about what is advantageous and just in their relations with each other.

Politics 7.9.1329^{a}28–34

No farmer or unrefined person should be appointed as a priest (for it is appropriate for the gods to be honored by citizens). But because the political element is divided into two parts, namely, the military and the deliberative, and because it is appropriate for those who are worn out with age to render service to the gods and find rest, it is to these that priesthoods must be assigned.

76. Wealth (*Pol.* 1.8.1256^{b}36), property, and slaves (4.1253^{b}31–33) are all instruments.

Politics 7.10.1330a11–13

One part of the communal land should be used to support public services to the gods . . . the other for expenditure on the communal messes.

Politics 7.12.1331a24–30

As for the buildings assigned to the gods, and the communal messes for officials with the most control, it is fitting for them to be located together in an appropriate place—except in the case of temples assigned a separate location by the law or some other prophecy delivered by the Pythian god.[77] And a place like this would be one that is such as to be a conspicuous enough setting for virtue[78] and also better fortified than the neighboring parts of the city.

Politics 7.12.1331b17–18

Temples must be distributed throughout the territory, some dedicated to gods and others to heroes.

Politics 7.14.1332b16–23

Now then, if they differed from each other as much as gods and heroes are believed to differ from human beings—straightaway having a great superiority first in body and then in soul, so that superiority of the rulers in

77. The oracle of Apollo (the Pythian god referred to) at Delphi was one of the most famous in antiquity; both cities and individuals consulted it in matters of importance, whether religious or secular. The inscriptions on the walls well convey the spirit the oracle stood for: know thyself; nothing in excess; observe the limit; hate wanton aggression; bow before the divine; glory not in strength.

78. Reading τὴν ἀρετῆς θέσιν. The thought, as at *Pol.* 7.11.1330b17–21, is that the qualities of places in the best city, which, as an aristocracy based on virtue, should match the virtue or merit of the citizens assigned to them, so that the best and best fortified places go to the most important officials.

comparison to those ruled was indisputable and evident—it would clearly be altogether better if the same people always ruled and the others were always ruled.

Politics 7.16.1335^{b}14–16

Even pregnant women should take care of their bodies and not stop exercising or adopt a meager diet. The legislator can easily accomplish this by requiring them to take a walk every day in order to worship the gods whose assigned prerogative is to watch over birth.[79]

Politics 7.17.1336^{b}14–23

Let the officials take care, then, that no statue or picture be an imitation of such |^{b}15| actions,[80] except in the precincts of certain gods[81] at whose festivals custom permits even licentious raillery[82] to occur. In addition to these, custom allows those of a suitable age to pay this sort of honor to the gods on behalf of themselves, their children, and their wives. But there must be legislation[83] that younger people not be spectators either of iambus[84] or of comedy |^{b}20| until they have reached the age when it is appropriate for them to recline at the communal table and drink wine, at which time their education will make them entirely unaffected by the harm resulting from such things.

---

79. E.g., Artemis and Eileithuia. See Plato, *Laws* 789e.

80. I.e., the unseemly ones imitated or represented in the forbidden stories or pictures.

81. Ritualized obscenity and scurrilous mockery played a role in certain religious festivals honoring Dionysus, Demeter, and other gods.

82. *Tôthasmon*: The verbal form *tôthazein* is used at *Rh.* 2.4.1381^{a}33, where it means to "mock" or "jeer" at someone, or "engage in a slanging match" with them. Here, though, the jeering seems to be of an obscene or licentious nature.

83. Reading νομοθητέον.

84. A figure named "Iambe" is mentioned in the *Homeric Hymn to Demeter*, who uses language so abusive that the goddess is overcome by laughter and forgets her sorrows. Iambus is associated especially with scurrilous personal humor of the sort exemplified by the work of Archilochus.

Politics 8.5.1339b4–8

The same argument also applies if music is to be used with a view to well-being and a free passing of the time, namely, why must they learn it themselves rather than having the enjoyment of other people's use of it? One may investigate the supposition we have about the gods; for Zeus himself does not sing or play the lyre to accompany the poets.

Politics 8.6.1341b2–8

The story told by the ancients about flutes is also reasonable. For they, as you know, say that Athena invented flutes but threw them away. Now, there is nothing wrong with saying that the goddess did this out of annoyance at how flute playing distorted her face, but the more likely explanation is that education in flute playing does nothing for thought, but it is to Athena that we attribute scientific knowledge and craft knowledge.

Rhetoric 2.9.1386b13–15

What happens contrary to what is deserved is unjust, which is why we ascribe indignation even to the gods.[85]

Rhetoric 2.17.1391a33–b3

Although people are more arrogant and more non-rationally calculating because of good fortune, there is one very good character trait that follows along with good fortune: that of being lovers of the gods, and of standing in a certain relation to the divine, namely, trusting in gods because of the things that have come about as a result of luck.

85. Compare: "The divine, however, cannot be envious" (*Met.* 1.2.983a2).

Rhetoric 3.7.1408^{b}19

Poetry is god-inspired.

Rhetoric 3.10.1411^{b}12–13

That "the god kindled the understanding as a light in the soul"[86] (for both understanding and light make something clear).

Poetics 1.15.1454^{b}2–6

But a deus ex machina must be used for what is outside the drama—either whatever things have happened beforehand and that no human being could possibly know, or whatever ones happen afterward that need to be foretold or announced (for we assign it to the gods to see all things).

86. Source unknown.

7. The Gods in the Fragments

Protrepticus B18–20

[B18] It is for the sake of this that we, among the things there are, were generated by the god and nature? What, then, is this? Pythagoras, when asked about this, answered, "to be a contemplator of the heaven," and he used to say that he himself was a contemplator of nature, and had come into life for the sake of this. [B19] And they say that when someone asked Anaxagoras for what's sake one might choose to come to be born and to live, he answered the question by saying, "to be a contemplator of the heaven and the stars, moon, and sun in it," since everything else, at any rate, is worth nothing. [B20] Therefore, according to this argument at least, Pythagoras was right in saying that every human being has been composed by the god in order to know and to contemplate. But whether the object of this knowledge is the cosmos or some other nature, we must investigate later; what we have said is enough for us as a first conclusion. For if wisdom is in accord with nature an end, exercising wisdom must be the best of all things.[1]

Protrepticus B28

A human being deprived of perception and understanding becomes pretty much like a plant; deprived of understanding alone, he turns into a wild beast; deprived of irrationality but retaining understanding, he becomes like a god.

Protrepticus B63–70

[B63] Further, when each thing completes in the most noble way that which—not coincidentally but intrinsically—is its natural function, that is

1. *Phronêsis* is usually "practical wisdom," but in *Protr.* seems not to be distinguished from wisdom generally, and is translated accordingly; "exercising wisdom" translates the cognate verb *phronein*.

also when one must say that it is good, and the virtue by which each thing can by nature accomplish this must be taken to have the most control. [B64] Now, what is composite and divisible into parts has several different activities, but what is by nature simple and does not have its substance [= essence] in relation to something else[2] must have one controlling virtue intrinsically.[3] [B65] If, then, a human being is a simple animal and his substance is ordered in accord both with reason and with understanding, he has no other function than this alone, namely, to arrive at the most exact truth about the beings. But if he is naturally co-composed of several capacities, and it is clear that he has by nature several functions to be completed, the best of them is always *his* function, as health is the function of the doctor, and safety of a ship's captain. But we can name no function of thought or of the thinking part of the soul that is better than truth. Truth, therefore, is the most controlling function of this part of the soul. [B66] And it performs this in accord with unconditional scientific knowledge, but more so in accord with what is more scientific knowledge, and in this knowledge the most controlling end is contemplation. For when of two things one is choiceworthy because of the other, the one because of which the other is choiceworthy is better and more choiceworthy—for example, pleasure than pleasant things, and health than healthy ones; for the latter are said to be productive of the former. Nothing, then, is more choiceworthy than wisdom, which we say is a capacity of the most controlling thing in us, when one state is judged in comparison to another. For the part of the soul that is capable of knowledge, both separately and in combination, is better than all the rest of the soul, and scientific knowledge is its virtue. [B68] Therefore, its function is none of the so-called particular virtues [of character]; for it is better than all of them, and the end produced is always superior to the scientific knowledge that produces it. But nor is every virtue of the soul a function in this way, nor is happiness. For if it is to be a productive science, it will be so of other things, as the science of housebuilding is of a house, but is not part of the house. However, wisdom is a part of virtue and of happiness; for we say that happiness either comes from this or is this.[4] [B69] According to this argument too, then, it cannot be a productive science. For the end must be better than the process of its coming to be, and nothing is better than wisdom. Therefore, we must say that this science is a theoretical one, if indeed it is impossible for a production to be its end. [B70] Therefore, exercising wisdom and contemplating

2. See *EE* 7.12.1245^{b}13–19.

3. See *NE* 7.14.1154^{b}20–31.

4. See *NE* 10.8.1178^{a}9–^{b}32.

are the soul's function, and this is the most choiceworthy of all things for human beings—comparable, I think, to seeing for the eyes, which one would choose to have even if nothing else were going to come into being because of it beyond sight itself.[5]

Protrepticus B110

For "the understanding is the god in us"—whether it was Hermotimus or Anaxagoras who said so—and "mortal life has a part of some god." So one must either do philosophy or say goodbye to living and depart from here, since all other things at least seem to be a lot of trash and folly.

F10 (Sextus Empiricus, *adv. dogm.* 3.20–22)

Aristotle said the concept of the gods came to be among human beings from two starting-points: from occurrences in the soul and from events in the heavens. The occurrences in the soul are due to inspiration of the soul in sleep and prophecy.[6] For whenever, he says, the soul comes to be in accord with itself in sleep, then, having received its own nature, it prophesizes and foretells what will come to pass. The soul is also this way when it is separated from the body at the point of death. At any rate, he accepts the poet Homer, as he relates this fact. For he made Patroclus, at the moment of his parting, foretell the departing of Hector, and Hector [at the moment of his parting] foretell the end of Achilles. From these things, he said, humans surmise that some god exists, similar to himself in his soul and wisest about all things. And also from the occurrences in the heavens: for, having observed the sun going round during the day and at night the well-ordered motion of the other stars, they thought some god existed, which was the cause of such motion and good order. Such was Aristotle's view.

5. See *Met.* 12.9.1074^{b}33–35.

6. See *Div. Somn.* 2.463^{b}12–464^{b}18.

F12 (Cicero, *de natura deorum* 2.37)

Thus Aristotle said brilliantly, if there were people who had always lived under the earth in good and respectable homes which were decorated with images and pictures and furnished with everything that those who are thought blessed held in abundance, but had never been above ground, but they receive by word of mouth a report that there is some kind of divine will and power, then if at another time a crevice is opened in the earth, and they go out from their hidden dwellings into those places which we inhabit and are able to leave, when they suddenly see earth, sea, and sky, know the great clouds and the power of the winds, and behold the sun and know both its size and beauty as well as its power, as it produces the day in the entire sky with its light spreading, and when night darkens the earth they discern the whole sky ornately decorated with stars and the multitude of light from the moon as it waxes and wanes and the risings and fallings of them all and the courses calculated and immutable for all eternity—when they see these things, they would certainly judge there to be gods and that these are all works of the gods. And he certainly said these things.

F14 (Seneca, *quaestiones naturales* 7.30.1)

That man [Aristotle] said most excellently that we should never be more reverent than when the subject turns to the gods. If we enter temples in an orderly way, [if when we approach the sacrifice, we change our countenance, tighten our toga, if we are instructed in every proof of propriety,[7]] how much more should we compose ourselves when we dispute about the stars and their nature, lest we are imprudent and either believe something rashly in ignorance or knowingly lie about something.

F22 (Cicero, *Academica* 2.38.119)

For as this wise Stoic of yours has meticulously spelled out these things for you, Aristotle shall come pouring forth a golden river of speech and would

7. Rose omits this clause.

say that man is foolish: "Never did the universe come to be, since there could be no beginning of such a brilliant work by a new intention entering. Further, the world is joined everywhere in such a way that no power could rouse such motions and changes, no old age can come to be by the passage of time, so that this world should ever fall into pieces."

F23 (Cicero, *de natura deorum* 2.15.42)

Thus since the place of some animate things is on the ground, while of others it is in water or the air, it seems absurd to Aristotle to think that no animal came to be in that region which is most suitable for animate things to come to be. But heavenly bodies occupy the place of ether. Since this is the finest of these [elements] and it is always moved in a lively way, it is necessary that some kind of animal comes to be in it and that it possesses penetrating perception and quick movement. That is why when stars come to be in ether, it is proper that perception and intelligence inhere in them. From this fact, one is led to believe that the stars number among the gods.

F24 (Cicero, *de natura deorum* 2.16.44)

And indeed Aristotle is to be praised for holding that all things which are moved are moved either by nature or force or will, and that the sun, moon, and all the stars are moved. However, what is moved by nature is either brought downwards by heaviness or elevated by lightness, neither of which befalls the stars, because their motion carries them in a circular orbit. Nor indeed can he say that the motion is generated by some greater force so that the stars are moved contrary to nature. For what force could be greater? It remains that the motion of the stars is willful. He who sees these things would be not only ignorant but also impious if he denied that the gods exist.

F26 (Cicero, *de natura deorum* 1.13.33)

And Aristotle in the third book of *On Philosophy* confuses many doctrines without disagreeing with his teacher Plato. For he assigns all divinity to mind at one point and at another he says that the world itself is a god, but then sets another god over the world and assigns it the role of directing and caring for the world's motion by a certain "winding." Then he says god is the heat of the heavens, even though he doesn't understand that the heavens are part of the world, which he himself in another place calls "god." But in what way can that divine perception of the heavens be preserved when it moves so quickly? Where then are all these gods, if we also count the heavens among the gods? But when he wants to say that the same god is without body, he strips it of all sense perception, even practical wisdom. Moreover, in what way can it be moved while lacking a body, and in what way can it be tranquil and blessed if it is always moving itself?

F49 (Simplicius, *Commentarius in de Caelo* 485.19–22)

Aristotle is clear that he can conceive of something above both intellect and substance, since he clearly says at the end of the book *On Prayer* that god is either reason or something beyond the understanding.

F61 (Cicero, *de finibus* 2.13.40)

. . . The human being is for two things, as Aristotle says: it is by nature for understanding and for acting, as if it were a mortal god.

F645 (Athenaeus 15.697a)

Nevertheless, Aristotle, in his *Defense against the Charge of Impiety*, if the speech isn't spurious, says "for I never proposed to sacrifice to Hermias[8] as an immortal, but rather prepared a memorial to him as a mortal and, wishing to immortalize (*athanatizein*) his nature, adorned it with funerary honors."[9]

8. Hermias of Atarneus was Aristotle's father-in-law and patron in the 340s BC.

9. See F675.

F652 (*Vita Aristotelis Marciana* 34–40 Gigon)

When he [Aristotle] was seventeen, he received an oracle from the Pythian god to become a philosopher in Athens. There he attended on Socrates, and stayed with him for the short time that remained before the latter's death; after him, he attended on Plato and stayed with him too until death, a period of some twenty years as he himself says in a letter to Philip.

F664 (Plutarch, *Peri Euthumias* 13)

Aristotle, writing to Antipater, says, "It is not just fitting for Alexander to be proud that he rules over many people. It is no less fitting for those people [to be proud] who are able to believe what they ought to about the gods."

F675[10] (Diogenes Laertius, 5.7–8)

O virtue, much labored for by mortal kind,

The noblest prey in life,

. . .[11]

For the sake of your dear form, Atarneus' nursling[12]

Left the rays of the sun bereft.

Which is surely why he will be sung of for his deeds

And the Muses, daughters of Memory,

Will exalt him into immortality,

Zeus, god of guest-friends, exalting,

And the last honors of steadfast friendship.

---

10. This song for Hermias, Aristotle's one lyric to survive complete, is fully studied in A. Ford, *Aristotle as Poet* (Oxford, 2011).

11. I omit some lines mentioning Leda, Achilles, and Ajax.

12. I.e., Hermias. See F645.

Aristotle's Will in Part (Diogenes Laertius, 5.16.185–187)

. . . And Nicanor, if he is saved (we have prayed for his sake), is to dedicate four-cubit stone statues to Zeus the Savior and Athena the Savior in Stagira.

Glossary

Account (*logos*): A *logos* in ordinary Greek is a word or organized string of words constituting an account, explanation, definition, principle, argument, reason or piece of reasoning, discussion, conversation, or speech; what such words or their utterances mean, express, or refer to, such as the ratio between quantities (*NE* 5.3.1131ᵃ31–32); the capacity that enables someone to argue, give reasons, and so on (*Pol.* 7.13.1332ᵇ5). One important sort of account is an "account of the substance corresponding to the name" (*Cat.* 1.1ᵃ2), so that "a definition is an account that signifies the essence" (*Top.* 1.5.101ᵇ38). In fact, *logos* is often used simply to mean "definition."

Action (*praxis*): The noun *praxis* (plural: *praxeis*; verb: *prattein*) is used in a broad sense to refer to any intentional action, including one performed by a child or wild beast (*NE* 3.1.1111ᵃ25–26, 2.1111ᵇ8–9), and in a narrower one to refer exclusively to what results from deliberation (*bouleusis*) and deliberate choice (*prohairesis*), of which neither beasts nor children are capable (1.9.1099ᵇ32–1100ᵃ5, *EE* 2.8.1224ᵃ28–29). A *praxis* in this second sense is usually contrasted with a *poiêsis* ("production"), and what distinguishes the two is that the latter is always performed for the sake of some further end, whereas a *praxis* can be its own end: "Thought by itself, however, moves nothing. But the one that is for the sake of something and practical does. Indeed, it even rules productive thought. For every producer produces for the sake of something, and what is unconditionally an end (as opposed to in relation to something and for something else) is not what is producible but what is doable in action. For doing well in action (*eupraxia*) [= *eudaimonia* or happiness] is the end, and the desire is for it" (*NE* 6.2.1139ᵃ35–ᵇ4). The frequent distinction between a *praxis* and a *poiêsis* is a special case of a more general distinction Aristotle draws between an *energeia* ("activity") and a *kinêsis* ("movement"; plural: *kinêseis*).

Activity (*energeia*): The term *energeia* is an Aristotelian coinage, which I have translated as "activation," when it is being predicated of something, and as "activity," when it is not. The dative or adverbial form *energeia[i]* is translated as "active" or "actively," in order to signal its relation to *energeia*. The etymology of the coinage is unclear, but Aristotle is explicit that it has been extended from movement to other things (*Met.* 9.1.1046ᵃ1–2,

3.1047ᵃ30–32), and that it is related to another term with an *erg-* root, namely, *ergon*: "The *ergon* ('function,' 'work') is the *telos* ('end'), and the *energeia* is the *ergon*, and that is why the name *energeia* is said [of things] with reference to the *ergon* and extends to the *entelecheian* ('actuality')" (9.8.1050ᵃ21–23). *Entelecheia* (for example, *Cael.* 1.12.283ᵃ26), which is mostly used as a synonym of *energeia*, but with a slightly different connotation, is also an Aristotelian coinage: *energeia* is action, activity, and movement oriented; *entelecheia*—as the *tel-* suggests—is end or *telos* or completion (*enteles*) oriented (*Met.* 5.16.1021ᵇ24–30). The dative or adverbial form *entelecheia[i]* is translated as "actual" or "actually." The *energeia of* is translated as "the activation of" and *entelecheia of* as "the actualization of." Putting all this together: the activation or actualization of X is an activity, which is X active or actual, which is X achieving its end, which—since "the for-the-sake-of-which is the function" (*Met.* 3.2.996ᵇ7)—is X fulfilling its function, and being actively or actually X, and so being complete. What exactly an *energeia* is, however, must be grasped from its contrast with a *kinêsis* ("process," "movement"): "Since, though, of the actions that have a limit none is an end, but all are in relation to an end (for example, making thin), and since the things themselves, when one is making them thin, are in movement in this way, [namely,] that what the movement is for the sake of does not yet belong to them, these [movements] are not cases of action, at least not of complete action, since none is an end. But the sort in which the end belongs *is* an action. For example, at the same time one is seeing [a thing] and has seen [it], is thinking and has thought, is understanding [something] and has understood [it], whereas it is not the case that [at the same time] one is learning [something] and has learned [it], nor that one is being made healthy and has been made healthy. Someone who is living well, however, at the same time has lived well, and is happy and has been happy [at the same time]. If this were not so, these would have to come to an end at some time, as when one is making [something] thin. But as things stand it is not so, but one is living and has lived. Of these, then, one sort should be called 'movements' and the other 'activities.' For every movement is incomplete, for example, making thin, learning, walking, building. These are movements and are certainly incomplete. For it is not the case that at the same time one is walking and has taken a walk, nor that one is building [something] and has built [it], or is coming to be [something] and has come to be [it], or is being moved [in some way] and has been moved [in that way], but they are different, as are one's moving and having moved [something]. By contrast one has seen and is seeing the same thing at the same time, or is understanding and has understood. The latter sort, then, I call an 'activity,' the former a 'movement'" (*Met.*

9.6.1048[b]18–35). Expressed linguistically, the contrast is one of aspect rather than tense. Roughly speaking, a verb whose present tense has imperfective meaning designates a *kinêsis*, while one whose present tense has perfective meaning designates an *energeia*. The distinction itself is ontological, however, not linguistic: *energeiai* and *kinêseis* are types of beings, not types of verbs. A *poiêsis* or *kinêsis* is something that takes time to complete and, like the time it takes, is infinitely divisible (*Ph.* 3.7.207[b]21–25, *Met.* 5.13.1020[a]26–32). It has a definite termination point or limit, before which it is incomplete and after which it cannot continue (*NE* 10.4.1174[a]21–23). An *energeia*, by contrast, does not take time to complete, and so does not really occur "in time" (*Ph.* 8.8.262[b]20–21) but is temporally point-like (*NE* 10.4.1174[b]12–13). Having no definite termination, while it may stop, it need never finish (*Met.* 9.6.1048[b]25–27).

Actuality, Actualization: *See* Activity.

Affections (*pathê*): The verb *paschein* means "suffer," "undergo," "be affected by," "have things happen to you," so that *pathê* are things that we are passive rather than active with respect to. A person's *pathê* are, in one sense, simply his attributes and, in another, his passions or feelings. Being pale or weighing ten pounds are *pathê*, but so are being angry or being friendly.

Agathon: Distinguished Athenian tragedian of the late 5th cent BC. Plato's *Symposium* memorializes his victory at the Lenaia (one of the annual Athenian dramatic festivals) of 416 BC.

All, the (*to pan*): *To pan* usually refers not to "the totality of things," but to what we (but not Aristotle) might refer to as "all of creation." That is why, for example, Aristotle can claim that everything (= everything that is a part of the All) has matter and a moving cause (*Met.* 12.5.1071[a]33–34)—something that is manifestly false of divine substances (6.1071[b]20–21).

Alteration (*alloiôsis*): (1) "There is alteration when the underlying subject remains and is perceptible but change occurs in the affections that belong to it, whether these are contraries or intermediates" (*GC* 1.4.319[b]10–12). (2) "Alteration is movement with respect to quality" (*Cael.* 1.3.270[a]27).

Anaxagoras: See DK 59 = TEGP pp. 271–325.

Appear to be so, things that (*ta phainomena*): *Phainomena* are things that appear (often to perception) to be so, but that may or may not be so. The corresponding verb *phainesthai* ("appear"), when used with a participle endorses what appears to be so and is translated as "it is evident that," "or it is seen to be that," or the like, and when used with an infinitive it neither endorses nor rejects what appears to be so and is translated as "appears." When it occurs without a participle or an infinitive, it may either endorse or reject. Aristotle often conjoins an appeal to appearances with an appeal to argument, or to things that are in accord with argument (*kata ton logon*) or in accord with reason (see, for example, *Ph.* 8.8.262^{a}17–19, *Mete.* 2.5.362^{b}14–19, *PA* 2.8.653^{b}19–30, 3.4.666^{a}13–18, *EE* 1.6.1216^{b}26–28, *Pol.* 7.4.1326^{a}27–28, 7.1328^{a}20–21).

Being (*to on*): The primary sort of being, on which all the others depend, is substantial being, since it alone is separable, and of substances the primary one is "the simple one and an activity" (*Met.* 12.7.1072^{a}31–32). For the mark of an activity—an *energeia*—is that it is never on the way to an end, but is at every moment fully achieving it—never becoming, always fully being (9.6.1048^{b}18–36). This substance is Aristotle's primary god, which is "the active understanding of active understanding" (9.1074^{b}34–35). (Notice "closest thing to substance" at *GC* 2.10.336^{b}33.) And it, therefore, is "the sort of starting-point on which the heaven and nature depend" (7.1072^{b}13–14). For it is the unmoved mover of the primary heaven, and so of all the other celestial spheres, including that of the sun, on which sublunary coming to be and passing away depend (*GC* 2.10.336^{a}32–^{b}3). Because the primary god—the activity of understanding or contemplating god, which god is—is the good that all other beings desire or aspire to (*Met.* 12.7.1072^{b}18–30). The difference between god and these other beings is that he is always actively being the very thing that they aspire to but are at different distances from reaching (*Cael.* 2.12.292^{a}22–28). Thus the primary heaven achieves the good (to the extent that it can) by eternally revolving in a circle ("one small action"); the second heaven (the sphere of the sun) requires two actions; whereas sublunary things require yet more actions.

Being (*einai*) **and not being** (*mê einai*): We think of the word "being" as having four different senses or meanings: (1) Existential "is"—where to say that something "is" means that it "exists." This is the sense captured by the existential quantifier. (2) "Is" of identity—where to say that A "is" B means that A "is identical to" B, or A "is one and the same thing as" B. (3) "Is" of predication—where to say that A "is" B means that "B belongs to A." (4) Veridical "is"—where to say that something "is" means that it "is the case" or "is true." In his account of being in *Met.* 5.7, Aristotle mentions a sort of being that corresponds to (2) at 1017^{a}8–30 and to (4) at ^{a}30–35, and in 5.9 and 10.3.1054^{a}32–^{b}3 he has much to say about identity and sameness, including that "everything that is a being is either distinct or the same" (1054^{b}25). (1), however, is absent from his discussion, although potential and actual being (5.7.1017^{a}35–^{b}9) surely bears on it, and it does seem to play some role in explaining what the separability distinctive of substance consists in (5.11.1019^{a}1–4). One reason for this is that a demonstrative science posits the existence of the genus it investigates, and proceeds to investigate it (*APo.* 1.10.76^{b}11–22), so that existence itself escapes the focus of the science—even of the science of being qua being.

Being for, the (*einai* + dative) A: What A is intrinsically; the essence of A (*Met.* 7.4.1029^{b}13–1030^{b}13).

Belief (*doxa*): Belief is "no less about things that are eternal and things that are impossible than about things that are up to us" (*NE* 3.2.1111^{b}30–33), the latter being the perceptible particulars we can change through our voluntary actions. At the same time, belief (or anyway mature belief) presupposes a capacity for rational calculation: "Perceptual imagination . . . also belongs to the other animals, but the deliberative sort exists [only] in the rationally calculative ones. . . . And this is the cause of these animals seeming not to have beliefs, namely, that they do not have the [imagination] that results from a deduction" (*DA* 3.11.434^{a}5–11). Hence the part of the soul that forms beliefs (*doxastikon*) is the same as the part that calculates or deliberates (*NE* 6.5.1140^{b}25–26, 13.1144^{b}14–15). Unlike calculation and deliberation, however, which are types of inquiry, what one believes is "already determined," since belief is "not inquiry but already a sort of affirmation" (9.1142^{b}11–14). That is why believing is of necessity done either falsely or truly. For it is a form of affirmation, and "to say of what is that it is not, or of what is not that it is, is false, whereas to say of what is that it is, or of what is not that it is not, is true, and so he who says of anything that it is, or that it is not, will say either what is true or what is false" (*Met.* 4.7.1011^{b}26–28). It is also why believing is not up to us.

Blessed, blessedly happy (*makarios*): *Makarios* is often a synonym for *eudaimôn* ("happy"), but sometimes with the implication of being extremely happy (*NE* 1.10.1101^{a}7) or in a condition like that of the gods (10.8.1178^{b}25–32).

Callippus of Cyzicus: Flourished c. 330 BC, studied with a friend of Eudoxus, and is said to have stayed with Aristotle in Athens helping him explore and criticize Eudoxus' views.

Capacity (*dunamis*): The term *dunamis* (plural: *dunameis*) is used by Aristotle to capture two different but related things. (1) As in ordinary Greek, it signifies a power or capacity something has, especially to cause movement in something else (productive *dunamis*) or to be caused to move by something else (passive *dunamis*). (2) It signifies a way of being, namely, potential (*dunamei*) being as opposed to actual (*entelecheia[i]*) or active (*energeia[i]*) being. Context usually makes clear which is intended. See also *Met.* 5.12.

Category: *See* Scientific knowledge (7).

Cause (*aition*): "Something is said to be a cause if it is: [1] That from which, as a component, a thing comes to be—for example, as the bronze is of the statue, the silver of the bowl, and also the kinds of these. [2] The form or paradigm, that is, the account of the essence, and kinds of this (for example, of the octave, the ratio 2:1 and number in general), and the parts included in the account. [3] Further, that from which the change or the resting from change first starts—for example, the deliberator is a cause [of the action] and the father of his child and in general the producer is a cause of the thing produced and the change maker of the change made. [4] Further, the end, and this is the for-the-sake-of-which—for example, health of someone's taking walks. For why does he take walks? 'In order that he may be healthy,' we say" (*Met.* 5.2.1013^{a}24–^{b}3). The four causes Aristotle recognizes (final, formal, material, efficient) are discussed in *Ph.* 2.3.

Chance (*automaton*): Things that come about by chance are the ones "whose cause is indefinite and that come about not for the sake of something, and neither always nor for the most part nor in an orderly way" (*Rh.* 1.10.1369^{a}32–34). Living things that come to be by chance are the so-called spontaneously generated ones. *See also* Luck.

Coincidents: A standard Aristotelian contrast is between what has an affection B coincidentally or contingently (*kata sumbebêkos* or *per accidens* in Latin), making the affection a coincident of it, and what has it intrinsically or non-contingently (*kath' hauto* or *per se*) (*Met.* 5.18.1022^{a}24–36). Affections that belong to something, such as the soul, contingently are of no interest to a science of it, since they cannot be demonstrated to hold of it, and all science is demonstrative (6.2.1026^{b}3–5). But some coincidents are demonstrable and so are of interest to science. These are the intrinsic coincidents or *per se* accidents—"the coincidents connected to the essences" (*DA* 1.1.402^{b}18)—that are not parts of a thing's substance or essence, but are demonstrable from it, as having internal angles equal to two right angles is demonstrable from the definition of a triangle's essence (*APo.* 1.7.75^{b}1, 22.83^{b}19).

Complete (*teleion*): The adjective *teleios*, which derives from the noun *telos* ("end," "goal") and can also be translated as "perfect," has a number of different senses: "What is said to be complete is: [1] one, that outside which not even one part is to be found—for example, the complete time of each thing is the one outside which there is no time to be found that is part of that time. [2] That which, as regards virtue or the good, cannot be surpassed relative to its kind (*genos*)—for example, a doctor is complete and a flute-player is complete when they lack nothing as regards the form of their own proper virtue. (It is in this way, transferring the term to bad things, we speak of a complete scandalmonger and a complete thief—indeed we even say that they are good, for example, a good thief and a good scandalmonger.) Also, virtue is a sort of completion; for each thing is complete and every substance is complete when, as regards the form of its proper virtue, it lacks no part of its natural magnitude. [3] Further, things that have attained their end, this being something excellent, are said to be complete; for things are complete in virtue of having attained their end. So, since the end is a last thing, we transfer the term to base things and say that a thing has been completely ruined and completely destroyed, when there is no deficiency in its destruction and badness but it has reached its last. That is why death, too, is by metaphorical transference said to be an end, because both are last things. And the end—that is, the for-the-sake-of-which—is a last thing" (*Met.* 5.16.1021^{b}12–30). Completeness is attributed to the city (*Pol.* 1.2.1252^{b}27–30, 3.9.1280^{b}40), to happiness (*NE* 1.7.1097^{a}25–^{b}21), to lives (1098^{a}18), and to virtues (1098^{a}18, 1.13.1102^{a}6, 5.1.1129^{b}30), as well as to actions (*Met.* 9.6.1048^{b}22), differences (10.4.1055^{a}16), and many other things.

Concoction: *See* Form.

Contemplate (*theôrein*): *See* Theoretical grasp on.

Contrary (*enantia*): "Said to be contraries are: Those things differing in genus that cannot belong to the same thing at the same time. The most different of the things in the same genus. The most different of the things in the same recipient. The most different of the things falling under the same capacity. The things whose difference is greatest either unconditionally or in genus or in species" (*Met.* 5.10.1018^{a}25–31; also 10.4.1055^{b}13–17).

Control, having (*kurios*): Control is fundamentally executive power or authority or the power to compel, so that a general has control over his army (*NE* 3.8.1116^{a}29–^{b}2) and a politician has control over a city and its inhabitants. Since what has control in a sphere determines or partly determines what happens within it, it is one of the most estimable or important elements in the sphere, so that what is less estimable than something cannot or should not control it (6.12.1143^{b}33–35, 13.1145^{a}6–7). When Aristotle contrasts natural virtue of character with the *kurios* variety (6.13.1144^{b}1–32), the control exerted by the latter seems to be teleological: the natural variety is a sort of virtue because it is an early stage in the development of mature virtue (compare *Met.* 9.8.1050^{a}21–23). Hence *kuria aretê* is "full virtue" or virtue in the full or strict sense of the term. *Ta kuria*, on the other hand, are the words that are in prevalent use among listeners: "By 'prevalent (*kurion*)' I mean [a name or word] a given group would use, and by 'exotic' one that others would. So it is evident that the same name can be both prevalent and exotic, although not for the same groups" (*Po.* 21.1457^{b}3–5). *Kuriôs* and *haplôs* ("unconditionally") are often used interchangeably, for example, *Cat.* 13.14^{b}24, as are *kuriôs* and *kath' hauta* ("intrinsically"), for example, *Cat.* 6.5^{b}8.

Craft (*technê*): "All productions come either from craft, or from some capacity, or from thought. But some of them, however, may come about from chance or from luck, in a way quite similar to the ones found in those that come to be from a nature. For sometimes there too some of the same things come to be either from (*ek*) seed or without seed. But we must investigate these later. From craft, though, come to be the things whose form is in the soul. And by 'form' I mean the essence of each thing and the primary substance" (*Met.* 7.7.1032^{a}27–^{b}2).

Cratylus: Little is known about Cratylus beyond what we can glean from Plato's *Cratylus* and what Aristotle tells us about him and at *Met.* 4.5.1010^{a}7–15, namely, that he "criticized Heraclitus for saying that it is not possible to step into the same river twice, since he thought that we could not do so even once." Other sources tell us that Plato's association with Cratylus occurred after the death of Socrates in 399 BC.

Define, definition (*horizein*, *horismos*, *horos*): (1) "One sort of definition is an indemonstrable account of the what-it-is; another is a deduction of the what-it-is, differing in mode [of arrangement] from a demonstration; a third is the conclusion of a demonstration of the what-it is" (*APo.* 2.10.94^{a}11–14). (2) "A definition is an account that signifies the essence" (*Top.* 1.5.101^{b}38). (3) "A definition is composed of a genus and a differentia" (1.8.103^{b}15–16). (3) "The ultimate differentia will be the substance of the thing and its definition" (*Met.* 7.12.1038^{a}19–20). (4) "A definition is a sort of number, since it is divisible, and indeed into indivisibles (for the accounts are not unlimited), and number is like that" (8.3.1043^{b}34–36). (5) "One sort [of definition] will be an account of what a name—or some other name-like account—signifies" (*APo.* 2.10.93^{b}30). Both sorts—both nominal and real definitions, as they are now called—say what something is, but do not assert that it is (1.2.72^{a}21–24). (6) "Every definition is always universal" (2.13.97^{b}25). (7) "In a definition nothing is predicated of anything else" (2.3.90^{b}34–35).

Defining mark (*horos*): A common meaning of the noun *horos*, from which the verb *horizesthai* ("define") derives, is "term," in the logical sense, in which a syllogism has three terms. But often a *horos* is a definition or a defining mark (a boundary marker is a *horos*) that gives definition to what would otherwise lack it. Hence the doctor's *horos* is the thing "by reference to which he discerns what is healthy for a body from what is not" (*EE* 8.3.1249^{a}21–22), "that is why too they make breathing the defining mark of being alive" (*DA* 1.2.404^{a}9–10).

Deliberate choice (*prohairesis*): We wish for the end or target, we "deliberate about and deliberately choose what furthers it" (*NE* 3.5.1113^{b}3–4). Deliberate choice (*prohairesis*) is thus a matter of choosing (*haireisthai*) one thing before or in preference to (*pro*) another (3.2.1112^{a}16–17), and so of deliberating about what things should be done earlier than or in preference to others in order to further the desired end: "someone with understanding chooses the better of two things in all cases" (*EE* 7.2.1237^{b}37–38).

Democritus (of Abdera): See DK 67–68 = TEGP pp. 516–685.

Differentia (*diaphora*): *See* Genus.

Element (*stoicheion*): A *stoicheion* was originally one of a row (*stoichos*) of things and later a letter of the alphabet or an element of any complex whole (Plato, *Theaetetus* 201e). Aristotle uses it in these ways, and to refer to the five primary elemental bodies (earth, water, air, fire, and ether), from which all others are composed. See *Cael.* 3.3.302^{a}15–19.

Empedocles (of Acragas): DK 31 = TEGP pp. 326–433.

Essence (*to ti ên einai*): Literally: "the what-it-was-to-be." A phrase of Aristotle's coinage, of which "essence," from the Latin verb *esse* ("to be") is the standard translation. The imperfect tense *ên* ("was") may—as in the Latin phrase *quod erat demonstrandum* ("which was to be proved")—stem from an original context (such as a Socratic conversation) in which someone is asked to say or define what something is, and concludes by giving his answer in the imperfect tense to signal that he is giving the answer that was asked for. Apart from that it seems to have no special significance, so we could equally well translate *to ti ên einai* as "the what-it-*is*-to-be."

Estimable (*timios*): The core sense of *timios* is captured in the remark that ordinary people "commonly say of those they find especially estimable and especially love that they 'come first'" (*Cat.* 12.14^{b}5–7). Something is thus objectively *timios* when—like starting-points and causes—it "comes first by nature" (14^{b}3–5). To say that something is estimable is thus to ascribe a distinct sort of goodness or value to it: "By 'estimable' I mean things of the following sort: the divine, the better (for example, soul, understanding), the more ancient, the starting-point, and things of this sort" (*MM* 1.2.1183^{b}21–23). Thus happiness is "something estimable and complete . . . because it is a starting-point . . . and the starting-point and the cause of goods is something that we suppose is estimable and divine" (*NE* 1.12.1102^{a}1–4).

Ether: See *De Caelo* 1.3.269^{b}18–270^{b}31.

Eudoxus of Cnidus: An important mathematician, astronomer, and philosopher (c. 390–c. 340 BC) who developed the general theory of proportion for incommensurable as well as commensurable magnitudes. He was acquainted with Plato and is thought by some to have been his colleague in the Academy. Parts of his astronomical theory are discussed in *Met.* 12.8.1073^{b}17–38.

Exactness (*akribeia*): In his focal discussion of exactness, Aristotle makes clear that a science's degree of it is measured along three different dimensions: "One science is more exact than another, and prior to it, if it is both of the that and the why, and not of the that separately from the why; or if it is not said of an underlying subject and the other is said of an underlying subject (as, for example, arithmetic is more exact than harmonics); or if it proceeds from fewer things and the other from some additional posit (for example, arithmetic is more exact than geometry). By 'from an additional posit' I mean, for example, that a unit is substance without position and a point is substance with position—the latter proceeds from an additional posit" (*APo.* 1.27.87^{a}31–37). The upshot is thus twofold. First, the most exact version or formulation of a science is the most explanatory one—the one consisting of demonstrations from starting-points. Second, of two sciences, formulated in the most exact way, one is more exact than the other if it demonstrates facts that the other deals with but does not demonstrate. Because a natural science has to posit sublunary matter in addition to such starting-points, the strictly theoretical sciences (theology, astronomy, and mathematics) are more exact than any natural science. Hence it is among these that the most exact one will be found. And it will be the one that explains what the others treat as a fact or undemonstrated posit.

Experience (*empeiria*): *Empeiria* is not quite what we mean by experience: for us experience gives rise to memory; for Aristotle memory gives rise to *empeiria*. Thus suppose A perceives that when X_1 is sick with a fever giving him honey-water is followed by a reduction in fever (*Met.* 6.2.1027^{a}23–24), and he retains this connection in his memory. Then he perceives that giving honey-water to X_2, X_3, . . . X_n is also followed by a reduction in their fever. A also retains these connections in his memory. When as a result of retaining them A associates drinking honey-water with fever reduction, he has "one experience," since "from memory—when it comes about often of the same thing—experience [comes about]; for memories that are many in number form one experience" (*APo.* 2.19.100^{a}4–6).

For the most part (*hôs epi to polu*): Aristotle associates what holds always with what holds by unconditional necessity: "*necessary* and *always* go together (for what it is necessary for there to be cannot not be)" (*GC* 2.11.337^{b}35–36). He associates what holds *hôs epi to polu* with what rarely fails to happen (*Top.* 2.6.112^{b}10–11) and attributes its existence to matter: "Nature tends to measure comings to be and endings by the regular movements of these bodies [the sun and moon], but cannot bring this about rigorously because of the indefiniteness of matter, and because many starting-points exist which impede coming to be and passing away from being according to nature, and often cause things to come about contrary to nature" (*GA* 4.10.778^{a}4–9). Since the "indefiniteness of matter" seems to be a standing condition, while the "many starting-points . . . which impede" are not, we should presumably divide things up as follows. The indefiniteness of matter explains why laws or theorems of natural science hold *hôs epi to polu*, and so have contraries that are rarely true, while impediments explain why what otherwise would occur rarely may occur quite often. All human beings are bipeds, and this would still hold *hôs epi to polu* even if some freak accident or genetic disorder resulted in all or most human beings having only one leg. For even under normal conditions a human offspring may be born with only one leg, simply due to facts about his father's seed (form) and his mother's menses (matter). See also *Met.* 6.2.

Force (*bia*): "By force and contrary to nature are the same" (*Cael.* 3.2.300^{a}23); "what is forced [is] contrary to natural impulse" (*Met.* 12.7.1072^{b}12; also 5.5.1015^{b}15).

Form (*eidos*): According to Aristotle we find in nature an apparently continuous scale of beings, in which, for example, animate beings—beings with souls—differ only very slightly from inanimate ones in their level of formation (*HA* 8.1.588^{b}4–12). The sublunary elements (earth, water, air, and fire) aside, the simplest beings on this scale are homoeomerous or uniform stuffs, such as wood, olive oil, flesh, and bone, whose parts have the same account as the whole (*GC* 1.1.314^{a}20). These are constituted out of the elements in some ratio, when the active capacities (hot, cold) in the elements master the corresponding passive ones (dry, wet) (*Mete.* 6.1.378^{b}26–379^{a}1). The fundamental form of such mastery is concoction (*pepsis*), which is responsible for producing a uniform stuff, and for preserving its nature thereafter: "Concoction, then, is a completion due to the natural and proper heat that comes from the underlying affectable things, these being the matter proper to the given thing. For when it has been concocted it is completed and has come to be. And the starting-point of the completion comes about due to the proper heat, even if certain external aids helped to accomplish it—for example, nourishment is helped to concoct even due to baths and due to other things of this sort. And the end in some cases is the nature—but nature, we say, as form and substance. . . . Concoction, in fact, is what everything is affected by when its matter—that is, its liquid—is mastered. For this is what is determined by the heat in its nature" (*Mete.* 4.2.379^{b}18–35). Natural heat is thus *formative* heat—the thing in nature partly responsible for the coming to be and preservation of things, like human beings, that are complex compounds of matter and form.

Uniform stuffs, as minimally formed, have a low level of such heat. As form is added, so that stuffs come to constitute the structural parts of animals (such as hands and eyes), and these to constitute whole animals of different degrees of complexity, natural heat increases: "the more complete ones are hotter in nature and wetter and not earthy" (*GA* 2.1.732b31–32). Such animals more completely pass on their form to offspring (733a33–b2). Since human beings are the most complete or most perfect of the sublunary animals (737b26–27), they are also hottest and most estimable of them (*Juv.* 19.477a13–23). Although male and female human beings both have formative heat, its level is not the same in each. This is revealed by the different roles played by their respective spermatic products in reproduction—semen (*gonê*) or seed (*sperma*) in the case of males, menses (*katamênia*) in that of females: "the male provides both the form and the starting-point of movement, while the female provides the body, that is, the matter" (*GA* 1.20.729a9–11).

What enables the transmission of such movements is that they are present in the male's blood—where, encoded in formative heat, they are responsible for the preservation of his form. When the male's formal movements are transmitted by concoction to menses, they first initiate the formation of the fetal heart. Once the heart is formed, the fetus then grows automatically, drawing its nourishment from its mother through the umbilicus, and in the process transmitting formative movements via the blood to the other developing parts (*GA* 2.1.735a12–26). While semen, as a concocted blood product, is a very purified type of nourishment, its natural heat, in which its formative movements are encoded, is of a quite special sort: "Now, the capacity of all soul seems to be associated with a body distinct from and more divine than the so-called elements. And as souls differ from each other in esteem and lack of esteem so too this sort of nature differs. For within the seed of everything there is present that which makes the seeds be fertile, the so-called hot. This is not fire or that sort of capacity, but the pneuma enclosed within the seed and within the foamy part—that is, the nature in the pneuma, which is an analog of the element belonging to the stars" (*GA* 2.3.736b29–737a1). Characterized as "connate" (*sumphuton*), because it is not drawn in from outside but produced and maintained inside the body (*PA* 2.2.648a36–649b8), it is the sort of pneuma that plays a fundamental role in nourishment and reproduction (*GA* 2.6.741b37–742a16). The reproductive system, indeed, is in many ways simply a means of transmitting the form-preserving digestive system (of which blood and the heart are parts) into new matter, thereby initiating the formation of a new self-maintaining creature. That is why both functions are assigned to the *threptikon* or nutritive part of the soul (*DA* 2.4.416a19–20).

Although many natural beings (for example, ones we think of as inanimate) do not preserve their form by means of nourishment, or transmit it by means of sexual reproduction, pneuma has a fundamental role to play in their existence too: "it is reasonable, indeed, for nature to make most things using pneuma as instrument. For just as some things have many uses where the crafts are concerned—as in blacksmithing are the hammer and the anvil—so does pneuma in those composed by nature" (*GA* 5.8.789ᵇ8–12).Yet despite its manifest importance, no focused discussion of pneuma occurs in Aristotle's extant works. This makes it difficult to determine his views with confidence. But by piecing together what he does say, a reasonably clear picture emerges.

From its role in embryology alone, for example, we can see that pneuma transmits movement by being itself in movement. The role accorded to it in animal movement confirms this fact: "[Pneuma] is evidently well disposed by nature to impart movement and supply strength. The functions of the movement, though, are pushing and pulling, so that its instrument must be capable of being expanded and being contracted. And this is just the nature of pneuma. For it is being both contracted [and expanded] without force, and is able to pull and push by force due to the same cause" (*MA* 10.703ᵃ18–23). Moreover, because the movements it imparts are formative, they must be complex and various—able to code for all an animal's parts. Since movements are "either in a circle, in a straight line, or in a mixture of the two" (*Ph.* 8.8.261ᵇ28–29), all the complex movements pneuma can produce must be some such combination. What makes this possible is that by actively expanding and contracting, and so pushing and pulling, it can cause not just rectilinear but also circular movements: "Spinning in a circle is a compound of pushing and pulling, since what causes something to spin must be pushing one part of it and pulling another, for it draws one part away from itself and another part toward itself" (*Ph.* 7.2.244ᵃ2–4). Hence all movements—rectilinear, circular, or a combination of the two—can be caused by pneuma in combination with earth, water, and the other elements (*DA* 3.10.433ᵇ25–26).

Initially pneuma is assigned a role in the transmission of form to noncontroversially animate beings. But its role also gets expanded to explain other phenomena: "For it is not insofar as something is water or insofar as it is air that it is visible, but because there is a certain nature in it that is the same in both of them and in the [eternal] body above" (*DA* 2.7.418ᵇ7–9). Then, because pneuma is involved in soul transmission, soul is to some extent itself attributed to anything in which pneuma is present: "Animals and plants come to be on earth and in liquid because in earth there is water present and in water pneuma, and in all pneuma there is soul-involving heat, so that in a certain way all things are full of soul" (*GA* 3.11.762ᵃ18–21). When "the capacity of all soul" is associated with the nature in the pneuma that is an analog of the element belonging to the stars, then, the point of the analogy is that the nature in question is both transparent and—when combined with other elements, whose movements are rectilinear—an appropriate transmitter of soul, form, and life. For the element that belongs to the stars, which is *ether* (*aithêr*) or primary body (*sôma prôton*), is a body "beyond the ones composed here, more divine and prior to all these" (*Cael.* 1.2.269a30–32), and is both transparent and in eternal circular movement (1.3.270a12–b25). Hence pneuma is a "body more divine than the so-called elements," because it is an analog of ether, which is in fact more divine than they.

Focusing now on pneuma, let us see how best to understand it. One thing we know is that, by being expanded and contracted, "it is able to pull and push by force" (*MA* 10.703a21–22), but another is that it is "hot air" (*GA* 2.2.736a1)—air that includes formative heat. Putting the two together we have air expanding and contracting due to heat. Pneuma is not a new element, then, but rather a construction from old ones introduced to explain the existence in the sublunary world of the circular movements crucial for the transmission and preservation of forms, and so for the coming to be and passing away of the matter-form compounds whose forms they are. But it is equally central to the explanation of animal movement, perception, and thought: "Just as automata are set moving when a small movement occurs: when the strings are released and the pegs strike against one another . . . so too animals are set moving. For they have instrumental parts that are of the same sort as these, with the nature of sinews and of bones . . . when these are relaxed or loosened they are set moving. . . . In an animal, however, [unlike in an automaton] the same thing can become both smaller and larger and change shapes, when the parts expand [and contract] because of heat, pneuma, and cold, and undergo alteration. These alterations, however, are caused by appearances, perceptions, and thoughts. For perceptions immediately have their being as alterations of a certain sort, and an appearance and a thought have the capacity of their objects. For in a way the form of something hot or cold or pleasant or frightening, when we think of it, is in being just like the thing itself. That is why we shudder and are frightened because of merely thinking of them. All these are affections and alterations; and of things in the body that are altered, some become larger and some smaller. And it is not hard to see that a small change occurring in a starting-point produces large and numerous changes at a distance from it—for example, by shifting the rudder a hair's breadth you get a large shift at the prow. Further, when under the influence of heat or cold or some other similar affection, an alteration is produced in the region of the heart, even in an imperceptibly small part of it, it makes a large difference to the body—causing instances of blushing, for example, or of turning white, as well as instances of shuddering, trembling, and their opposites" (*MA* 7.701^{b}1–32). Form of every variety, one might almost say, then, just is a sort of movement. That is why Aristotle is able to identify it with actuality or activity, which is itself a special sort of movement.

Function (*ergon*): A function is (1) an activity that is the use or actualization of a state, capacity, or disposition; (2) a work or product that is the further result of such an activity (*NE* 1.1.1094^{a}5–6). It is intimately related to its possessor's end or final cause: "The function is the end, and the activity is the function" (*Met.* 9.8.1050^{a}21–22). Moreover, a thing's good or doing well "seems to lie in its function" (*NE* 1.7.1097^{b}26–27). But this holds only when the thing itself is not already something bad (*Met.* 8.9.1051^{a}15–16). Finally, a thing's function is intimately related to its nature, form, and essence. For a thing's nature is "its for-the-sake-of-which" (*Ph.* 2.2.194^{a}27–28), its form is more its nature than its matter (1.193^{b}6–7), and its essence and form are the same (*Met.* 7.7.1032^{b}1–2). Hence "all things are defined by their function" (*Mete.* 4.12.390^{a}10), with the result that if something cannot function, it has no more than a name in common with its functional self (*Met.* 7.10.1035^{b}14–25, *Pol.* 1.2.1253^{a}20–25, *PA* 1.1.640^{b}33–641^{a}6). Functions are thus attributed to a wide variety of things, whether living or non-living. These include plants (*GA* 1.23.731^{a}24–26) and animals generally (*NE* 10.5.1176^{a}3–5), parts of their bodies and souls (*PA* 2.7.652^{b}6–14, 4.10.686^{a}26–29), instruments or tools of various sorts (*EE* 7.10.1242^{a}15–19), crafts, sciences (2.1.1219^{a}17), philosophies (*Met.* 7.11.1037^{a}15) and their practitioners (*NE* 6.7.1141^{b}10), cities (*Pol.* 7.4.1326^{a}13–14), and nature itself (1.10.1258^{a}35). When a thing has many functions, one is singled out as *its* proper function (*Protr.* B63–65). Thus contemplation can be a human being's function, even though he has others as well.

Genus (*genos*): "Genus" (plural: "genera"), "differentia" (plural: differentiae"), and "species" are the traditional Latinate translations of *genos*, *eidos*, and *diaphora*, and they are best thought of as near transliterations, with no independent semantic content beyond that conveyed by Aristotle's uses of the terms, which are many and various. In his own philosophical lexicon, for example, we find the following entry on *genos*: "Something is said to be a *genos* if: [1] The coming to be of things with the same form (*eidos*) is continuous—for example, 'as long as the *genos* of human beings lasts' means 'as long as the coming to be of human beings is continuous.' [2] It is the first mover that brought things into existence. For it is in this way that some are said to be Hellenes by *genos* and others Ionians, because the former come from Hellen and the latter from Ion as their first begetter. And more so when from the male begetter than when from the matter, although the *genos* is also sometimes named from the female—for example, the descendants of Pyrrha. [3] Further, as the plane is said to be the *genos* of plane figures and solid of solids. For each of the figures is in the one case a plane of such-and-such a sort and in the other a solid of such-and-such a sort, this being the underlying subject for the differentiae. [4] Further, as the first constituent in accounts is said to be—the one said in the what-it-is. For this is the *genos*, whose differentiae the qualities are said to be" (*Met.* 5.28.1024^{a}29–^{b}5). A *genos*, then, is [1–2] a race or bloodline and [3–4] the kind of thing—the genus—studied by a single science. Similarly, he uses *eidos* to refer to the species of a genus, but also to form (as opposed to matter) and to a separate Platonic Form. By the same token *diaphorai* are sometimes the differentiae that divide a genus into species, and so figure in their essential definitions: "species are composed of the genus and the differentiae" (*Met.* 10.7.1057^{b}7). But sometimes they are simply the different features that distinguish one kind of thing from another, without necessarily suggesting that the kinds are genera or species in the strict sense or that the differences are differentiae.

God (*theos*): Aristotle recognizes the existence of a number of different divine beings or gods, among whom he distinguishes a primary god, usually referred to as *ho theos* ("the god"), discussed in *Met.* 1.2, 12.8–10, and who is defined as the "active understanding of active understanding" (12.9.1074^{b}34–35). When *theos* occurs with the definite article, it is sometimes natural to treat it as referring to *a* god, sometimes to *the* god.

Heaven, the: See *Cael.* 1.9.278^{b}8–21.

Heraclitus of Ephesus: See DK 22 = TEGP pp. 135–200.

Hermias (of Aterneus): See F645, F675.

Hermotimus of Colophon: A mathematician associated with Plato.

Immovable (*akinêton*): Verbals ending in *-ton*—of which *akinêton* is an example—sometimes (1) have the meaning of a perfect passive participle ("unmoved") and sometimes (2) express possibility ("immovable"). Although it is clear that the primary mover discussed in *Ph.* 8.10 is not just unmoved but immovable, it (he) is traditionally—but not in this book—referred to as "the unmoved mover."

Increase and decrease (*auxêsis kai phthisis*): "Movement with respect to quantity, as regards its common feature, has no name, but with regard to each of its two varieties it is called 'increase and decrease'—that to the complete magnitude being increase, that away from it being decrease" (*Ph.* 5.2.226ᵃ29–32). *Auxêsis kai phthisis* often means "growth and withering," especially when applied to living things.

Induction (*epagôgê*): See Scientific knowledge (5).

Intelligible (*noêton*): An intelligible object or content (*noêma*) is a form (*eidos*) (as at 1.1 *Met.* 981ᵃ10), which is usually encoded in an appearance, and can be grasped by the understanding (*nous*) when it contemplates (*theôrein*) that appearance: "To the understanding soul appearances are like perceptual contents. . . . The part that understands, then, understands the forms in the appearances" (*DA* 3.7.431ᵃ14–ᵇ10). It differs from an appearance in being part of an affirmation, evaluable as true or false: "when someone contemplates, he must at the same time contemplate an appearance. . . . However, imagination (*phantasia*) is distinct from affirmation and denial, since truth and falsity involve a combination of intelligible objects" (8.432ᵃ8–12).

Intrinsically (*kath hauta*): See Coincidents.

Leisure (*scholê*): Aristotle's way of thinking about leisure overlaps with ours but differs from it in important ways. We think of leisure time as time off from work in which we can do as we choose. Aristotle agrees that leisure time and work time are distinct (*Pol.* 1.8.1256ᵃ31–35), but thinks that activities that are entirely leisured must be choiceworthy solely because of themselves. Among these he includes such scientific activities as the exercise of theoretical wisdom or mathematical knowledge, which we might think of as work. In these, he thinks, complete happiness consists (*NE* 10.7.1177ᵇ19–26). Entirely unleisured activities, he thinks, are choiceworthy solely because of some additional end, such as producing or providing the necessities of life (10.6.1176ᵇ2–3)—included among these are the canonical productive crafts (*Met.* 9.6.1048ᵇ18–35). Activities which are choiceworthy in part because of themselves, and in part because of an additional end, include activities in accord with practical wisdom and the virtues of character. These too constitute happiness, but of a less than complete or secondary sort (*NE* 10.7.1177ᵇ4–18, 8.1178ᵃ9–22). Most people would include amusing pastimes as leisured activities par excellence

(10.6.1176^{b}6–17), but Aristotle does not agree: "Happiness is not found in amusement, since it would be absurd indeed for the end to be amusement, and our life's labors and sufferings to be for the sake of amusement. For we choose almost everything, except happiness, for the sake of something else, since it is the [unconditional] end. To work hard and toil [just] for the sake of amusement, however, appears a silly and entirely childish thing to do. Rather, 'play to be serious,' as Anacharsis puts it, seems to have it right. For amusement is a form of relaxation, and it is because we cannot toil continuously that we need relaxation. Relaxation, then, is not an end, since it occurs for the sake of activity [in accord with virtue]" (10.6.1176^{b}27–1177^{a}1). Nonetheless, because humans do have to engage in unleisured practical and productive activities, a good political constitution "should permit amusement, but be careful to use it at the correct time, dispensing it as a medicine for the ills of unleisure" (*Pol.* 8.3.1337^{b}35–42; also 8.5.1339^{b}31–42).

Leucippus: See DK 67–68 = TEGP pp. 516–685.

Life (*zôê*): Two Greek words correspond to the English word "life": *zôê* and *bios*. *Zôê* refers to the sorts of life processes and activities studied by biologists, zoologists, psychologists, and so on, such as growth, reproduction, perception, and understanding. *Bios* refers to the sort of life a natural historian or biographer might investigate—the life of the otter, the life of Pericles—and so to a span of time throughout which someone possesses *zôê* at least as a capacity (*NE* 1.13.1102^{b}5–7). Thus, in the conclusion of the famous function argument, we are reminded that a certain *zôê* will not be happiness for a human being unless it occurs "in a complete *bios*" (1.7.1098^{a}18–20). And so it is *zôê* that the primary god enjoys.

Logico-linguistically (*logikôs*): (1) The adjective *logikos* is used to distinguish a set of propositions and problems from those belonging to natural science or ethics: "Propositions such as this are ethical—for example, whether one should obey our parents or the laws, if they disagree. *Logikos*, whether contraries belong to the same science or not. Natural scientific, whether the cosmos is eternal or not. And similarly for the problems" (*Top.* 1.14.105^{b}21–25). Since the question about a science of contraries is a philosophical one (*Met.* 3.2.996^{a}18–21), *logikos* problems overlap with philosophical ones. At the same time, "if an argument depends on false but reputable beliefs, it is *logikos*" (*Top.* 8.12.162^{b}27), suggesting that *logikos* arguments overlap with dialectical ones, since both may rely on reputable beliefs (*endoxa*) or—more or less equivalently—on things said (*legomena*) about the topic. Indeed, the question about a science of contraries is itself identified as one for dialectic (*Met.* 13.4.1078^{b}25–27).

Luck (*tuchê*): What happens by luck in the broad sense is what happens coincidentally or contingently (*APo.* 1.30.87^{b}19–22), so that luck in that sense is pretty much the same as chance. But in a narrower sense, which is contrasted with chance, what happens by luck is what has a coincidental final cause: "Luck is a coincidental cause in things that come about in accord with deliberate choice for the sake of an end" (*Met.* 11.8.1065^{a}30–31). Thus if a tree's being by the back door is the sort of thing that might be an outcome of deliberative thought, it is a candidate final cause of action—an end we aim at (*Ph.* 2.5.197^{a}5–14, 6.197^{b}20– 22). If wish, which is the desire involved in deliberation and deliberate choice, is what causes it to be there, the tree's being by the back door has a genuine final cause. If not, its being there has a coincidental final cause. Unlike chance, then, which applies quite generally to whatever results from coincidental efficient causes, narrow luck applies only to what could come about because of action and deliberate choice. Hence it is the sphere relevant to action: "Luck and the results of luck are found in things that are capable of being lucky, and, in general, of action. That is why indeed luck is concerned with things doable in action" (*Ph.* 2.5.197^{b}1–2). The sphere of narrow luck is also that of the practical and productive sciences (*Rh.* 1.5.1362^{a}2). *See also* Chance.

Matter (*hulê*): "Some matter is [1] perceptible, however, while [2] some is intelligible—perceptible matter being, for example, bronze, wood, and any matter that is movable, and intelligible matter being the sort that is in the perceptible things but not insofar as they are perceptible, such as the objects of mathematics" (*Met.* 7.10.1036^{a}9–12). Perceptible (as opposed to intelligible) matter comes in a variety of different sorts. [1a] Movable matter (*kinêtê hulê*), mentioned at *Met.* 7.10.1036^{a}10, is the sort something needs if it is to be capable of moving from place to place. Hence it is also referred as *hulê topikê* (8.2.1042^{b}6). [1b] Matter for alteration (*alloiôtê*) is the sort that things need if they are to change in quality (9.8.1050^{b}16–8). [1c] Then there is matter needed for movement with respect to magnitude, or increase and decrease (*auxêtê kai phthitê*) (*Ph.* 8.7.260^{a}27). [1d] And finally the matter needed for coming to be and passing away (*gennêtê kai phthartê*), which is most of all and in the full sense matter (*GC* 1.4.320^{a}2). Things that have [1a] but not [1d] include the various heavenly bodies (*Met.* 9.8.1050b22–28, 12.2.1069b24–26). *Hulê noêtê* is mentioned by name only in [2], at 7.11.1037a5, and at 8.6.1045a33–35: "Some matter is intelligible, and some perceptible, and of the account always one part is the matter and the other the actuality [= the form]—for example, the circle is shape + plane (*ho kuklos schêma epipedon*)." But "the matter of the objects of mathematics (*hê tôn mathêmatikôn hulê*)" (*Met.* 11.1.1059b15–16) is fairly certainly a reference to the same sort of thing.

Methodical inquiry (*methodos*): A *methodos* is a *tropos tês zêtêseôs*—a way of inquiry (*APo.* 1.31.46a32–b36). *Hodos* means "way," "route," or "road," as at *NE* 1.4.1095a33. Sometimes the *met-* prefix is omitted, as at *GC* 1.8.324b35–325a2.

Name (*onoma*): An *onoma* is not always what we call a "name," but a word more generally, or—when contrasted with a verb—a noun: "A noun or name is a composite significant voiced sound, without [a reference to] time, the parts of which are not intrinsically significant. . . . A verb is a composite significant voiced sound, involving [a reference to] time, the parts of which are not intrinsically significant" (*Po.* 1.20.1457a10–15). A name, however, often signifies an account or (in some cases) a definition (*Met.* 4.7.1012a22–24, 8.6.1045a26) of the form (7.10.1035a21) or essence (4.1029b20) of the thing named.

Nature (*phusis*): (1) In the primary and full way, a being that is or does something by nature has a nature—an internal starting-point of movement and rest (*Ph.* 1.2.192b20–23, *Cael.* 3.2.301b17–18, *Met.* 5.4.1015a13–15). The world of nature, investigated by natural science, is a world of such beings, all of which have perceptible matter as a constituent (*Met.* 6.1.1025b30–1026a6). This world is roughly speaking the sublunary one. Beyond it lies the world of the heavens studied by astronomy and theology (1026a7–22), where beings either have no matter, or matter of a different sort (*Cael.* 1.2.269b2–6, 3.270b19–25, *Mete.* 1.3.339b25–27). Although, strictly speaking, these beings do not have natures, since "nature is the proper order of perceptible things" (*Cael.* 3.2.301a5–6), Aristotle nonetheless speaks of them as if they do (3.1.298b23, *Met.* 6.1.1026a20, 25 are nice examples). We use the term "nature" in a similar way when we speak of the nature of the numbers or the nature of fictional entities, not meaning to imply at all that these things are parts of the natural world (compare 13.4.1078a10). (2) Sometimes, instead of using *phusis* to refer to the or a *phusis of* X, Aristotle uses the term and its plural *phuseis* to mean something we translate as "a nature" (Greek has no indefinite article) or "natures." The thing or things referred to may or may not have natures in the strict sense; they are pretty much just entities of some sort. (3) He also speaks of *phusis* or *hê phusis* in agentive terms—for example, when he says, as he frequently does, that nature does nothing pointlessly (for example, *Cael.* 1.4.271^{a}33, *DA* 2.5.415^{b}16–17, 3.9.432^{b}21, 12.434^{a}31, *PA* 1.1.641^{b}12–29) or that it does something correctly (*Cael.* 1.3.269^{b}20), or for the best (2.5.288^{a}3). Just as when he speaks of "the nature of the All" (1.2.268^{b}11) or "the nature of the whole" (*Met.* 12.10.1075^{a}11) it is not entirely clear how exactly or how literally these words are to be taken. He also speaks of it as having psychological attitudes, such as wish (*boulêsis*) (*Sens.* 3.441^{a}3, *GA* 4.10.778^{a}4, *Pol.* 1.6.1255^{b}3), but in these cases *bouleuesthai* is usually, and best, translated as "tend."

Many natural things are said to desire (*oregesthai*) the good, in the shape of immortal and eternal existence (*DA* 2.4.415^{a}25–^{b}2). Even to the celestial spheres such a desire is attributed (*Met.* 12.7.1072^{a}21–29). But then these spheres are themselves living things (*Cael.* 2.12.292^{a}18–22). Moving from the heavenly bodies to the sublunary elements we find even them imitating the divine: "The things that cannot pass away are also imitated by things that are involved in change—for example, earth and fire. For these too are always active; for they have their movement both intrinsically and within themselves" (*Met.* 9.8.1050^{b}28–30).

Noble (*kalon*): The adjective *kalos* is often a term of vague or general commendation ("fine," "beautiful," "good"), with different connotations in different contexts: "The contrary of *to kalon* when applied to an animal is *to aischron* ["ugly in appearance"], but when applied to a house it is *to mochthêron* ["wretched"], and so *kalon* is homonymous" (*Top.* 1.15.106^{a}20–22). (Similarly, the adverb *kalôs* often means something like "well," or "correct.") Even in the general sense, however, *kalos* has a distinctive evaluative coloration suggestive of "order (*taxis*), proportion (*summetria*), and definiteness (*hôrismenon*)" (*Met.* 13.3.1078^{a}36–^{b}1), making a term with aesthetic connotation, such as "beauty," seem a good equivalent: to bear the stamp of happiness one must have *kallos* as opposed to being "very ugly (*panaischês*)" (*NE* 1.8.1099^{b}3–4; also *Pol.* 5.9.1309^{b}23–25). Moreover, just as a thing need not have a purpose in order to be beautiful, a *kalon* thing can be contrasted with a purposeful one: a great-souled person is one "whose possessions are more *kalon* and purposeless (*akarpa*) than purposeful and beneficial" (*NE* 4.3.1125^{a}11–12). At the same time, it seems wrong to associate *kalon* with beauty in general, since to be *kalon* a thing has to be on a certain scale: "greatness of soul requires magnitude, just as *to kallos* ('nobility of appearance') requires a large body, whereas small people are elegant and well-proportioned but not *kaloi*" (1123^{b}6–8); "any *kalon* object . . . made up of parts must not only have them properly ordered but also have a magnitude which is not random, since what is *kalon* consists in magnitude and order (*taxis*)" (*Po.* 1.7.1450^{b}34–37; also *Pol.* 7.4.1326^{a}33–34). It is this requirement that makes "nobility" in its more aesthetic sense, or "noble beauty," a closer equivalent than "beauty."

Opposites (*antikeimena*): "One thing is said to be opposed to another in four ways: as relatives, as contraries, as privation and state, or as affirmation and denial" (*Cat.* 10.11^{b}17–19); "The sorts of opposition are contradiction, privation, contrariety, and relatives, and of these the primary sort is contradiction" (*Met.* 10.5.1055^{a}38–^{b}1).

Particular (*kath' hekaston*): (1) *Ta kath' hekasta* are often things that are severally one in number and jointly many (*Met.* 3.4.999^{b}34–1000^{a}1). (2) Sometimes, though, what is *kath' hekaston* is what is less universal than something else. Thus while true particulars are indefinable (*Met.* 7.15.1039^{b}27–29, 1040^{a}27–^{b}4), it is "easier to define *to kath' hekaston* than the universal" (*APo.* 2.13.97^{b}28), and a definition of a universal "divides it into *kath' hekasta*" (*Ph.* 1.1.184^{b}2–3), where these are things that are particular in the sense of being "indivisible in species" (*PA* 1.4.644^{a}30–31).

Philosophy (*philosophia*): Aristotle sometimes applies the term *philosophia* (or sometimes just *sophia*) to any science aiming at truth rather than action (*Met.* 2.1.993^{b}19–21). In this sense of the term, all the broadly theoretical sciences count as branches of philosophy, and *philosophia* is more or less equivalent in meaning to *epistêmê* in its most exact sense. *Philosophia* also has a narrower sense, however, in which it applies exclusively to sciences providing knowledge of starting-points (11.1.1059^{a}18, *NE* 6.7.1141^{a}16–18), and it is among these that theology, as the science of being qua being, belongs (*Met.* 6.1.1026^{a}6–30).

Phocylides: A 6th-cent-BC poet from Miletus.

Place (*topos*): "The limit of what encompasses" (*Cael.* 3.3.310^{b}7–8).

Pneuma: See Form.

Practical (*praktikos*): What makes something *praktikos* for Aristotle is that it appropriately involves *praxis* or action, considered as an end choiceworthy because of itself, and not—as with "practical"—that it is opposed to what is theoretical, speculative, or ideal. That is why, paradoxical as it may sound, *theôrêtikos* activities are more *praktikos* than those that are widely considered to be most so: "It is not necessary, as some suppose, for a *praktikos* life to be lived in relation to other people, nor are those thoughts alone *praktikos* that arise for the sake of the consequences of doing an action, rather, much more so are the acts of contemplation and thought that are their own ends and are engaged in for their own sake. For doing well in action is the end, and so action of a sort is the end too" (*Pol.* 7.3.1325ᵇ17–21).

Practical wisdom (*phronêsis*): The virtue of the deliberative part of the rational part of the soul (*NE* 6.1.1139ᵃ15–17) that involves all of the virtues of character (*NE* 6.13.1144ᵇ14–17).

Priority: "What is said to be prior is [1] that without which the other things will not exist, whereas it can exist without them, and there is also [2] priority in time and [3] with respect to substance" (*Ph.* 8.7.260ᵇ17–19). In his focal discussion of priority and posteriority in *Met.* 5.11, however, Aristotle makes [1] equivalent to [3]: "Others, however, are said to be prior in nature and substance, when it is possible for them to be without other things, but not the others without them" (1019ᵃ2–4). And there [2] is explained as follows: "Others things are prior in time, some by being further from now, as in the case of things that come to be (for the Trojan Wars are prior to the Persian because they are further from now), some by being closer to now, as in the case of things that are to come (for the Nemean Games are prior to the Pythian because they are closer to now, treating now as starting-point and first)" (1018ᵇ14–19). In *Ph.* 8.7, however, [1] and [3] are distinguished, with [3] (explained at 261ᵃ13–26) and [2] (explained at 260ᵇ29–261ᵃ12) understood differently. Finally, A is prior in account to B if the account of A figures in the account of B, but not vice versa (*Met.* 7.1.1028ᵃ34–36).

Puzzle (*aporia*): "A dialectical problem is a speculation, directed either to choice and avoidance or to truth and knowledge (either by itself or when working together with something else of this sort), about which [1] people believe nothing either way, or [2] ordinary people believe in a contrary way to the wise, or [3] the wise to ordinary people, or [4] each of them to themselves. . . . Problems also exist [5] where there are contrary deductions (for there is a puzzle as to whether it is so or not so, because there are persuasive arguments concerning both sides), as well as [6] those we have no arguments about, because they are so large, thinking it difficult to give the why of them (for example, whether the cosmos is eternal or not). For one could also inquire into things of that sort" (*Top.* 1.11.104^{b}1–17). Thus a problem is [5] a *puzzle* just in case there are strong arguments on one side of it and strong arguments on the other: "A certain sophistical argument constitutes a puzzle. For because they wish to refute in a way that is disreputable (*paradoxos*) in order to be clever when they engage in ordinary discussions, the resulting deduction turns into a puzzle. For thought is tied up when it does not wish to stand still, because what has been concluded is not pleasing, but cannot move forward, because of its inability to refute the argument" (*NE* 7.2.1146^{a}21–27).

Pythagoreans: "Among these thinkers and before them, the so-called Pythagoreans were the first to latch on to mathematics. They both advanced these inquiries and, having been brought up in mathematics, thought that its starting-points were the starting-points of all beings. Since [1] among these starting-points the numbers are by nature primary, and since [2] they seemed to get a theoretical grasp on many similarities to beings in the numbers, and to things that come to be, more so than in fire, earth, or water (for example, that such-and-such an affection of numbers is justice, that such-and-such an affection is soul and understanding, whereas another one is appropriate time, and—one might also say—each of the rest likewise), and, further, [3] seeing in harmonies affections and ratios that are found in numbers—since, then, [2] the other things seemed to have been made like numbers in the whole of their nature, and [1] numbers were primary in the whole of nature, they took the elements of numbers to be the elements of all beings, and [3] the whole heaven to be harmony and number" (*Met.* 1.5.985^{b}23–986^{a}3).

Science, scientific knowledge (*epistêmê*): (1) Aristotle usually divides sciences (*epistêmai*) into three kinds: theoretical (contemplative), practical (action-involving), and productive (crafts) (*Top.* 6.6.145^{a}15–16, *Met.* 11.7.1064^{a}16–19). But sometimes a more fine-grained classification is employed, in which theoretical sciences are divided into natural sciences (such as physics and biology) and strictly theoretical sciences (such as astronomy and theology) on the basis of the kinds of beings with which they deal (*Ph.* 2.7.198^{a}21–^{b}4, *Met.* 6.1.1025^{b}18–1026^{a}32). The term *epistêmê* is sometimes reserved for the unconditional scientific knowledge provided exclusively by the strictly theoretical sciences (*NE* 6.3.1139^{b}31–34), but typically it is used in the looser sense, which encompasses the practical and productive sciences as well. To understand what a science—whether theoretical, productive, or practical—is like we must begin a few steps back.

(2) A *statement* (*logos apophantikos*) is the true (or false) predication of a single predicate term A of a single subject term B, either as an affirmation (*kataphasis*) (A belongs to B) or a denial (*apophasis*) (A does not belong to B) (*Int.* 5, 8). What makes a term a single subject term, however, is not that it is grammatically singular or serves as a grammatical subject but that it designates a substantial particular—a canonical example of which is a perceptible matter-form compound, such as Socrates. Similarly, what makes a term a predicate is that it designates a universal (man, pale)—something that can have many particular instances. When the role of predicate is restricted to universals, therefore, while that of subject is left open to both particulars and universals, it is more on ontological or metaphysical grounds than on what we would consider strictly logical ones. Subjects and predicates are thus ontological items, types of beings, rather than linguistic or conceptual ones, and logical principles, such as the principle of non-contradiction, are very general ontological principles, truths about all beings as such, or qua beings. Particular affirmations (Socrates is a man) and general affirmations (Men are mortal) have the same subject-predicate form, but when the subject is a universal, the affirmation may itself be either universal (All men are mortal) or particular (Some men are mortal)—that is to say, the predicate may be affirmed (denied) of the subject either universally (*katholou*) or in part (*kata meros*) or, if the quantifier is omitted (Men are mortal), indefinitely (*adioristôs*). General affirmations, as a result, which are the only ones of interest to science (*Met.* 7.15.1039^{b}27–31), are of four types: A belongs to all B (**a**AB), A belongs to no B (**e**AB), A belongs to some B (**i**AB), and A does not belong to all B (**o**AB).

(3) A *science* is a state of the soul that enables its possessor to give demonstrative explanations—where a demonstration (*apodeixis*) is a special sort of deduction (*sullogismos*) from scientific starting-points and a deduction is "an argument in which, certain things having been supposed, something different from those supposed things necessarily results because of their being so" (*APr.* 1.2.24^{b}18–20). The things supposed are the argument's premises; the necessitated result is its conclusion; all three are affirmations of one of the four types we looked at. In Aristotle's view, such deductions are *syllogisms* (*sullogismos*, again) consisting of a major premise, a minor premise, and a conclusion, where the premises have exactly one "middle" term in common, and the conclusion contains only the other two "extreme" terms. The conclusion's predicate term is the *major term*, contributed by the major premise; its subject is the *minor term*, contributed by the minor

premise. The middle term must be either subject of both premises, predicate of both, or subject of one and predicate of the other. The resulting possible combinations of terms yield the so-called figures of the syllogism:

	First figure		Second figure		Third figure	
	Predicate	Subject	Predicate	Subject	Predicate	Subject
Premise	A	B	A	B	A	C
Premise	B	C	A	C	B	C
Conclusion	A	C	B	C	A	B

Systematic investigation of the possible combinations of premises in each of these figures results in the identification of the *moods* or modes that constitute valid deductions. In the first figure, these are as follows:

Form	Mnemonic	Proof
aAB, **a**BC | **a**AC	B**a**rb**a**r**a**	Perfect
eAB, **a**BC | **e**AC	C**e**l**a**r**e**nt	Perfect
aAB, **i**BC | **i**AC	D**a**r**ii**	Perfect
eAB, **i**BC | **o**AC	F**e**r**io**	Perfect

A mood is perfect when there is a proof of its validity that is *direct*, in that it does not rely on the validity of any other mood. Only first figure syllogisms have perfect moods.

(4) Besides their logical interest as admitting of direct proof, perfect syllogisms in Barbara are also of particular importance to science. First, because "of the [syllogistic] figures, the first is most scientific. For the mathematical sciences carry out their demonstrations through this figure—for example, arithmetic, geometry, optics—and so do pretty much all those that investigate the why. For whether it is in general or for the most part and in most cases, a deduction of the why is carried out through this figure. That is why it is the most scientific; for getting a theoretical grasp on the why is most in control of knowledge" (*APo.* 1.14.79^{a}17–24). Second, "only through this figure is it possible to hunt down scientific knowledge of the what-it-is" (79^{a}24–25): essences hold universally, only perfect syllogisms in Barbara have universal conclusions, and definitions of essences, which are scientific starting-points, must hold universally.

(5) Specifically scientific starting-points are of just three types (*APo.* 1.10.76^{a}37–^{b}22). Those special to a science are definitions (*Rh.* 2.23.1398^{a}15–27) of the real (as opposed to nominal) essences of the beings with which

the science deals (2.3.90b24, 2.10.93b29–94a19). Because these are definitions by genus and differentia (2.13.96a20–97b39), a single science must deal with a single genus (*APo.* 1.7.75b10–11, 1.23.84b17–18, 28.87a38–39). Other starting-points (so-called axioms) are common to all or many sciences (*APo.* 1.2.72a14–24, 1.32.88a36–b3). A third sort of starting-point posits the existence of the genus with which the science deals, but this may often be left implicit if the existence of the genus is clear (1.10.76b17–18). The source of these starting-points, in turn, is perception and experience, which lead by induction to a grasp by understanding of them: "From perception, then, memory, as we say, comes about, and from memory—when it comes about often of the same thing—experience; for memories that are many in number form one experience. And from experience, or from the entire universal having come to rest in the soul, the one beyond the many (this being whatever is present as one and the same in all of them), comes a starting-point of craft knowledge and scientific knowledge—of craft knowledge if it concerns production, of scientific knowledge if it concerns being" (*APo.* 2.19.100a3–9).

(6) To constitute a *demonstration* (*apodeixis*) a deduction must be a valid syllogism in the mood Barbara, whose premises meet a number of conditions. First, they must be immediate or indemonstrable, and so must be reached through induction. Second, our confidence in them must be unsurpassed: "Anyone who, on the other hand, is going to have scientific knowledge though demonstration must not only know the starting-points more and be more persuaded of them than of what is being proved, but also nothing else must be more persuasive or more known to him among the opposites of the starting-points from which there will be a deduction of the contrary error, if indeed someone who has unconditional scientific knowledge must be incapable of being persuaded out of it" (*APo.* 1.2.72a37–b4). Finally, they must be necessary (and so, of course, true) in a special sense: the predicates in them must belong to the subjects in every case, intrinsically, and universally (*APo.* 1.4.73a24–27):

(6a) *In every case:* A predicate A belongs to every subject B if and only if there is no B to which it fails to belong and no time at which it fails to belong to a B: "for example, if animal belongs to every man, then if it is true to say that this thing is a man, it is also true to say that it is an animal, and if the former is the case now, the latter is also the case now" (73a29–31).

(6b) *Intrinsically:* A predicate A belongs intrinsically to a subject B just in case it is related to B in one of four ways: (i) A is in the account or definition of what B is, or of B's substance, or essence (73a34–37); (ii) B is a complex subject φB_1, where φ is an intrinsic coincident of B_1—for example, odd number or male or female animal (*Met.* 13.3.1078a5–11)—and A is in the definition of φB_1's essence; (iii) A just is B's essence; (iv) A is not a part of B's essence or identical to it but stems causally from it, so that being B is an intrinsic cause of being A ($73^a34–^b24$).

(6c) *Universally:* A predicate A belongs to a subject B universally just in case "it belongs to it in every case and intrinsically, that is, insofar as it is itself" ($73^b26–27$).

(7) Because intrinsic predicates stem in various ways from essences, the subjects to which they belong must have essences. In other words, they must be *intrinsic beings*, since—stemming as they do from essences—intrinsic predicates identify them or make them clear: "The things said to be intrinsically are the very ones signified by the figures of predication" (*Met.* 5.7.$1017^a22–23$). These figures of predication are the so-called *categories*: "Anything that is predicated (*katêgoroumenon*) of something must either be . . . a definition . . . if it signifies the essence . . . or, if it does not, a special affection (*idion*) . . . or one of the things in the definition, or not; and if it is one of the things in the definition, it must signify the genus or the differentia since the definition is composed of genus and differentia. If, however, it is not one of the things in the definition, it is clear that it must be a coincident; for a coincident was said to be that which belongs to a thing but that is neither a definition nor a genus nor a special affection. Next we must distinguish the kinds (*genos*) of predication in which one will find the four mentioned above. These are ten in number: what it is, quantity, quality, relation, when, where, position, having, doing, and being affected. For the coincidents, the genus, the special affections, and the definition will always be in one of these kinds of predication [or *categories*]" (*Top.* 1.8–9.$103^b7–25$). For each of the intrinsic beings in these ten *categories* we can state what it is (*Met.* 7.4.$1030^a17–24$), even if strictly speaking only substances have definitions and essences (5.$1031^a7–24$). Specifying these beings is one of the tasks of *Categories*, where Aristotle explains how beings in categories other than that of substance are ontologically dependent on those in the category of substance. The list of categories itself, however, has a somewhat provisional status, as Aristotle's remark about the category of *having* indicates: "Some further ways of having might perhaps come to light, but we have made a pretty complete enumeration of those commonly spoken of" (*Cat.* 15.$15^b30–32$).

(8) What all four types of intrinsic beings have in common, what makes them worth the attention of someone inquiring into starting-points and causes, is that they are the ontological correlates or truth-makers for scientific theorems—the beings responsible for the necessary truth of those theorems. Moreover, they would seem to be the only sorts of being that can play this role, since they constitute an exhaustive catalog of the necessary

relations that can hold between a subject (A) and something (B) predicated of it: B is part of the essence of A; A is part of the essence of B; B is the essence of A; the essence of A (being A) is an intrinsic cause of (being) B.

Self-sufficient (*autarkês*): (1) Something is *autarkês* if it has no needs, or none that it cannot satisfy itself (*Cael.* 1.9.279ᵃ21, *Met.* 14.4.1091ᵇ15–20, *NE* 3.3.1112ᵇ1, 4.3.1125ᵃ12, 8.10.1160ᵇ4, 9.9.1169ᵇ5). (2) Also, if it satisfies all of a relevant set of needs of something else. Thus happiness is something *autarkês* because it, "on its own, makes a life choiceworthy and lacking in nothing, and this, we think, is what happiness is like" (*NE* 1.7.1097ᵇ14–15, 10.6.1176ᵇ5).

Separable (*chôriston*): Verbals ending in *-ton*—of which *chôriston* is an example—sometimes have the meaning of a perfect passive participle ("separated") and sometimes express possibility ("separable"). When *chôriston* is applied to substances "separable" often seems to better capture its sense, especially that of its negative (see *Met.* 7.1.1028ᵃ23–24). For things, such as the form and matter of a matter-form compound, are not just not separated, in that they are always found together (11.1036ᵇ3–4)—they cannot be separated. Moreover, things that are separable, such as the understanding and the other parts of the soul, do not become actually separated until, for example, death (*DA* 3.5.430ᵃ17–23). Just what the separability of substance amounts to is another question.

(1) Walking and being healthy are characterized as "incapable of being separated," on the grounds that there is some particular substantial underlying subject of which they are predicated (*Met.* 7.1.1028ᵃ20–31). Often, separability is associated with being such a subject: "The underlying subject is prior, which is why the substance is prior" (5.11.1019ᵃ5–6); "If we do not posit substances to be separated, and in the way in which particular things are said to be separated, we will do away with the sort of substance we wish to maintain" (13.10.1086ᵇ16–19). Similarly, not being separable is associated with being predicated of such a subject. Being predicated of a substance—being an affection—seems, then, to be a sufficient condition of not being separable. Moreover, not being separable seems itself to be a sufficient condition of being ontologically dependent: (1a) "All the other things are either said of the primary substances as subjects or in them as subjects. So if the primary substances were not, it would be impossible for any of the other things to be" (*Cat.* 5.2ᵇ3–6).

(2) Couched in terms of priority, what is attributed to primary substances in (1a) is *substantial* priority, or priority in nature, which Aristotle defines in two ways: (2a) "[Things] are said to be prior in nature and substance,

when it is possible for them to be (*einai*) without other things, but not the others without them" (*Met.* 5.11.1019ᵃ3–4); (2b) "Those things are prior in substance [to others] which, when separated, surpass [them] in being (*tô[i] einai huperballei*)" (13.2.1077ᵇ2–3). Moreover, in a text apparently expressing an idea similar to (2b), the form of a matter-form compound is said to be "prior to the matter and more (*mallon*) of a being" (7.3.1029ᵃ5–6). Since existence, like identity, does not come in degrees, the use of the verb *huperballein* and the adverb *mallon* makes it difficult to understand *einai* ("being," "to be") as having an exclusively existential sense. At the same time, *einai* does seem to have some existential import, as it surely does in (2c): "if everyone were well, health would be (*estai* = exist) but not sickness, and if everything were white, whiteness would be (*estai*) but not blackness" (*Cat.* 11.14ᵃ7–10). It seems reasonable, therefore, to think that to be is to be a being of some sort, and that to be a being entails existing. To be a being, however, is to be either a coincidental being (the pale human) or an intrinsic being, something with an essence (the human). To be an intrinsic being, in turn, is to be either an intrinsic coincident, a matter-form compound, or simply a substantial form (*Met.* 6.1.1025ᵇ28–1026ᵃ15). As identical to its tightly unified essence (7.12.1037ᵇ10–27), a substantial form is an intrinsic being of the highest order—a primary substance (11.1037ᵃ33–ᵇ4). A matter-form compound, by contrast, since it is never identical to its essence (1037ᵇ4–7), is an intrinsic being of a lower order (12.7.1072ᵃ30–32), since it is always a complex thing—a this in this (7.5.1030ᵇ18)—whose essence is complex in a structurally parallel way (10.1035ᵇ27–30). Similarly, an intrinsically coincidental being, while it follows from an essence, is still a complex of two intrinsic beings, one a substance with an essence, the other an affection. For it to be more of a being than Y, or to exceed Y in being, we might reasonably conclude is for it to be closer to a substantial form on this scale. It is, as we might put it, for it to be more intrinsic a being than Y. Degrees of being are degrees of intrinsicality, then, not degrees of existence.

(3) Affections depend for their existence on substance, but not on that of some particular substance, any substance that has them will do: white exists if something is white, but the something does not have to be Bucephalus. Hence the parallel claim about substances should not be that a substance can exist without any affections, suggesting that substances are bare particulars, but that substances in general can exist whether or not affections do. On an *ante rem* (or Platonist) theory, affections can exist uninstantiated by particulars. On an *in re* theory, like Aristotle's, they cannot. That is the message of (2c). Hence the ontological dependence of affections—and the cognate ontological independence of substances—must be formulated

differently by these theories. It seems, then, that if *in re* affections were ontologically independent of substances, it could only be because *they were instantiated by something else*, since they cannot exist uninstantiated by particulars of some sort. This is the way we see Aristotle thinking in the following text: "Heat and straightness [and whiteness] can be present in every part of a thing, but it is impossible for all of it to be hot, white, or straight [and nothing else]. For then the affections would be separated" (*Long.* 3.465^{b}12–14). Whiteness would be separate from substance, notice, not if it existed entirely uninstantiated, but if it were instantiated by a being that was wholly and exclusively white. Such a being is obviously not an Aristotelian substance, but something more like the Platonic Form of whiteness, which does seem to be white and nothing else (Plato, *Phaedo* 78d5–7). Aristotelian substances can exist, then, whether or not their affections exist by being instantiated by something else. Affections, on the other hand, cannot exist unless they are instantiated by Aristotelian substances, since such substances are (in Aristotle's view) the only ultimate subjects of predication. The separability of substance from affections, on this way of looking at it, is entirely of a piece with their inseparability from it.

(4) The verb *chôrizein* derives from *chôra* ("place"), and means "to separate, part, sever, or divide" things by causing them (roughly speaking) to be in separate (or disjoint) places (*Met.* 3.2.998^{a}17–19, 11.12.1068^{b}26–27). Thus when Aristotle describes Plato as separating the Forms from perceptible particulars (13.4.1078^{b}30–34), a view he adverts to in our text, the primary connotation is that of putting them in separate places: perceptible particulars are "here (*entautha*)," Forms are "over there (*kakei*)" (1.9.990^{b}34–991^{a}1). For a Form is "a particular, they say, and separable" (7.15.1040^{a}8–9) and "place is special to particular things, which is why they are separable by place" (14.5.1092^{a}18–19). Moreover, the fundamental objection Aristotle makes to such separable Forms is that they are an incoherent mixture of universals and of the particulars needed for their instantiation and existence: "they say that there is man-itself and horse-itself and health-itself, and nothing else—like those who introduce gods, but say that they are human in form; for those people were making the gods nothing but eternal human beings, and these are making the Forms nothing but eternal perceptibles" (3.2.997^{b}9–12); "They at the same time make the Forms universal and contrariwise treat them as separable and as particulars . . . that this is not possible is a puzzle that has been gone through before" (13.9.1086^{a}32–35; 3.6.1003^{a}5–17). We might expect, therefore, as (4) implies, that the separability Aristotle accords to his own substances, but denies to affections, would be the separability he denies to

Platonic Forms: affections are in substances around here not in substances (= Forms) that are elsewhere.

(5) Though separability is often characterized in terms of existential independence, in some cases this seems not to be required: "Of things that reciprocate as to implication of being (*einai*), that which is in some way the cause of the other's being might perfectly sensibly be called prior in nature. And that there are some such cases is clear. For there being a human reciprocates as to implication of being with the true statement about it: if there is a human, the statement whereby we say that there is a human is true, and reciprocally—since if the statement whereby we say there is a human is true, there is a human. And whereas the true statement is in no way the cause of the thing's being, the thing does seem in some way to be the cause of the statement's being true. For it is because of the thing's being or not being that the statement is called true or false" (*Cat.* 12.14^{b}11–22). What lies at the bottom of separability, then, seems rather to be a sort of ontological independence that is causal or explanatory in nature. In any case, this is clearly what we find in the following texts: "This [vegetative soul] can be separated from the others, but the others cannot be separated from it, in the case of the mortal ones. This is evident in the case of plants, since they have no other capacity of soul" (*DA* 2.2.413^{a}31–^{b}1; also 1.1.403^{a}10–16, ^{b}17–19); "Bodily parts . . . cannot even exist when they are separated. For it is not a finger in any and every state that is the finger of an animal, rather, a dead finger is only homonymously a finger" (*Met.* 7.10.1035^{b}23–25). For what makes perceptual soul inseparable from nutritive soul, or a finger inseparable from an animal, are the causal relations that make the former dependent on the latter. Again, this makes the separability accorded to substances, but denied to affections, the same as the separability denied to Platonic Forms. For the latter too were intended to play an explanatory role: "the Forms are the causes of the what-it-is of other things, as *the one* is of the Forms" (1.6.988^{a}10–11).

(6) The separability of substance and the inseparability of affections, while obviously essential to the account of both, is a special case of a more general phenomenon. For substance as form is not just separable from affections but from matter as well. But if this is the sort of separability characterized in (1)–(6), it must be anti-symmetrical, so that form can exist apart from matter but not matter apart from form. In the case of the forms of form-matter compounds, whether their matter is perceptible or intelligible, this is clearly not the case: like snub, but unlike concavity, they cannot exist apart from matter (*Met.* 6.1.1025^{b}28–1026^{a}15). But in the case of other forms, those that are like concavity, it is possible (1026^{a}15–16, 12.6.1071^{b}20). These are the primary intelligible substances, on which all

others—including matter-form compounds—causally depend for their existence (9.8.1050ᵇ19) and order (11.2.1060ᵃ26–27). Matter, by contrast, cannot exist apart from form of some sort (14.2.1089ᵇ27–28), since without form it is not intrinsically anything at all (7.3.1029ᵃ20–21).

(7) In (1) separability is tied to being a particular subject of predication, and so seems to be somehow logical or logico-linguistic in nature. (6), on the other hand, seems to tell a different sort of story, in which separability has more to do with causation and explanation than with logic. To bring the two together we need only reflect that Aristotle's logic is primarily a logic of science, and that whenever we have a subject-predicate proposition there is always a question as to why the predicate holds of the subject. The target of scientific explanation, indeed, is always just that: Why does predicate P hold of subject S (*Met.* 7.17.1041ᵃ10–11)? If P holds of S coincidentally, or by luck or chance, science has nothing to say about it (6.2.1026ᵇ3–5). There is no explanation. But if P is an intrinsic coincident of S, or if P is part of S's essence, or is S's essence, science does have something to say about it. What this implies is that the primary explanatory entities cannot themselves have a subject-predicate structure (*Met.* 9.10.1051ᵃ34–ᵇ5). They cannot be expressed as one thing said of another—they are not thises-in-thises. Instead, in comparison to things with such a structure, they are simple—forms, not form-matter compounds. The problem is—and it is one of the deepest—is how separable forms, which, like all forms, are universals (7.11.1036ᵃ28–29), can indeed be primary subjects and this somethings—separable "in the way in which *particular things* are said to be separated."

Aristotle's answer is the following: "The fact that all scientific knowledge is universal, so that the starting-points of beings must also be universal and not separate substances, involves the greatest puzzle of those mentioned. But though there is surely a way in which what is said is true, there is another way in which it is not true. For scientific knowledge, like knowing scientifically, is twofold, one potential, the other active: the capacity [or potential], being as matter, universal and indefinite, is of what is universal and indefinite, whereas the activity, being definite, is of what is definite—being a this something of a this something. But it is only coincidentally that sight sees universal color, because this [particular instance of] color that it sees is *a* color, and so what the grammarian theoretically grasps, namely, this [particular instance of] A, is *an* A. For if the starting-points must be universal, what comes from them must also be universal, as in the case of demonstrations. And if this is so, there will be nothing separable and no substance either. However, in one way scientific knowledge is universal, but in another it is not" (*Met.* 13.10.1087ᵃ10–25).

Sign (*sêmeion*): Aristotle often declares something to be a sign of something (more than thirty times, for example, in *Rh.*). But just what a sign is takes a bit of working out. The first thing to note is that signs are of two sorts: related as (1) particular to universal or (2) as universal to particular (*Rh.* 1.2.1357^{b}1–3). An example of (1): "if someone were to say that since Socrates is wise and just it is a sign that the wise are just" (1357^{b}11–13); an example of (2): "if someone were to say that there is a sign that a person is feverish, since he is breathing rapidly" (1357^{b}18–19). Both of these are refutable (1357^{b}13, 19–20). Yet, as Aristotle puts it in the *Prior Analytics*, "truth may be found in signs whatever their sort" (2.27.70^{a}37–38). The question is what sort of truth? Not necessary truth: signs are not proofs or demonstrations. But is it contingent truth or the sort of necessary truth found in things that hold for the most part (*APr.* 1.13.32^{b}4–21)? And if it is the latter, are signs distinct from things that hold for the most part or the very same thing? The answer becomes clear once we reflect on the fact that only a universally quantified proposition can hold for the most part, as in the examples Aristotle gives about crabs: "for the most part all crabs have the right claw bigger and stronger than the left" (*HA* 4.3.527^{b}6–7). For it certainly cannot hold for the most part that *some* crabs have their right claw bigger than their left. Their right claw is either bigger than the left or it isn't. The same goes for any particular crab. With signs, by contrast, there are some that are related as particular to universal, as the fact that Socrates is wise and just is a sign that the wise are just. Therein lies the difference we were seeking. A sign can be a particular proposition; one that holds for the most part cannot. At the same time, though, it is not just a contingent fact that Socrates is both wise and just, as it might be that he was married to Xanthippe, but something (putatively) more robust or necessary than that.

Simonides: A poet from Iulis on Ceos (c. 556/532–466/442 BC). None of his surviving poems explain the allusion to him. He did, however, have a reputation for acquisitiveness, and this may be what Aristotle has in mind.

Sleep (*hupnos*): "Sleep is not every incapacity of the perceptual part, but rather this affection arises from the evaporation that attends eating food. For that which is vaporized must be driven on to a given point and then must turn back and change just like the tide in a narrow strait. And in every animal the hot is made by nature to move upward, but when it has reached the upper parts, it turns back, and moves downward in a mass. That is why sleepiness mostly occurs after eating food; for, then, a large watery and earthy mass is carried upward. When this comes to a stop, therefore, it weighs down and makes drowsy; but when it has actually sunk downward, and by its return has driven back the hot, then sleepiness comes on and the animal falls asleep" (*Somn.* 3.456^b^17–28).

Solon: Athenian statesman and poet (c. 640–560 BC), and architect of the Athenian constitution.

Soul (*psuchê*): Unlike souls as we conceive them, which are found only in "higher" beings like us, Aristotelian souls are found wherever there is life and movement: souls are animators. Thus all plants and animals, however primitive or simple, have some sort of soul. Moreover, unlike Cartesian or some religious conceptions of the soul, Aristotelian souls (the understanding aside) are tightly tied to the bodies whose souls they are. The account of them makes this apparent: "It is necessary, then, for the soul to be substance, as form, of a natural body that has life potentially. But substance is actuality. Therefore, it is the actuality of such a body. But something is said to be actual in two ways, either as scientific knowledge is or as contemplating is. And it is evident that it is as scientific knowledge is. For both sleep and waking depend on the presence of the soul; waking is analogous to contemplating, and sleep to having but not exercising [scientific-knowledge]; and in the same individual scientific knowledge is prior in coming to be. That is why the soul is the first actuality of a natural body that has life potentially" (*DA* 2.1.412^a^19–28). Thus an ensouled body is a matter-form compound whose body is matter and whose soul is form.

Although the various sorts of soul are found separated from each other in other living things, they are also found hierarchically organized within the human soul, with higher ones presupposing lower ones (*Pol.* 7.14.1333^a^21–30, 15.1334^b^15). On the lowest rung in the hierarchy is nutritive soul, responsible for nutrition and growth. It is the only sort of soul possessed by plants. The next rung up is perceptual soul, responsible for perception and for the feeling and appetite that cause animal movement. Together with nutritive soul it is found in all animals. In human beings, both are constituents of the non-rational part of the soul. The third sort of soul, found only in human beings, is rational soul, which comprises the part of the soul that has reason and the understanding.

Looked at from the bottom up rather than from the top down, this hierarchy is teleological: lower sorts of soul and their functions are for the sake of the higher ones. For example, the homoeomerous parts, such as flesh, and their functions exist for the sake of the non-homoeomerous or structured parts and their functions. Among the latter parts, the sense organs are particularly important with regard to survival, which is essential for all other functioning (*DA* 3.12.434^a^22–^b^27). In animals with rational soul, the senses (especially smell, hearing, and sight) "inform us of many distinctions from which arise wisdom (*phronêsis*) about intelligible objects as well as those of action," and so also exist "for the sake of doing well" or being happy (*Sens.* 1.436^{b}10–437^{a}3). Finally, *phronêsis*, though it exists for its own sake, also exists for the sake of the understanding (*NE* 6.13.1145^{a}6–9). Understanding, then, is at the teleological peak of the organization, and so is the final or teleological cause of everything else in it.

Special (*idion*): "A special affection (*idion*) is one that does not make clear the essence of a thing yet belongs to that thing alone and is predicated convertibly of it. Thus it is a special affection of a human to be receptive of grammar, since if someone is human he is receptive of grammar, and if he is receptive of grammar he is human" (*Top.* 1.5.102^{a}18–22).

Species (*eidos*): See Genus.

Speusippus: The son of Plato's sister Potone and of Eurymedon of Myrrhinous. A member of Plato's Academy, he became its head on Plato's death in 348/7 BC, and remained such for eight years.

Starting-point (*archê*): An *archê* is a primary cause: "This is what it is for something to be a starting-point, that it is itself the cause of many things, with nothing above it being a cause of it" (*GA* 5.7.788^{a}14–16).

Substance (*ousia*): *Ousia* is a noun, perhaps formed from the present participle *ousa* of the verb *einai* ("to be"). "Substance" is the traditional translation. (1) The substance *of* something is its essence, whereas (2) *a* substance, on the other hand, is something that has the fundamental sort of being possessed by an ultimate subject of predication—a *tode ti* ("this something")—which is not itself ever predicated of anything else (*Met.* 5.8.1017^{b}23–26). It is usually but not always clear which of (1) or (2) is intended.

Supposition (*hupolêpsis*): *Hupolêpsis* is like belief but unlike scientific knowledge, in that it can be false as well as true (*NE* 6.3.1139^{b}15–18). But whereas belief must be based on rational calculation, *hupolêpsis* need not be: "*hupolêpsis* is that by which we play a double game (*epamphoterizomen*) with everything, as to whether it is so or not so" (†*MM* 1.34.1197^{a}30–31). The idea, then, is that *hupolêpsis* is what allows us to entertain a proposition without asserting or denying it.

Synonymous: "Things are said to be synonymous when they have a name in common and when the account of the essence that corresponds to the name is the same—for example, both a human and an ox are animals. Each of these is called by a common name 'animal,' and the account of the essence is also the same, since if we are to give the account of what-it-is for each of them to be an animal, we will give the same account" (*Cat.* 1.1^{a}6–12).

Theoretical grasp on, get a: The verb *theasthai*, with which *theôria* is cognate, means "to look at" or "gaze at." Hence *theôria* itself is sometimes what someone is doing in looking closely at something, or observing, studying, or contemplating it. *Theôria* can thus be an exercise of understanding (*nous*), which is the element responsible for grasping scientific starting-points (*NE* 6.6.1141^{a}7–8), such as (the definition of) right angle in the case of geometry, or (the definition of) happiness in the case of politics. Hence the cognate verb *theôrein* sometimes means "to be actively understanding" or "to be actively contemplating" something. "Get a theoretical grasp on" often seems to convey the right sense. See also Practical.

Theoretical wisdom (*sophia*): Theoretical wisdom, which is the virtue of the scientific part of the soul (*NE* 6.1.1139^{a}15–17) and "the most exact of the sciences" (6.7.1141^{a}16–17), is "understanding plus scientific knowledge—scientific knowledge, having a head as it were, of the most estimable things" (7.1141^{a}19–20). See also *Met.* 1.1.982^{a}1–2.983^{a}23.

This something (*tode ti*): *Tode ti* involves a particularizing element and a generalizing element. I take the demonstrative pronoun *tode* as particularizing (as suggested by *Met.* 7.4.1030^{a}5–6) and the indefinite pronoun *ti* as generalizing, but since *tode* need not be particularizing and *ti* may be, it is possible to go the other way and translate as "thing of a certain sort." Often *tode ti* appears in translations simply as "a this," and in at least one place Aristotle himself suggests that *tode* and *ti* are interchangeable (12.2.1069^{b}9, 11).

(1) In very many cases, being a *tode ti* is a distinctive mark of *ousia* ("substance"), and so has some share in the ambiguity of the latter, as between (1a) an ultimate subject of predication and (2a) the substance or essence of something. This is reflected in the fact that (1b) a particular man and a particular horse are primary substances (*Cat.* 5.2^{a}11–14), so that "it is indisputably true that each of them signifies a *tode ti*" (3^{b}10–12), while at the same time (2b) what is separable and a *tode ti* is "the shape or form of each thing" (*Met.* 5.8.1017^{b}24–26; also 7.1.1042^{a}27–29, 9.7.1049^{a}35). Some

things, to be sure, are one and the same as their forms or essences—which would remove the ambiguity at least in their cases—but it is not true that all are (7.11.1037a33–b7).

(3) As strong as the connection between substance and being a *tode ti* is the disconnection between being a *tode ti* and being a universal—"no common thing signifies a this something, but rather a such-and-such sort of thing" (*Met.* 3.6.1003a8–9; also 7.13.1039a15–16)—and the connection between being substance and being a *kath' hekaston*: "If we do not posit substances to be separate, and in the way in which the *kath' hekasta* are said to be separate, we will do away with the sort of substance we wish to maintain" (13.10.1086b16–19). Apparently, then, a form that is (2b) a primary substance—as some are explicitly said to be (7.7.1032b1–2)—must be a *kath' hekaston.*

(4) A *kath' hekaston*, in turn, is "what is numerically one" (*Met.* 3.4.999b34–1000a1), and so, (4a) taking "numerically one" to mean that no two things can be one and the same *kath' hekaston*, as no two things can be you or Socrates (7.14.1039a34), it is translated as "particular"—the argument in 7.15.1040a27–b1 hinges crucially on *kath' hekaston* having this sense. But it is also possible to take "numerically one" to mean (4b) "indivisible" or "individual," so that like an ultimate differentia—identified with form and substance at 7.12.1038a25–26—something is *kath' hekaston* because it cannot be further divided or differentiated.

(5) As we try to disambiguate *tode ti*, then, we run into ambiguities that parallel the initial one in substance itself, or that are related to it. That this may be no accident, but rather the heart of the issue, is suggested by *Met.* 13.10.1087a19–21.

(6) Finally a point about matter. What *Ph.* 1.7.190b24–26 refers to as "countable matter (*hulê arithmêtikê*)," and treats as a generalization of such things as the human and the bronze, is "more of a this something," as, no doubt, is the "this wood (*todi to xulon*) of this [box]" at *Met.* 9.7.1049a24 and the "this (*toudi*), which is bronze" at 7.8.1033b2, from (some or all of) which the smith makes this brazen sphere. But these are particular identifiable and countable parcels of matter—minimally shaped up by form, perhaps, but enough to count as (anyway low-grade) *tade tina*. Matter taken more generally, however, is "what not being actually a this something, is potentially a this something" (8.1.1042a27–28).

Underlying subject (*hupokeimenon*): In addition to being (1) what underlies or persists through every change, whether in affections (as a substantial subject) or in the coming to be or passing away (as matter), a *hupokeimenon* can be (2) a subject of predication, or (3) the subject matter of a science or body of knowledge (*NE* 1.3.1094^{b}12).

Understanding (*nous*): In the broadest sense of the term, someone with *nous* is someone with sound common sense and the cognate verb *noein*, like *dianoeisthai*, means "to think" (*Mete.* 1.3.340^{b}14, *Ph.* 4.1.208^{b}25, *NE* 3.1.1110^{a}11). *Nous*, in this sense, is what enables a soul to suppose, believe, deduce, calculate, reason, and believe, so that it is possible to *noein* something false (*DA* 3.3.427^{b}9). In the narrow sense, *nous* is what makes possible a type of knowledge of universal scientific starting-points that, unlike scientific knowledge proper, is not demonstrable from anything further: "About the starting-point of what is scientifically known there cannot be scientific knowledge . . . since what is scientifically known is demonstrable . . . the remaining alternative is for *nous* to be of starting-points" (*NE* 6.6.1140^{b}33–1141^{a}8); "*nous* is of the terms or definitions (*horoi*) for which there is no argument (*logos*)" (8.1142^{a}25–26). This *nous* is a divine substance (*NE* 10.7.1177^{b}19–1178^{a}8), or anyway the most divine one, present in human beings (10.7.1177^{a}16), which, as such, shares in the immortality that is characteristic of gods (*DA* 3.5.430^{a}23). Consequently, it alone of these parts is separable from the human body and can survive its death (1.4.408^{b}18–25; also *Long.* 2.465^{a}26–32). Among sublunary animals this *nous* is fully possessed only by human beings (*PA* 2.10.656^{a}7–8, *NE* 10.8.1178^{b}24–25), and thus is special to them. In fact, a human being is most of all his *nous* (*NE* 9.8.1168^{b}31–32, 10.7.1178^{a}2–8).

Universal (*katholou*): "What is universal, or in general what is taken as such when we say 'as a whole,' is universal as encompassing many things by being predicated of each of them, and by all of them—each one of them—being one thing, as human, horse, and god are, because all are living things" (*Met.* 5.26.1023^{b}29–32).

Virtue (*aretê*): Anything that has a function (*ergon*) has a correlative *aretê*, which enables it to perform that function well. Thus it is possible to speak of the *aretê* of thieves, scandalmongers, and other bad things that are good at doing what they do (*Met.* 5.16.1021^{b}12–23), as well as of the *aretê* of non-living tools and instruments. For this reason *aretê* is nowadays sometimes translated as "excellence."

Void (*kenon*): See *Cael.* 1.9.279^{a}13–14.

What-it-is, the (*to ti esti*): When we ask, *Ti esti A?*, we ask, What is A? The correct answer defines or makes clear the what-it-is of A, or—a related notion—the being for A, or—another related notion—the essence or what-it-is-to-be of A. Any intrinsic being, regardless of its category, has a what-it-is, although not all in the same unconditional way (*Met.* 7.4.1030^{a}17–27).

Wish (*boulêsis*): Wish is a desire whose proper object is "unconditionally and in truth . . . the good, but to each person it is the apparent good" (*NE* 3.4.1113^{a}33–34). On what we might call the *official view*, wish seems to be the quintessential thought-involving desire (*NE* 6.2.1139^{b}5). For wish is "always found in the rationally calculative part" (*Top.* 4.5.126^{a}13; also *DA* 3.9.432^{b}5–7, *Rh.* 1.10.1369^{a}2–4), so that "when something is moved in accord with rational calculation, it is moved in accord with wish" (*DA* 3.10.433^{a}23–25). Thus when wish is attributed to the heavenly bodies (*Met.* 12.7.1072^{a}26–^{b}4), only rational soul is involved: the stars and planets have rational calculation and understanding, but not the sort of soul needed for growth and perception. Elsewhere, however, Aristotle seems to deviate from the official view: "spirit and wish, and furthermore appetite, are present in children straight from birth, whereas rational calculation and understanding naturally arise as they grow" (*Pol.* 7.15.1334^{b}22–25). But the explanation for the deviation is not far to seek. When Aristotle discusses wish in the process of trying to explain deliberate choice, he writes: "[Deliberate choice] is not wish either, although it appears to be a close relative of it. For there is no deliberate choice of impossible things, and if someone were to say he was deliberately choosing them, he would seem silly. But there is wish for impossible things (*adunatôn*)—for example, immortality. There is also wish concerning the sorts of things that could never come about through ourselves—for example, that a certain actor or athlete should win a victory prize. No one deliberately chooses things like that, but things he thinks can come about through him. Further, wish is more for the end, whereas deliberate choice is of the things that further the end" (*NE* 3.2.1111^{b}19–27). Understood in this way, there seems to be nothing especially rational about wish, which makes it easy to see why children are said to have it. This suggests that *boulêsis* is being used in two different ways, the first technical, the second loose and popular. But there is a way to reconcile the two, which lies in the very definition of wish itself as a desire that is "unconditionally and in truth . . . [for] the good" but in each individual for "the apparent good" (*NE* 3.4.1113^{a}23–24). So what we should say, presumably, is that wish, as a desire for the apparent good, is present in children straight from birth, but that with the proper habituation and training it can come to be for the real good, and so to be properly responsive to the deliberation that best furthers it.

Xenocrates of Chalcedon: A follower of Plato, and head of the Academy from 339 to 314 BC.

Zeno of Elea: See DK 29 = TEGP pp. 245–270.

Further Reading

Detailed and regularly updated bibliographies of works on Aristotle's *Metaphysics* (compiled by Marc Cohen and myself), on his ethics (compiled by Richard Kraut), and on his philosophy generally (compiled by Christopher Shields) are available online at:
plato.stanford.edu/entries/aristotle-metaphysics/
plato.stanford.edu/entries/aristotle-politics/
plato.stanford.edu/entries/aristotle-ethics/
plato.stanford.edu/entries/aristotle/

Thesaurus Linguae Graecae (http://www.tlg.uci.edu) has excellent searchable Greek texts and English translations of Aristotle's writings, with linked dictionaries and grammars.

General

Laks, A. "Theories of Religion." In J. Brunschwig and G. Lloyd, eds., *Greek Thought; A Guide to Classical Knowledge* (Cambridge, MA, 2000), pp. 511–535.

Lear, J. *Aristotle: The Desire to Understand* (Cambridge, 1988).

Schofield, M. "Theology and Divination." In J. Brunschwig and G. Lloyd, eds., *Greek Thought: A Guide to Classical Knowledge* (Cambridge, MA, 2000), pp. 498–510.

Sedley, D. *Creationism and Its Critics in Antiquity* (Berkeley, 2007).

Aristotle's Theology

Baghdassarian, F. *La Question du Divin chez Aristote: Discours sur les Dieux et Science du Principe* (Louven, 2016).

———. *Aristote: Métaphysique Lambda* (Paris, 2019).

Bodéüs, R. *Aristotle and the Theology of the Living Immortals* (Albany, 2000).

Bordt, M. *Aristoteles' "Metaphysik XII"* (Darmstadt, 2006).

Elders, L. *Aristotle's Theology: A Commentary on Book Λ of the Metaphysics* (Assen, 1972).

Frede, M., and D. Charles, eds. *Aristotle's Metaphysics Lambda. Symposium Aristotelicum* (Oxford, 2000).

Horn, C. *Aristotle Metaphysics Lambda—New Essays* (Berlin, 2016).

Judson, L. *Aristotle: Metaphysics Book Λ* (Oxford, 2019).

Kontos, P. *Aristotle on the Scope of Practical Reason: Spectators, Legislators, Hopes, and Evils* (Abingdon, 2021).

Kosman, A. *The Activity of Being* (Cambridge, MA, 2013).

Menn, S. *Plato on God as* Nous (Carbondale, 1995).

——— "Aristotle's Theology." In C. Shields, ed., *The Oxford Handbook of Aristotle* (Oxford, 2012), pp. 422–464.

Van Riel, G. *Plato's God* (Farnham, 2013).

On Ethics and Politics

Aufderheide, J. *Aristotle's Nicomachean Ethics Book X: Translation and Commentary* (Cambridge, 2020).

Walker, M. *Aristotle on the Uses of Contemplation* (Cambridge, 2018).

Relevant Works of Mine

Substantial Knowledge: Aristotle's Metaphysics (Indianapolis, 2000).

Action, Contemplation, and Happiness: An Essay on Aristotle (Cambridge, MA, 2012).

Aristotle: A Quick Immersion (New York, 2019), Spanish edition (Barcelona, 2020).

"Aristotle on Women: Diminished Deliberation and Divine Male Rule." *Revue Roumaine de Philosophie* 64 (2020): 1–36.

"Aristotelian Immortality." In P. Destrée and M. Zingano, eds., *Theoria: Studies in the Status of Contemplation in Aristotle's Ethics* (Louvain, 2014), pp. 334–343.

"Good and Bad in Aristotle." In Pavlos Kontos, ed., *Evil in Aristotle* (Cambridge, 2018), pp. 17–31.

"Human Happiness as a Political Achievement in Aristotle." *Kronos Philosophical Journal* 7 (2019): 61–84.

"Hylomorphic Explanation and the Scientific Status of the *De Anima*." In Caleb Cohoe, ed., *Aristotle's De Anima: A Critical Guide* (Cambridge, 2022), pp. 14–31.

Index of Quoted Passages

*Starred * passages appear with annotation in the body of a chapter; others appear in the Glossary, the Introduction, or notes.*